As history keeps
the world interesting,
we as humans are
rarely bored, often
agitated, to make the
future safer for those
we love.

The Sxykins
1990

THE PRIEST

and

THE POLICEMAN

THE COURAGEOUS LIFE
AND CRUEL MURDER
OF FATHER JERZY POPIELUSZKO

John Moody
·
Roger Boyes

SUMMIT BOOKS · NEW YORK

Published by SUMMIT BOOKS
A Division of Simon & Schuster, Inc.
Simon & Schuster Building
1230 Avenue of the Americas
New York, New York 10020
First published in Great Britain in 1986
by Victor Gollancz Ltd
as The Priest Who Had to Die
SUMMIT BOOKS and colophon
are trademarks of Simon & Schuster, Inc.
Designed by Edith Fowler
Manufactured in the United States of America

10 9 8 7 6 5 4 3 2 1

Library of Congress Cataloging in Publication Data

Moody, John.
  The priest and the policeman.

  Originally published: The priest who had to die.
London : Gollancz, 1986.
  1. Poland—Politics and government—1980–
  2. Popiełuszko, Jerzy, 1947–1984. 3. Church and
state—Catholic Church. 4. Catholic Church—Poland—History—20th century. 5. Poland—Church
history—20th century. 6. Police—Poland. 7. Internal security—Poland.
  I. Boyes, Roger. II. Title.
DK4442.M66   1987   943.8'056   86-22993
ISBN: 0-671-61896-2

To Kate Alexandra and Philip Adam,
who were conceived and born
at the same time as this project

Contents

Cast of Characters (*with a pronunciation guide*)   9

1 The Priest Who Had to Die   13
2 Beginnings   25
3 New City, New Name   39
4 Whose Church Is It Anyway?   56
5 Solidarity   68
6 Martial Law   83
7 God Who Watches Over Poland   94
8 Bomb Through the Window   103
9 Return of a Hero   109
10 Negotiating with the Devil   122
11 Amnesty   132
12 Preparations   152
13 Trial Run   158
14 "It's the Water for Him"   168
15 End of the Chase   189
16 Laying Blame, Laying to Rest   203

8 CONTENTS

17 The Defendant, Popieluszko 214
18 Who Ordered the Killing? 228

Cast of Characters

WITH A PRONUNCIATION GUIDE

EDWARD BABIUCH (bī′-book) Former prime minister of Poland

FATHER TEOFIL BOGUCKI (tā′-o-feel bo-gut′-ski) Pastor of St. Stanislaw Kostka parish

LIEUTENANT WALDEMAR CHMIELEWSKI (val′-da-mar chimlev′-ski) Codefendant in Popieluszko murder trial

WALDEMAR CHROSTOWSKI (kros-tov′-ski) Popieluszko's bodyguard and driver

GENERAL WLADYSLAW CIASTON (vwad′-i-swav chas′-ton) Deputy Interior Minister

EDWARD GIEREK (gear′-ek) Former Party chief

ANDRZEJ GWIAZDA (on′-jay gvee-azh′-da) Solidarity regional leader

FATHER HENRYK JANKOWSKI (yan-kov′-ski) Walesa's confessor

GENERAL WOJCIECH JARUZELSKI (voy′-chek yahr-a-zel′-ski) Party leader

SEWERYN JAWORSKI (sev'-er-in ya-vor'-ski) Solidarity regional leader

KAZIMIERZ KAKOL (kazh'-i-meerzh kon'-kul) Former head of the Council for Religious Affairs

GENERAL CZESLAW KISZCZAK (ches'-wov kees'-chak) Interior Minister

BISHOP ZBIGNIEW KRASZEWSKI (zbig'-nhev krash-ev'-ski) Popieluszko's former professor

ARTUR KUJAWA (koo-ya'-va) Presiding judge at Popieluszko murder trial

JACEK KURON (yat'-sek koor'-on) Solidarity activist

ADAM LOPATKA (wo-pat'-ka) Head of the Council for Religious Affairs

STANISLAW MALKOWSKI (mal-kov'-ski) Activist priest

MIROSLAW MILEWSKI (meer'-a-swav meel-ev'-ski) Former Interior Minister

BISHOP WLADISLAW MIZIOLEK (vwad'-a-swav meezh-ol'-wek) Auxiliary Bishop of Warsaw

MIECZYSLAW MOCZAR (meesh'-a-swav moat'-zahr) Party hardliner

LIEUTENANT LESZEK PEKALA (lesh'-ek pen-kahl'-a) Codefendant in Popieluszko murder trial

COLONEL ADAM PIETRUSZKA (pee-a-troosh'-ka) Deputy director of Department Four of Interior Ministry; Codefendant at Popieluszko murder trial

CAPTAIN GRZEGORZ PIOTROWSKI (zheg'-gosh pee-a-trov'-ski) Codefendant at Popieluszko murder trial

GENERAL ZENON PLATEK (pwat'-ek) Director of Department Four of Interior Ministry

FATHER JERZY POPIELUSZKO (yehr'-zhy pop-e-yoosh'-ko) Solidarity's chaplain, murdered October 19, 1984

ANDRZEJ PRZEKAZINSKI (on'-jay shek-a-zhin'-ski) Popieluzko's friend

LECH WALESA (lek va-when'-sa) Solidarity leader

EDWARD WENDE (ven'-da) Popieluszko's lawyer until his death; Chrostowski's lawyer at trial

KAROL WOJTYLA (voy-tee'-wah) Former cardinal of Krakow; elected Pope John Paul II

LIEUTENANT LESZEK WOLSKI (lesh'-ek vol'-ski) Warsaw regional secret police

1
•
The Priest
Who Had to Die

THE DEMONSTRATION was doomed from the beginning. Perhaps, if there had been a way of muffling the siren, that long sinister caterwauling siren, the protest would have developed differently, broken out of the street rituals of chaser and chased. But May Day, the Worker's Holiday, was not a time for the Communist authorities to take chances. The day was one of finely choreographed reverence, a day when Politburos remember, briefly, that they are at the helm of a workers' state and pay tribute to the state of the workers.

May 1, 1984, was a warm day in Warsaw, the first real day of spring. It was much the same across Central and Eastern Europe. In Prague, the radio served up brave songs about gallant Communist heroes. In East Berlin, Erich Honecker was rehearsing a speech about fraternal solidarity. In Moscow from daybreak, teachers barked at the Young Pioneers and the more languid but still excited teenagers from the Young Communist League. Marchers prepared for the long parade through Red Square and a snatched glimpse of the huddled old men on top of the Lenin Mausoleum.

In Warsaw there were signs of activity, too. Dusty buses from the provinces parked askew outside the smaller hotels and disgorged awed hayseeds who had been selected to take part in the celebration. Few of the marchers viewed this as an honor. With little warning and no explanation, entire factory units, school classes, and typing pools were simply ordered to appear. Since the declaration of martial law in Poland in the winter of 1981, the official May Day parades resembled ghost marches, line after line of lost souls tramping through Victory Square.

At the same time, another Polish tradition, only four years old but already ingrained in millions of hearts, was taking shape. Thousands of people, studiously ignoring the official celebrations uptown, began to filter into Warsaw's Old Town in time for nine o'clock mass. The sun was already high enough in the morning sky to cast a shadow down the narrow cobblestoned streets. Sweat was beginning to show through the dresses of the *babcie* and their middle-aged daughters. The mass would be celebrated in St. John's Cathedral, rebuilt from the rubble of World War II, as was the whole of the Old Town. Inside the cathedral, about three thousand believers could be accommodated. On politically sensitive occasions, the church was a natural focus, a source of information and consolation, and the congregation would spill out into Swietojanski Street, listening to the priest's voice relayed with the help of booming, faulty electronics. May Day in Orwell's year was one of those days, a spillover day, a day for demonstrations.

The troops of the Polish People's Militia who were splayed across Krakowskie Przedmiescie, the old royal way that leads into the Old Town, the cathedral and the palace, were at their most discriminating. Later, in the heat of the riot, the militia would not make fine distinctions between young and old, innocent bystander and involved protester. For the moment, though, there was a polite alertness. The instructions read out to company commanders on the previous day were explicit. First priority: ensure that any Solidarity demonstration does not merge with the officially sanctioned Communist procession. No Solidarity banners, no V-for-victory signs must be seen by the Party leadership, or by their distinguished Russian guests. That had happened once before, to everyone's chagrin. Second priority: prevent as many young potential Solidarity protesters as possible from entering the Old Town. The second objective was uttered more in hope than in reasonable expectation.

"Documents, please," was the usual laconic conversation opener. There was not much "please" about the request.

"Documents, why? We're just going to church." The younger ones, the *smarkacze*, might snigger, but a glance from under the peaked gray cap was usually enough to end the interchange.

"The area is off limits today to all except residents of the Old Town. Turn around and go home." This pretty speech was one of several drummed into the policemen, who were given a kind of Berlitz for dealing with potential demonstrators. They were not schooled in further debate. Anyone who argued or tried to push past was arrested immediately. This rarely happened. Everyone remembered his script and role from the last May Day protest. While the policeman collected each youth's identity card and, laboriously spelling out the names with his lips, copied them into a small blue spiral notebook, the teenagers decided among themselves which street corner to try next. They knew, or could deduce from the caravans of water cannon, jeeps, paddy wagons, and troop carriers parked in the side streets, that the Old Town would be completely sealed off within the hour, as hermetically as if the police were guarding against an outbreak of anthrax. In that time, while the police were still reasonably civil, there were holes and cracks in the security through which one could squeeze and, still rejoicing in the game, arrive at the church in time.

By 8:55 the devout were in their pews; the devious were in the street, clad in scuffed leather jackets, jeans, and steel-toed workers' boots. From inside, the organ music and cracked contralto voices sounded like a radio fixed on a faraway station. A sense of imminent action was spreading as each hymn brought the mass closer to its end.

From the altar came the priest's remote voice: "Go in peace to love and serve the Lord." "Thanks be to God," was the response. The organist began the standard hymn at the end of May Day mass, "God Who Watches Over Poland." The words are as familiar to every Polish child as "Jack and Jill." It is a hymn of sweet succor for the wounds of life. It is balm. It was also the hymn unofficially adopted by the Solidarity trade union during its legal existence, from August 1980 to December 1981. When the decree of martial law suspended Solidarity, the hymn became an act of defiance. When Poles sing it, their right hands shoot into the air, their index and middle fingers spread into the V that was Solidarity's symbol. Victory. This was the first May Day since martial law had been lifted on July 22, 1983. The "state of war" was over, but special penal regulations were still in effect. And so the forest of hands pushed up, and out came the V-sign that so enraged General Wojciech Jaruzelski, the leader of the Polish Communist Party and the country's prime minister. "There is no letter V in the Polish alphabet," he once shouted while looking at police films of a demonstration.

The hundreds in Swietojanski Street knelt for the blessing. In the small apartments opposite the cathedral, listeners also fell to their knees. Even with the windows closed every word of the service could be heard.

Leaflets tumbled from one of the high gables into the crowd. A young boy climbed onto the scaffolding around the Jesuit church adjoining the cathedral and unfurled a banner: "Solidarnosc," it read, in playful red lettering. There were cheers, rebel yelps.

The voices were building, but suddenly they were overwhelmed by a shrill dissonance coming from the next street. It was a deep, howling siren, the kind used to turn away ships that have strayed too close. It was not an accident; it was a first warning. At 9:45 precisely, the police operation began. One end of Swietojanski Street, leading into Castle Square and onto Krakowski Przedmiescie, was cut off by a hundred officers of the motorized militia known as ZOMO. Dressed in gray-green battle fatigues and protected by visored helmets that look like something from an astronaut's footlocker, the ZOMO had been cooped up in paneled vans since before seven o'clock that morning. Their mood was testy. The hours of waiting, the sweat, the bad jokes, the tension, all came to a head now. For a month before May Day, the ZOMO units had thrown themselves at sandbags, run around assault courses in full gear, shouted sounds without meaning. Some people thought they were on amphetamines. But this was probably a way of answering the question, How can one Pole beat, kick, mistreat another with such vigor in the name of an alien political philosophy?

The Old Town, which had been off limits an hour before, was now a mousetrap. No one could get past the ZOMO without taking a severe beating with the white rubber, lead-filled truncheons they carried. The only way out was the other end of the street, which fed into the Old Market Place, the main attraction of Warsaw's pitifully small tourist trade.

There was no time to think. A blast of blue-tinted water from one of the French-made cannons shot over the ZOMO and spilled through Swietojanski Street like a flash flood in a gulley. The shouting, pushing crowd took only seconds to cross to the southeast corner of the market square and regroup. The ZOMO dashed down the street, joined by reinforcements who knew that this was how the action was supposed to proceed.

The police occupied one quadrant of the market. Cater-cornered to them were the bravest of the cathedral crowd, waving white and red Solidarity banners that had been concealed inside shirts, handbags, even wrapped around fishing rods. Between the two armies sat a few dozen pensioners who had ordered ice cream from the outdoor pavillion restaurant and were watching with the partiality of season ticket holders. The square was cleared for action: the waitresses from the Basilyczek restaurant craned out the windows; in the doorway of the post office a distinguished-looking lady clutched a poodle; at the Krokodil wine bar there was a debate whether to close for an hour. Alcohol sales had in any case been banned over the sensitive days. The ZOMO began to beat their shields, a menacing sound, a tribal Zulu gesture supposed to strike fear in the heart of the enemy.

The siren sounded again. This time it was a signal of attack. Like legions of lancers, the ZOMO pounded across the cobblestone marketplace, their white clubs overhead. The Solidarity supporters knew they had no chance. The ZOMO were under orders to use the minimum amount of force necessary to disperse the troublemakers. Brutality was acceptable, but it was not supposed to produce martyrs. The demonstrators leaked through the narrow opening of the marketplace that breaks onto a stone staircase. The stairs lead down a grassy embankment to the meadows near the Vistula River. Pushing and shoving in panic, they fell helter-skelter down the hill, like children following the Pied Piper to the River Weser. Those who tried other routes of escape were hounded through the hot streets by twos and threes of policemen. Once grabbed or tackled, they were roughed up and led to the blue patrol wagons that in Polish slang are called bitches. Many bitches howled, their red strobes tracing crazy circles. Inside, the ZOMO troops relieved some of their frustrations.

The scattered demonstrators at the bottom of the hill were not out of it yet. Dozens of mounted militia bore down on them, sending them into chaos. The horses were not usually used for strenuous duty, and the shock of spurs dug into their ribs startled more than aroused them. Horses and rider were intended to disperse groups of more than two, and this they did with an effectiveness that surprised all sides in the fracas. From above, on the crest of the hill, the incident resembled a classic nineteenth-century tableau: a cavalry skirmish, perhaps, on the fringes of the Crimean War.

Just as the riverside protesters had been broken up, a tremendous explosion sounded from the other side of the river, bringing everyone to a stunned silence. It had the muffled crack of artillery, the shock of a jet breaking the sound barrier. For that blink of an eye, the question hung: Have they opened fire? A second time, the sky seemed to rip open, and with that eruption all became clear. The ceremonial cannon on the other side of the Vistula, in the battered Praga District, were announcing the beginning of the official marchpast.

The demonstrators used the interruption of the cannon to advantage. Some scurried along the riverbank, weaving between parked cars, moving north. Others managed to climb the steep hill leading to the northeastern fringe of the Old Town. There they regrouped. Several hundred other people who had not been at the mass were also milling around. So were the police, but as long as there were no knots of demonstrators in the Old Town itself, they were satisfied. Their instructions had been to clear the Old Town. They were following orders, no more, no less. Prime Minister Jaruzelski, who was also a general of the Polish Army, was fond of saying that Poland was a nation of laws. This was the final logic of Communist rule: power backed up by force, or the threat of force.

To those who had taken part in the short-lived demonstration, such distinctions carried little weight. To most of them, the Communist Party leadership were quislings, executives whose head office was in Moscow. Jaruzelski's was the guiding hand of martial law, that guillotine of dreams. The symbol of his system, the red flag of socialism, was everywhere: hanging from windows, jutting out of gates that surrounded official buildings, waving from telephone poles. It hung next to the red and white Polish flag. Whenever they got a chance, the demonstrators tore the flags out of their stanchions. The red flags were dragged along the street and jammed head first into trash cans and sewer gutters. The Polish flags, too, were pilfered. These were waved reverently aloft, next to banners proclaiming, "Solidarity lives."

As a political manifestation, the May Day protest was a piddling thing, twenty minutes of taunts against superior force, then a quick run for safety. It would change nothing. Solidarity was still banned, the Communists were still in power. But as they nursed their bruises, the Poles who had been a part of the action on that day could console themselves with the knowledge that nowhere else in the Soviet empire could even such pitiful affrontery as theirs have gotten as far as it did. A few of the rowdier marchers tried to reach for broader themes: "Soviets out of Afghanistan," they shouted, but they received little encouragement. How could Poles worry about such things when they saw all around them the evidence of Soviet occupation of their own country?

Like a fresh wind sweeping across the flat plains for which Poland is named, a voice carried: "To Kostka!" "To Kostka!" replied three others. "To Kostka," chimed in a dozen more. The new destination was nowhere as strategic as the Old Town. In fact, it was three miles north, a long walk on such a day for several hundred people who already had been pelted with water, menaced by clubs, and chased through streets. Yet the word was like elixir: Kostka.

Their destination was a gray stone church with twin yellow

bell towers that overtop the maple and oak trees of a park across the street. The parish of St. Stanislaw Kostka occupies a choice piece of land in Zoliborz, one of Warsaw's most affluent and diverse neighborhoods. At the northern tip of Zoliborz sits the squat and squalid Huta Warszawa steel works, a mile-long caldron of hissing smokestacks and conveyor belts. To the east lies the Gdansk Railway Station. Yet Zoliborz is also a holdout against the twentieth century. There are houses with history and fortunes behind them. A flower farmer on the outskirts of the city made so much money that he literally had no place to store it. But his fortune was in zloty, the Polish currency that is worthless in any other country. So he bought thirty acres of land in Zoliborz and hired craftsmen to build him a palace on the grounds. Such things can be accomplished in Communist Poland. Andrzej Wajda, the renegade filmmaker whose documentaries *Man of Iron* and *Man of Marble* made him both the talk of the Cannes Film Festival and filthy rich, lives in Zoliborz.

Wajda could easily have watched the ragtag band of demonstrators as their forced march came to an end. The church was packed, and there were three thousand more people standing outside. The newcomers arrived just as the eleven o'clock mass was finishing, in time to hear the parish's youngest resident priest give his final blessing.

"I bless you, fellow Poles, in the name of the Father, and of the Son, and of the Holy Spirit," said Father Jerzy Popieluszko. The answering "Amen" reverberated from the church, echoed into the street and across the park. It was a bond of togetherness, the sealing of a spiritual bargain with the thin, green-robed priest at the altar. Some of the youths who had come from the Old Town hoped that another demonstration might erupt at the conclusion of this mass as it had at the cathedral. They were primed for another encounter with the ZOMO.

Father Jerzy knew and shared their gnawing anger. But he did not want the sacred service that he had just completed to become an incitement to violence. It was not his way. "The mass is ended, go in peace," he said, and added: "He who does not, he who shouts slogans or makes a disturbance, is not one of us. He is a provocateur."

There had been nothing extraordinary about the mass that Father Jerzy celebrated that day. Liturgically, it was indistinguishable from those offered by twenty-two thousand other Polish priests, good men who for the most part cared just as deeply about the nation. Why then did the mass at St. Stanislaw Kostka attract five thousand people? They had come because of him, to hear what he thought of the country's predicament. No priest in Poland was better known than Jerzy Popieluszko; none was more beloved.

There were other Poles interested in what Father Jerzy would say, and although they did not attend his May Day mass, it did not take them long to find out. His sermon was recorded, transcribed, typed, and waiting the next morning on the desks of half a dozen officers of the Polish Interior Ministry, located on Rakowiecka Street in Warsaw. The Interior Ministry controlled every policeman in the country, from traffic wardens to the hard-eyed young men who had mixed into the crowd outside the cathedral earlier in the day, and at St. Stanislaw Kostka during Father Jerzy's mass. The secret police, known variously as the SB, UB, Ubeks, and Tanjiaks, had guessed that the Old Town demonstration would take place and be easily dispersed. Some scoffed at the lack of imagination the pro-Solidarity crowd had shown: gathering in the same narrow street as they had the year before, running at the first charge of the ZOMO.

They were surprised and disturbed, however, to hear about the regrouping and the march north to Zoliborz. They knew well enough that Popieluszko was a constant danger, a rallying point for civil disobedience. They did not care what he said at his masses, but only about the effect of the words.

One agent in particular read the report ("To Kostka! To Kostka!") with alarm and disgust. He was younger than Popieluszko, taller, heavier, in better health. His name was unknown to Popieluszko, but there was a thick file bearing the priest's name in the agent's desk. He read on. At least there had been no illegal demonstrations after the mass at Kostka. That was not always the case. Popieluszko was a slick crowd pleaser who incited his listeners and then withdrew behind the sanctity of the church walls.

Grzegorz Piotrowski sighed. He had tried once before to take care of this misguided citizen. Clearly, the lesson had gone un-learned. When he thought about Popieluszko, he was surprised that he felt almost no emotion. No hatred, no anger, just weari-ness brought on by a sense that it was all so pointless. The pro-tests, the clever sermons, the proud sounding, patriotic words. Such perverted passion. He saw himself as a hand of justice. And of course, as a Pole who loved his country.

So Popieluszko, after all, had outgrown himself. Piotrowski traced his initials on the May Day report. That too was part of his job. But not the part at which he excelled.

On May 14, Archbishop Bronislaw Dabrowski was driven to Okecie Airport to board the Polish airline flight to Rome. Da-browski was the secretary of the Polish Episcopate, the body of Roman Catholic bishops in Poland that guides the Church's ac-tions. The country's spiritual welfare was nominally under the charge of the primate of Poland, Jozef Cardinal Glemp. But it was Dabrowski who made the paper move from the dead letter pile to the office where it could be stamped for approval.

Dabrowski did his job well because he did it so quietly. He met regularly with the State Council for Religious Affairs, whose purpose was to curb, not enhance the role of the Catholic Church. And he shuttled to Rome to report directly to the most powerful Pole in the world, Karol Wojtyla, who had once been the archbishop of Krakow, but who in 1984 was Pope John Paul II. Dabrowski had to be driven to the airport by a deputy, and he was always seen off at the airport by a delegation of the Council for Religious Affairs. The ritual was unnecessary, but for both Church and government it maintained the taut thread of politeness with which their relations were precariously stitched.

One face was new to Dabrowski as he scanned the small cir-cle. He let his eyes trail for an extra second over the wide cheeks, the set mouth, and the dark brown eyes that shone in the weak sun. Dabrowski looked away just as the introductions were coming to an end. Occasionally, his bureaucratic training deserted him, and he listened but did not hear as the names were droned out. The other government representatives were a known quantity to him. He assumed this latest addition was a young and rising prospect, someone to plague a future archbishop. He stretched his smile automatically, put out his hand, his eyes already directed toward the waiting plane. Fingers locked for a second, no more.

"And this is Mr. Piotrowski, from the Ministry."

Piotrowski had gone to observe. It paid to learn the routines and habits of one's enemy, and he regarded the Church as just that. So much of his job consisted of dull chores: reading and signing reports, assigning agents to listen to priests' sermons, and ensuring that they turned in accurate descriptions of them. Now and then, Piotrowski liked to get out and see for himself. He hated the deskbound routines of the Ministry. In another week, Grzegorz Piotrowski would celebrate his thirty-third birthday and he would tell a co-worker that he wondered whether he had made a mistake in becoming a secret policeman. He wanted to serve his country, to make it once again a working cog in the engine of socialism, to help it ward off the menace posed by the Church. When, Piotrowski asked plaintively, would he get to see some action?

Exactly five months after that birthday outburst, Piotrowski's wish had been granted. His name was still not widely known, as befitted a secret agent. Nevertheless, he was the most sought-after man in Poland. Frustrated by failure and fortified with a hatred that he could not explain, he had taken a step that he was convinced was not only correct but courageous, an action that he felt compelled as a patriot, and entitled as a policeman, to carry out. He murdered Father Jerzy Popieluszko.

To Poland and to the rest of Communist Europe, the killing of Popieluszko had a percussive effect similar to that of John Kennedy in the United States. Father Popieluszko was not the leader of the country. But he was at the time of his death the embodiment of two passionate ideals for which Poles have been giving their lives for more than a thousand years: a fierce loyalty to the Catholic Church; and an inflexible and, for the most part, unfulfilled struggle to rule their own country without outside interference.

He was stalked like a game animal in the last years of his life, hunted by agents like Piotrowski, who knew that the priest had to be silenced. Murder was not the only solution. It would have been enough to persuade the Church to transfer him to an obscure rural parish, or bring him to Rome. It would have sufficed to put him on trial and sentence him to prison for his political preaching, or to strain his delicate health to the breaking point, so that his death could be passed off, in the words of one agent, as "a beautiful accident." The police tried all these methods but found it was impossible to silence the priest, who declared modestly, "I am only saying aloud what people are thinking privately."

So they killed him, with confidence and a clumsiness that provided the most detailed account of a political assassination behind the Iron Curtain. Never before have so many facts about the activities of a Soviet-controlled secret police force been exposed so thoroughly.

The murder and the events that followed it also created confusing questions: Who stood to gain from Father Popieluszko's murder? Who directed the killers and who inspired the directors? The clues are hidden in the tangled weave of Polish politics, of secret police dynasties, in the confidential dealings of the Catholic Church, and in the secret diary in which the victim recorded his own suspicions, fears, and resolve. This book tries to follow the trail before it goes cold. It hunts the hunters.

2
•
Beginnings

ON THE LAST SUNDAY of May 1984, every inch of space in St.
Stanislaw Kostka Church in Zoliborz was claimed by 6 PM.
Those who had been to previous masses for the fatherland knew
about the crowds, knew how long it could take for thousands of
people to receive the wafer on their tongues and the word of
God in their hearts. The wise ones arrived an hour before the
start of the ritual to assure themselves seats, or failing that, at
least a slice of wall against which to stand. Not that the entire
congregation would keep blessed vigil through the entire mass.
Many were here to pray, a few to expiate their sins. But most
came to evening mass on that last Sunday of May 1984 to hear
Father Jerzy Popieluszko speak aloud their thoughts, to touch
on the brutality and indifference of their lives, and to offer hope
that someday—perhaps not soon, but eventually—it would end.

There would be no demonstrations here, except for the fervor
wrapped around their prayers. (May Day, May 3, August 31,
which commemorated the birth of Solidarity in 1980, December 13, that black day when martial law swept away their hopes
for change: these were the days when youths wearing thick
boots and carrying banners swarmed through the streets for a
few heady minutes before the police, armed with shields and

25

truncheons, descended.) Fatherland masses were a different kind of protest and provoked a different atmosphere. There was tension, but it was less anticipation of colliding with the police than the realization that one was taking part in a historical ritual.

Prayers on behalf of the nation had risen from altars in times of crisis since the middle of the nineteenth century. During the 1863 Polish uprising against tsarist rule, for which the rebel general Romauld Traugutt was executed, masses were regularly offered for the eventual deliverance of the country from its oppressors. A message from the royal court in Moscow to the provincial governors of Poland ordered the removal of all symbols of resistance and nationalism from the churches. During the five years of Nazi occupation, the masses went on with a self-imposed caution that kept them just inside the border of acceptability. The end of World War II left Poland once again a victim of its neighbors, this time a neighbor that had extracted the support of the Western allies for its land grab. The Soviet leader Joseph Stalin wanted a wide buffer strip between his nation and the first inch of German territory, crumpled by defeat though it was. The Nazis had chosen Poland as their main extermination grounds; Stalin selected the flat, humbled nation as a shield and set about hammering it to his specifications. The United States and Britain had agreed at the Yalta conference to rearrange Poland's borders to Stalin's liking; thus five million Poles who lived in the easternmost reaches of the country suddenly found themselves in a newly expanded Soviet Union. It was not forced migration, it was migration by fear. Despite its willingness to let Stalin have his way with Poland, the West kept an eye on the promised free elections of 1947. Their outcome was largely determined by the national referendum sponsored by the "democratic" bloc—the People's Party, the Socialists, the Peasants Party, and the Democratic Party. They asked citizens of the newly reshaped nation to answer three questions: Are you in favor of Poland's new borders? Are you in favor of agricultural reform? Are you in favor of a two-house legislature? It was understood that by approving the referendum, Poles were approving the democratic bloc as their leaders. For families just reunited after an experience of incalculable horror, for workers

unsure of how they would live, for farmers who feared that
Stalin would try to impose his mad idea of collectivized agri-
culture on the fields they had worked for generations, the distinctions between parties and men were haphazard. Who could
they believe? To whom could they turn for credible advice? For
a country that had once had more standing churches than any
other in Europe, almost all of them Roman Catholic, the answer
was clear. Many of Poland's bishops saw Stalin as a threat of
nearly equal magnitude to Hitler. It was important, the bishops
agreed, that Catholic voters knew their choices and knew how
God's earthly shepherds regarded those decisions. Their episco-
pal statement said in part:

> Catholics may not vote for candidates whose programs or
> methods of ruling are hostile to common sense, the national
> welfare, Christian morality, or Catholic faith. Catholics
> may vote only for those candidates and election platforms
> which do not contradict Catholic teachings and morality.
> Office or power can only be held by people of good moral
> character. Catholics may not belong to organizations or po-
> litical parties whose principles conflict with Christianity.

The bishops were fighting a losing cause and knew it. The
letter was read out from altars, at masses for the fatherland, its
message was heard, and then seven out of ten Poles went to
their voting places and said, three times, "Yes." (Years later
Jakub Berman, a Communist Party leader from that era, admitted that the results of the referendum were fixed to show more
support for the bloc than actually existed.)

On this spring evening in May 1984, Poland was again being
prepared for local council elections, although the results themselves were not important. June 17 had been designated as the
first election day since the declaration of martial law on December 13, 1981, and some fifteen thousand village, township, and
county positions would be filled according to the will of the
people. In most cases, of course, the people were offered a
choice of one. The ballot papers were designed so that voters
did not have to make any mark on them. The preordained win-
ners, who had the support of the Polish United Workers or
Communist Party, were listed first. Voters were told that if

they wished to elect the Party's choice, they need only collect their ballot paper after registering their name at the poll, cross the room, and drop the ballot into a red and blue metal drum. Anyone who wished to vote for someone else was required to announce that intention when registering, then go into a curtained booth to select alternative names further down the list, or to write them in by hand. A number of groups and individuals, some of whom sympathized with the government, had made the point that this system intimidated anyone who wished to vote for any but the approved choices. Their efforts were ignored. The fugitive underground leadership of Solidarity called for a boycott of the elections as the only way to undercut the regime's assertion that life in Poland had returned to normal. But many people feared that a boycott would be punished. Jobs and university admission for their children could be at stake; what should a patriotic Pole do?

About five thousand of them had come to St. Stanislaw Kostka to hear what Father Jerzy Popieluszko would tell them. No one doubted that he wanted the elections to flop spectacularly, both to deny legitimacy to the government and to prove to the outside world that Solidarity still commanded the hearts and loyalty of Poles.

The opening bell rang once, the organ struck its chords, those who had been able to squeeze into seats rose, the rest stood straighter. Father Jerzy had chosen as the opening hymn the Polish national anthem.

"Lord have mercy," the celebrant sang.

"Christ have mercy," the people answered. The Epistle and Gospel followed, and then Popieluszko mounted the pulpit to deliver his sermon. With characteristic shyness, he took from under his green vestment a folded sheet of paper and raised his eyes, saw the thousands looking back at him, and began to read:

"Catholics may not vote for candidates whose programs or methods of ruling are hostile to common sense, the national welfare, Christian morality, or Catholic faith," he said. His voice was as flat as he could keep it. He fought down the temptation to emphasize a word here, a word there.

Poles knew their history. By the end of Popieluszko's second sentence, his listeners knew from what document he was reading. The tittering rose, was shushed, came alive elsewhere in the church. "Poles may not belong to organizations or political parties whose principles conflict with Christianity," he concluded.

Without a word of explanation—was any needed?—he left the pulpit and began the next part of the mass: "I believe in God, the Father Almighty. . . . " There was no sermon, only the careful, unambiguous statement.

By midnight, the thousand or so people intimately involved in Poland's political tug-of-war knew about Popieluszko's gesture. Lech Walesa, the chairman of Solidarity, and the fugitive underground chieftain Bogdan Lis were delighted when they heard of Popieluszko's advice to voters. Although the authorities trumpeted victory with a turnout figure of some seventy-five percent, Solidarity later claimed that a third of Poland had boycotted the elections.

The priest's words had reached other ears, and the response was not one of amusement. Popieluszko knew his fatherland sermons were monitored by the secret police. He recorded regularly his own words to guard against an edited version of a sermon being used against him. The faithful at these masses became accustomed to seeing leather-jacketed toughs holding pocket-sized recorders near the amplifiers which carried the priest's voice, then hurrying away to make their reports.

Any priest could have recited from the bishops' 1947 decree, any priest could have delivered the words with more or less drama. Their effect at St. Stanislaw Kostka was largely due to the authority of Father Jerzy and the fact that his words drew nationwide attention. Only the week before, he and thousands of Polish priests had received a letter from the primate, Jozef Cardinal Glemp, which reminded them that they were ordained not to preach politics but the word of God. Even if Father Jerzy had read out Glemp's letter, the message would have carried from home to home, from workshop to foundry. The message itself was less important than its utterance by this man, this servant of God and Poland. That he possessed this influence over his countrymen says more about the man than all the family portraits, all the testimonies of courage, all the political utterances after his death.

Who was this priest?

From a distance, he looked an adolescent boy. Popieluszko was slender, had an acne-scarred face, with high cheekbones, large ears flanked by sideburns, eyes rounded rather than slanted, hinting of candor and honesty. His smile, not seen frequently, produced long vertical dimples on his face and crinkled his brown eyes. His chestnut hair was receding and his forehead was high. He was short—five feet seven inches—and walked with his shoulders hunched. His soft voice was one of his few artful devices; he spoke to hundreds of people as if they were all seated with him at a corner table. He spoke a spare, direct kind of Polish, a language which offers countless derivatives, diminutives, slang words, and euphemisms.

Flowery speech would not have been in keeping with his background. He carried a peasant simplicity from the Okopy farm where he was born in 1947 until thirty-seven years later, when he shouted a plaintive "Spare my life."

Children did not shout in the home of Wladyslaw and Marianna Kalinowska Popieluszko. "My children asked my permission before they did anything," said Marianna, "whether it was to go to a dance or to rosary circle." And she added, "And I didn't always say yes." Her air of authority contrasted with the informality all around: chickens wandering in and out of the kitchen, remnants of meals preserved on numerous plates, a chintz curtain across the front doorway. Marianna's determined leadership marked the family. Her husband came from a clan that had farmed the uncooperative Okopy soil for more than two hundred years. But there was no doubt who made the house function. During her bereavement for her son, she appeared wraithlike, with hollowed cheeks and shadowed eyes. That concealed her domineering presence at home. She was a woman who ordered rather than invited visitors into the house. "Go into the second room and sit down. I'll have my son bring you something to drink." This was her unpretentious welcome.

The first of her five children, Jazdia, died before her second birthday. Jazdia was delicate. Her mother recalled that she died on Christmas Eve, first kissing and hugging her parents and closing her eyes as a prayer was recited. Marianna claimed that Jazdia would have been the most intelligent of her children had she lived. Teresa, her second child, was thickset and with a flashing smile. Her brother Jozef, as firstborn son, knew from the time he could lead a cow to pasture that he was being prepared to take over the farm, after first putting in two or three decades as his father's apprentice. When the family sat down to dinner, the father would sometimes indicate that Jozef should serve the others; the symbolic act of distributing food grown by their own hands was not lost on the family.

Popieluszko was born in a street with no name. The family address is simply number 17. Okopy is so small that it has only one thoroughfare and house numbers speak for themselves. The nearest town is Suchowola, a dozen miles from the Soviet frontier. The local joke is that border guards need watch only for Russians trying to sneak into Poland; anyone attempting to enter Soviet territory illegally is immediately placed in a psychiatric hospital. The reality is that travelers in both directions are scrutinized closely. Dirt roads are rolled so that footprints can be spotted. Infrared sensors are triggered several times daily by the flight of birds. Russian soldiers who sometimes cross the border en route to Warsaw are cautioned to keep their car doors locked. They know they are not popular in a region that is otherwise considered most genial. Poles say that the further east one travels the friendlier the people. The proximity of such a traditional enemy pulls the frontier Poles together, fosters the good will and kindness of neighbors.

It was into this atmosphere that a traveling band of monks arrived in the spring of 1947 and announced that they would conduct a one-week mission at the Church of Sts. Peter and Paul in Suchowola. Marianna, pregnant for the fourth time, attended the mission every evening, listened to the prayers, and heard the monks' words of reassurance: these were terrible times, Poland had been betrayed, the end of the Nazi occupation signaled not a release from oppression but only a transfer to another sort. As she recited her rosary, an idea began to form. She promised God that one of her children would become a priest.

When her baby was born that September, Marianna wondered if he would live long enough to become anything. Weak at birth, he appeared in such imminent danger of dying that he was baptized just two days later. Marianna named him Alfons, after her brother. The child survived, but relatives could tell at a glance that this was no future farmer. Too small, too thin, and with a wracking cough, Alfons, who was to become Jerzy, also had double nipples, the "witches' teat." Taunting children called it the mark of the devil. Not surprisingly, the young boy grew up shy, introspective, with a preference for books and quiet corners over rowdy games. "He had some friends at school, but none particularly close," recalled Jozef. "He wasn't the most popular boy at school, but he got along with everyone."

Alfons Popieluszko read, but he also worked. His father was finding it harder than before to plant out his twenty-hectare farm and harvest the crops in time to sell them to the newly established state-purchasing agencies. With help from his wife and neighbors, he could bring in whatever harvest had survived his sometimes casual supervision during the summer. As Teresa, Jozef, Alfons, and one final son, Stanislaw, grew up, they too had to join in the weeding of rows of wheat, barley, potatoes, and corn. "Mostly," said Wladyslaw, "we grew weeds."

Farming families in Poland start their day early. Roosters were startled from slumber by the slamming of doors, the harnessing of horses to plows. Marianna Popieluszko rose between 3 and 4 AM and went to her kitchen stove in the corner of the back room, which was where her baby son slept. There she began, eight hours in advance, to prepare the meal her family would eat at noon, the main meal of the day. As she peeled potatoes, fried meat, stirred the thick soup, she hummed the hymns she heard in church each week. The house was filled with her imperfect singing. By four-thirty, her husband had turned the cows out to graze and was leading the one carthorse to work in the fields. Jozef, who left school before his twelfth birthday, worked full time with his father, learning the character of the land, knowing that violent thunderstorms would wash all the soil out of the sloping barley field. Teresa, who rose at about four-forty-five, was charged with bringing in four large buckets of water from the outdoor well for washing, cooking, and cleaning. Only after all this, when the sun was moving across the Soviet border, the young Alfons woke, rose, dressed, washed, greeted his mother, and asked her permission to leave the house. That was a request that Marianna never refused, despite her dominant manner. From the age of seven, Alfons was a regular altar boy at the 6:30 AM mass at Sts. Peter and Paul. Father Stefan Poczyk, the pastor, was just rising at about the same time, moving stiffly down the two flights of stairs of the rectory, past the common kitchen shared by four other priests, past a room full of desks cluttered with official church documents, death notices, mass cards, correspondence from the Bialystok Diocese, newspapers, letters from barely literate parishioners. As he walked down the stone path from the rectory to the street, to his right was a huge oak that flowered early and stayed in leaf well past the first frost. To his left was a vast field of trampled grass and earth that served as a makeshift car park. Through the gate of the iron fence topped with crosses, he moved across Bialystok Street—not only the roadway to the only major city in northeast Poland but the only proper street in Suchowola.

The church stood across the street. Made of gray stone and surrounded by a verdant lawn and well-kept iron fence, Sts. Peter and Paul looks like a church of tradition. Its two bell-towers rise above the tree tops and form a natural center for a town that otherwise seems to begin and end without reason.

While the priest was moving slowly through his house and across the street, young Popieluszko was completing a two-mile hike from his home to Suchowola. Entering the church by the back door, he would slip on the black cassock and white surplice that made him a vital and visible part of the Holy Mass.

Inclusion in that ritual is more significant in Poland than in any other country in Europe. To those who attend mass every Sunday, or even every day, the parish priest becomes a central figure of authority. For a boy already judged too physically limited to become a farmer in a part of the country where farming is the mainstay of the population, each mass must have confirmed this to young Popieluszko. As he knelt at the celebrant's side, as he held the patten during mass, as he heard a thousand sermons delivered and watched how the words affected the congregation, as he saw this part of Polish society which Communists could never destroy, the boy must have imagined himself in the role of the all-knowing, beneficent priest. And slowly he must have realized that there lay in that idealized profession a calling to which he would be suited, which would demand the one thing in which he was strongest—faith in God and the justice of his teachings.

It was not a straight path. The problems began with his name, Alfons. He had never known the uncle for whom he was named. Alfons Kalinowski died before his birth; the passing on of his unusual name was one of Marianna's unexpected gestures of sentiment. But he hated the name and persuaded the priests of Sts. Peter and Paul and his older brother to call him Alek. Finally, the name caught. By the time he entered primary school, he was Alek Popieluszko; teachers who did not know that this was merely an accommodation to the boy's sensitivity and assumed that Alek was a diminutive called him Alexander. He never complained.

He did not complain either when, shortly after he began school, a female doctor came from the Bialystok health ministry to vaccinate all the children of Suchowola against smallpox. Marianna remembered being assailed by the whelps of fearful children when she entered the building with Jozef. "They were all afraid of the doctor with the needle, and when one of them would be vaccinated and start to cry, it would start all the other ones crying out of fear." It was more, she recalled, like a menagerie of nervous caged animals than a place of education. She and Jozef waited at the back of the queue, and so she was able to see her other two children. Teresa let out a yelp of pain, but Alek watched steadily as the needle scratched his skin and said nothing. He pulled down his sleeve and walked away, not smiling, but neither did he betray pain. His mother wondered that day about her devout, bookish son.

She pondered deeper the next year, when Alek was nine. Chestnut trees dot the land of northeastern Poland, and the teacher at the primary school told each pupil to collect some chestnuts to be used for carving. The students were given sharp implements; some had knives, some scissors, some like Alek had to make do with a carpenter's nail. Not clever with his hands, Alek lost control of the nail as he was cutting a design on his chestnut and drove it into his palm with such force that it came out on the other side of his hand. For a time he sat silently. Then, when the blood began pumping out, he walked up to the teacher and showed her the wound. "She nearly fainted," Marianna recalled. "She took him to a nurse at the school and the nurse took him to a doctor, where the nail was removed." Alek never said a thing, except to thank the doctor for her efforts.

His mother only learned of the accident when a neighbor asked after her son. It was one of the few times Marianna was angry with her son. "When I threatened to hit him, he looked at me and said, 'Mother, if you want to beat me, I must have done something wrong. Go ahead.' " She did not, of course, but she rebuked him for being casual about his health.

The gulf between mother and son was one of intellect, not affection. By the age of thirteen, Alek had shown no interest at all in farming; his older brother, too, was having second thoughts about the life that had been planned for him since birth. The amount of land plowed each year declined, and the farm was increasingly used for grazing. There was a temptation to press Alek into staying on the farm. But his mother put an end to that when she saw her second son parading down the street of Suchowola in red cassock and white surplice in the annual Corpus Christi procession. "I always knew after that that he would be a priest," Marianna said.

The thin boy who imagined himself at the center of the altar was moving toward the realization of his fantasy.

Stalin was dead, but his political legacy would be felt for another decade. Purges were common at all levels of educational institutions throughout the Soviet Union and its Eastern European allies. The curriculum was supposed to shape the New Socialist Man. Top-level Communist Party decisions were to be accepted and applauded enthusiastically without reflection or analysis. But in the mid-1950s, no one could be bothered installing and institutionalizing those new schools in remote spots like Suchowola. It was quietly conceded that those unfortunates would have to eke out an education as best they could with minimal guidance from the Party. For a pious young altar boy, a rigid Communist education might have had one of two effects:

it could have brought him into early and ineradicable conflict with the system, or it could have won him over to its message, and quite possibly set him out on a much different mission of proselytism.

But Alek went instead to the less doctrinaire secondary school established just at the end of the war by Father Kazimierz Wilczewski in Suchowola. The school could hardly have been tailored more to the needs of a country boy who had already lived through a crucial transition in his nation's history but knew little of the rest of the world.

In the autumn of 1961, when he entered the school, the curriculum included a non-Marxist variant of Polish history, literature, and science. With one exception the teaching staff was made up of Roman Catholics who had lived through the Nazi occupation and saw a different period of domination descending on their country. Children came to the school not just from Suchowola and satellite villages like Okopy but from small towns closer to Bialystok, where they could have obtained a more modern education. Most country people, themselves instructed in Catholic schoolrooms with a crucifix on the wall, distrusted the idea of entrusting children to instructors whom they did not see in church each Sunday. For Marianna, already convinced that her son's future lay in the Church, there was no question of where he would complete his education.

There was doubt for a while if he would complete it at all. The one non-Catholic teacher at the school was not even Polish, but Byelorussian, and she taught mathematics. During Alek's second year at the school, Marianna received a summons from the teacher, who told her that it was well known her son attended Friday night rosary sessions at Sts. Peter and Paul Church. Perhaps Alek could instead attend school dances? Marianna demurred with something less than Christian good grace. The teacher shifted the grounds of attack, saying that if Alek's rosary nights continued, she could not guarantee that he would pass mathematics and would therefore be ineligible for a diploma.

This was too much. Marianna protested to the school and repeated the conversation. Alek passed mathematics. The teacher was dismissed at the end of the school year.

Had the teacher not engaged Marianna in ideological black-mail and merely failed Alek in her subject, no one would have been shocked. He was a mediocre student, favoring Polish liter-ature, the history of Poland, and Russian language courses, which were mandatory. Alek almost constantly carried with him a book, but it was not an academic text. Rather it was a re-ligious book: the life of a saint, church accounts of Poland's reli-gious development, a collection of sermons by the Primate of Poland, Stefan Cardinal Wyszynski, who for devout Catholics had already taken on larger-than-life proportions, treatises on Maximilian Kolbe, the Franciscan priest who had been interned in Auschwitz and offered to die in place of another prisoner. Kolbe's martyrdom was only one of thousands of individual acts of heroism by Poles during their country's occupation by the Nazis. But it symbolized for an adolescent the courage of his countrymen, their unreasonable willingness to die rather than concede control of their tortured land. Kolbe became for Alek Popieluszko the sort of symbol that Marshal Josef Pil-sudski was for other boys whose heroes were swords and scab-bards rather than soutanes and dog collars.

In the spring of 1964, Alek Popieluszko told—did not ask but told—his mother that he was going to Niepokalanow, the vil-lage near Warsaw where Kolbe had founded a friar's commu-nity. Marianna correctly understood her son's trip as a rite of manhood, a declaration of independence. She also saw in it the completion of her vow to offer one of her children to God's ser-vice. After seeing the friary, but before boarding the bus to re-turn to Okopy, Alek took a decisive step without his mother's counsel. He visited for the first time the seminary of St. John the Baptist in Warsaw and applied for admission to it in one year's time. His choice of vocation was a logical one. He re-turned to Okopy and in the spring of 1965 received news of his acceptance, along with about two hundred other young men to that summer's class of seminary studies at St. John the Baptist's in Warsaw. In choosing to leave home, Popieluszko was assert-ing his independence not only from his parents but from the one authority to which he had been subordinating himself for ten years: the parish priest of Sts. Peter and Paul. Father Po-czyk counseled his longest-serving altar boy to change his mind and enroll instead at Bialystok seminary, close to home, close to the reassuring presence of his childhood parish. The priest wanted Popieluszko to return and work in Suchowola.

But he was determined to go to Warsaw. On June 23, 1965, he and his mother walked the two miles to Suchowola. He carried two black cardboard suitcases. She carried a lunch she had prepared for him. Mother and son's farewell was a quick one. They had only a few minutes of waiting at the corner of Bialystok Road within the shadow of the church until the bus appeared. Alek kissed his mother and got on the bus without looking back. She had begun walking back to Okopy before the smoking vehicle was out of sight.

The first thing she saw when she entered the house where Alek had eaten, slept, prayed, and asked her permission for eighteen years was the framed picture of the Sacred Heart of Jesus in her kitchen. She knelt before it and said two prayers for her son: the first, that he would fulfill the vow she had made while he was in her womb; the second, that God would let no harm come to him.

3

•

New City, New Name

ON JUNE 24, 1965, Alfons Popieluszko began a career and lost a name. He made an unwelcome and mortifying discovery—in Warsaw Alfons was slang for a pimp. The new arrival from the cornfields of eastern Poland provided some of his fellow students with a chuckle as he was introduced to everybody. It was a long, long day, and there were more than two hundred people to meet.

The seminary of St. John the Baptist encapsulated the history of the Church in Poland. Built in the eighteenth century by the Carmelite religious order, it is a vast red brick warren of hallways, small and smaller sleeping cells, airless lecture rooms, dark chapels, reading rooms, and library. After the unsuccessful Polish uprising against the Russian tsar in 1863, the Carmelites were evicted for giving encouragement to the Polish rebels. Earlier, in the eighteenth century, after the partitioning of Poland by Russia, Prussia, and Austria, the building had been converted into a school, and afterwards a seminary. It operated as such virtually untouched by the Nazi occupation. After World War II, the seminary found itself the next-door neighbor to a building occupied by the government, the Council of Ministers. A high wall next to the main church separated them.

If he expected that by coming from Okopy to Warsaw he would be running from rural obscurity to urban glamour, Popieluszko received a tremendous shock. The Warsaw of 1965—fully twenty years after the end of the war—was only getting down to repairing the vast damage it suffered for being in the center of Europe. A few months before Popieluszko left his parents' house, which had no running water, construction was just beginning on a central hot water supply system for the capital, which had to draw on the output of three heating plants. Targowa Street, a nearly impassable pile of rubble when the Nazis left, was finally being recognized as in need of modernization. The completion of the hundred-thousandth apartment in a city of one million had just been celebrated.

Popieluszko, who by the end of his first day as a Warsaw student was already contemplating the demise of Alfons and was toying with the idea of telling fellow seminarians and teachers that his name was Jerzy, found that following the path of God was in no way a guarantee of escaping the housing crisis. He was lucky and was initially assigned a room in the new part of the seminary, half of which was taken up by a reference library that was the second largest in Warsaw. Being assigned the room did not mean it was his to arrange as he wished. First-year students were packed twenty to a room, with just enough space for their clothes and few personal belongings to fit under the narrow bed on which they slept. Some of the older students obtained the comparative luxury of rooms in which just two young men slept. But even they could not stake claim to that privilege for more than six months. At the beginning of each new term there were housing lotteries, and a student who had spent the previous six months in a room for two might suddenly be posed with the task of learning the names of nineteen new roommates. Coming from the loving bedlam of a small farm, young Popieluszko took the seminary's rooming arrangements in his stride. Besides, there were even greater surprises ahead. He had only the vaguest ideas of the curriculum at the seminary, and when he finally learned what he was expected to study, he was suitably pleased.

Andrzej Przekazinski, one of Popieluszko's closest friends and now the head of Warsaw's archdiocesan museum, knew what the course of studies would be like. A seminarian five years older than Popieluszko, he remembered how imposing the academic requirements for ordination first sounded.

The first two years are philosophical studies and the remaining four years are theological studies. Theology is divided into sections and a given section is taught to four different classes at the same time. In addition to general theological problems, there are specific issues, which have to be taught individually to each class. The history of theology is taught separately to each new class, and at the same time moral theology is further divided into sections like the theology of love. Every year, every student sits through these lectures. Then there were the classical languages. The basic ones, Latin, Greek, and Hebrew, are taught from the first through to the fifth year. And then each man has to select a foreign language: French, German, English, Italian, or Spanish.

It was a closed, self-sufficient world. But it was difficult to shelter completely from the chill political winds outside the seminary.

Wladyslaw Gomulka had taken power in October 1956 and had ushered Poland through its post-Stalinist thaw. For the first two years it seemed as if the Gomulka era would bring about lasting reform; he reassured the private farmers, censorship was eased, workers were given a greater say in running factories. It was to be a national, a Polish—as opposed to Soviet—road to socialism. But within a few years the hopes of the Poles were dashed. By the mid-1960s he had become increasingly autocratic. The Party leadership was losing credibility, and it began to cast about for scapegoats. The Roman Catholic Church, powerful and proud, was an obvious target: it would fit well into Soviet-style orthodoxy to persecute the most influential nongovernment institution behind the Iron Curtain. To cause rifts within the Church and, if only for a short time, to put the Pope's legions on the defensive—those were the aims of the Party. The logical place to start the campaign was in the cradle of the priesthood: the seminary of St. John the Baptist made its students as welcome as possible and tried to nourish them spiritually. But the novices were left in no doubt that in addition to learning how to preach the word of God they would have to fight for themselves in the temporal world of shortages and queues. There was no well-stocked refectory, no cosy coffee room where students could prop their heads on their books. Father Przekazinski added the necessary perspective: "The seminarians in Warsaw had only what they earned or gained themselves. After all, we were going through Gomulka's time of tough treatment of the Church—the years when the remnants of church land and properties were finally and completely confiscated. We had neither meat nor vegetables to eat, and to a large extent we lived on parcels sent us by our families. Nobody kept his provisions for himself. They were all shared."

And because Gomulka was attempting to tax the seminaries as places of business, its students, far from receiving stipends, were required to take outside jobs to contribute to the seminary's upkeep. They became odd job men in various parishes and rotated among themselves a series of low-paying, hardworking jobs as office cleaners, road sweepers, window cleaners. Przekazinski, as one of the senior students, was in charge of allocating these jobs, ensuring that each student not only did his fair share of work but also had sufficient time to concentrate on his studies. Seminarians had to pass courses in public elocution and as a corollary to that essential part of their job had to learn to write well and to the point. They were encouraged to compose their sermons on paper, in advance, and to practice delivering them to their colleagues. This was a habit that Popieluszko picked up early and used repeatedly, and to great effect, until the end of his life. The youths were also instructed in psychology (Why do people act unjustly? Why do two people regard the same act differently?) and philosophy (What is sin?). When Popieluszko entered the seminary at its head was Wladyslaw Miziolek, later a bishop in the Warsaw Curia. Miziolek had a radical view of what priests should know and ensured that their curriculum also included healthy doses of sociology, social sciences, non-Biblical literature, and, because they were to be priests in the Warsaw archdiocese, the history of Warsaw.

For the boy from Okopy, this mental workload together with

the necessary outside work for wages might have proved over-whelming. But Popieluszko was used to such double duties from childhood. Father (later Bishop) Zbigniew Kraszewski was one of Popieluszko's professors and a tutor during his first year. He viewed the pale young man as an indifferent student but one filled with enthusiasm about the nature of the things he was learning and would someday do. Kraszewski was struck by the teenager's clear-cut attitude of reverence for God and country. And in spite of his difficult life, the youth seemed to blossom in the rarefied seminary atmosphere. It was by no means a universal reaction. Przekazinski, the product of a Warsaw intellectual family, combined praise and wonder at Popieluszko's ability to flourish at St. John's. "I found the seminary a very closed institution. I felt bad there. I even considered ways of backing out of it. I believe that for a young man who had been in high school, has his own friends, can go to the cinema, to a cafe, can freely spend his time, the move to a seminary, which is a closed place, is always a shock. It is a new life, completely new—meals on time, bells ringing, getting up on time, etc. It is not a simple matter to find oneself in these organizational rigors."

Another son of a Warsaw intelligentsia family who attended St. John's was Stanislaw Malkowski, although it was not an easy matter for him to get there. Malkowski, whose fiery sermons warning of the evils of the "red dragon" and the sickness of Communism would unite him with Popieluszko twenty years later, at first could see little that he had in common with the boy from Okopy when they met in the seminary. "I knew that Popieluszko was not intellectually exceptional, and in fact I thought that he was very average intellectually, simple, straightforward, sincere, open, and friendly. This was no doubt a result of his peasant background. At that time the majority of seminarians were peasants. This situation made me feel a bit foreign at the seminary. Being of intelligentsia background I felt at the seminary as if I was at a boarding school. I felt as if I was being treated like a child."

But Popieluszko was living a life that few of his fellow residents of Okopy could ever have visualized. The same picture of him is drawn by everyone who met him during his first days in

Warsaw: uncultured and unspoiled, not very bright but bound-lessly enthusiastic, limited in his knowledge but sure of the things he knew.

Possibly no other decade in the last five hundred years was so fraught with change and experimentation for the Roman Cath-olic Church. The same year that Popieluszko decided to become a priest, Pope John XXIII convened the Second Vatican Coun-cil to plot the course of the Church for the rest of the century. A church with nearly two thousand years of history was being told it had lost touch with its people, that its priests were too remote from the lives and concerns of the flock they presumed to lead, and that the incense-laden rites of Catholicism must allow the fresh air of the postwar years to sweep through. This was not an easy message for a generation of Catholics (among them a Polish bishop named Karol Wojtyla) which clung to ro-saries and rituals, the weekly rebirth through water of the Asperges Me, the breast-beating penance of the Confiteor. They were used to the sedative effects of mass in largely in-comprehensible but familiar Latin, of seeing little more than the back of the celebrant as he carried on his private dialogue-in-code with Heaven, of flinging themselves to their knees to re-ceive a wafer of bread and being reminded, again in that foreign, comforting tongue, that they were ingesting the body of Christ. The aging Pope was insisting that there should be changes: mass should be celebrated in the language of the locality, the vernacular; altars and the priests bowing before them must turn around and face the people.

Poles were still adjusting unwillingly to terminology such as "five-year plan" and "people's council." Wholesale changes in their religion were hardly welcomed with enthusiasm. The Vat-ican reforms were also skeptically received by the clergy of Po-land, which sensed correctly that its previously safe position was about to change. It was not eager to see the foundations of church life being uprooted without reason. But one of the par-ticipants of the Council in Rome had been Stefan Cardinal Wyszynski, the Primate of Poland, whose personal endorse-ment of the Council's decisions was all that was needed to make them acceptable to Polish Catholics. Wyszynski oversaw the transition with the same mixture of authoritarianism and pastoral compassion that he brought to all aspects of his demanding job. That did not, however, mean that he intended to burden himself with the practical, time-consuming aspects of ecumenism. Who, for instance, would translate the practically endless rituals of Roman Catholicism from Latin into Polish? How should one priest address another? In Polish, in Latin, in some appropriate combination? Father Przekazinski recalled the time:

> It was only after we became students that Polish marked its presence at the seminary. That was difficult for both students and lecturers. For example, there were no appropriate textbooks in Polish. Latin prevailed in the life of the seminary. When Polish started to take over, we had a lot of work. We had to think of ways in which all the customary Latin greetings and titles normally used in our everyday contacts would be properly replaced by Polish equivalents, keeping in mind the fact that the religious nature of our communications had to be preserved. During our stay in the seminary, all prayers were translated into Polish. The whole transition was in fact carried out by us, the seminarists. We discussed our ideas and translations with our professors, and then waited for the approval of Cardinal Wyszynski. For us, the whole problem of change was essential. We were aware that if those texts were properly translated and formulated, they would help shape a certain type of (Catholic) personality: an open personality, with broad horizons and perspectives.

Popieluszko was eagerly involved in these changes. To him they would come to have a much larger meaning: they were equipping him for his special role in a Communist state. They were making Poland's major religion comprehensible to its people and, in so doing, giving them a source of comfort for times of oppression and a weapon, albeit a passive one, to use when the time for defiance was ripe.

The oppression came first, in double measure, in 1966, less than a full year after Popieluszko had entered St. John the Baptist. Popieluszko acclimatized quickly and promisingly to seminary life; he was enthusiastic about his work and was beginning to make the contacts in Warsaw that he could draw on for the rest of his life. One of the great advantages of being accepted into the Warsaw seminary was that it put a young man in a position to meet and talk with the top stratum of the Polish Church hierarchy. This included Cardinal Wyszynski, who was fond of visiting St. John's without advance notice and mingling with the young men. Wyszynski could be sour-tongued, abrupt, imperious, and unresponsive both to Communist Party leaders and to seminarians. His place in Polish history and in Polish hearts was already more than secure. He had endured interrogation and house arrest for two years and had emerged as a hardened combatant. The commemoration of the millenium of Christianity in Poland in 1966 was to him a justification of his efforts to keep the Church structurally and emotionally alive, to make it the strongest nongovernmental institution in Poland and thus a force with which the Party would have to negotiate. Just as the Communists hoped to eradicate its influence by controlling the education of the postwar generation, Wyszynski was determined to win that generation over, to make it the bedrock of opposition to Moscow's European empire. For this task he needed intelligent, devoted young priests, a whole crop of them who could shoulder the task of educating their parishioners.

St. John's was the key, and Wyszynski molded it to his aspirations. His visits to the seminary were not so much to inspect as to inspire and encourage. As a contemporary of Popieluszko recalled: "Wyszynski was concerned that we know history, and the history of Warsaw in particular, as we were after all going to work in his city. We had many contacts with him. He often gave lectures, but also he visited us informally, sat together with us, and made us see the problem of genuine communication with people."

The primate found in Popieluszko what others had seen: not a great mind, but a receptivity to new ideas and enthusiasm for trying them. He was one of the young men selected to greet and accompany the visiting bishops and priests who arrived in Warsaw that May for the enormous millenium celebration at St. John's Cathedral. The festivities had taken nine years to plan, under Wyszynski's direction, the culmination of his efforts to make his Church (and no one doubted that it was "his" Church) a beacon of freedom and light in the Communist world. It should have been his finest hour. Instead it turned into a near riot, a physical confrontation between believers and bully-boys dispatched by the regime to sully the special day.

The bishops walked to the cathedral from the primate's residence in Miodowa ("Honey") Street. After the mass, however, their return was cut off by a mob of youths shouting, "Down with Wyszynski," and looking drunk. The seminarians could hardly believe that the celebrations of the Polish Church could be marred by violence. The toughs blocking the streets claimed to be workers but had been ferried to Warsaw in special buses. Throughout the fracas, Wyszynski maintained his composure. Urging the bishops to take courage, he led them through a back entrance, along side streets to his residence. He waited for each bishop to pass through the gate, some so old they needed assistance to climb the stairs. Przekazinski and Popieluszko were among the seminarians who guided the bishops to safety. "We stayed another several hours to be able to come back safely home after the whole commotion died down," Przekazinski recalled. "The primate himself kept coming down to see us every half-hour to make sure everything was all right. And at the same time we knew he had so many more important things to take care of. I think they all spent the night in Miodowa Street, and I remember vaguely that they slept on mattresses on the floor. What struck us most about Wyszynski was his constraint, dignity, and composure."

For an idealistic teenage seminarian, it was a shock to see Church leaders humiliated that way. But Wyszynski's handling of the situation made him the winner in the test of wills. And Popieluszko saw in this the inspiration for his own style of coping with physical threats, hostile groups, bully-boys.

But he could not dwell on that memory exclusively, for he was at that time undergoing another rite of passage that would bring him into conflict with the state. Less than a year after arriving at St. John's, Popieluszko was drafted into the army. The Communist authorities, in no mood to grant any concessions to the Church, were certainly not about to exempt priests-in-training from military service. They hoped to use the army experience to dissuade seminarians from pursuing their vocation. At the same time, they were worried that the young religious men might sow the Word of God throughout the rest of the corps.

Various solutions had been attempted. The first had been to put a maximum of one seminarian in a barracks full of soldiers and wait for the greater numbers of nonreligious recruits to scorn, chide, and bully him into conformity. Instead, the seminarians were invariably popular in the barracks and were conducting catechism classes, leading rosary sessions, and reading from the Bible. The second attempt was the creation of "special" brigades for seminarians. Located in remote corners of the country, the special brigades were often little more than punishment cadres designed to shake them out of their beliefs. Ground down from the moment they arrived, like all army recruits, the seminarians had the added psychological baggage of representing an institution that was portrayed officially as an enemy of Poland's national interests. Reality was the baiting by the drill sergeant, and abuse heaped upon them. Some found it convenient to put on a mask of comradeship for two years.

By the time Popieluszko put on a military uniform for the first time the regime's handling of seminary recruits was noticeably harder. One priest drafted at about the same time as Popieluszko remembered being given a first-day indoctrination speech. "Remember, father," the sergeant said, with no attempt to disguise the threat, "your collar won't protect you here." It was in the army that Popieluszko first displayed the tenacity, physical courage, and patient sufferance that were to become his personal hallmarks in the 1980s.

Popieluszko was assigned to a special brigade in Bartoszyce, in northern Poland, where he saw a brutal face of Communism that he would oppose for the rest of his life. Popieluszko was not naturally drawn to conflicts, and in fact tried to avoid them. But he responded fiercely to instances of oppression, threats, and physical retribution. It was during his time in the army that a new Popieluszko showed his metal: a young man who found it almost impossible to compromise his beliefs under pressure from atheistic authority. Like many fervent Catholics, Popieluszko, since his first Holy Communion, wore a scapular medal which proclaimed his devotion to the Blessed Virgin Mary. The traditional promise behind the medallion is that by wearing it faithfully the bearer assures himself a plenary indulgence at the moment of death; that is, he is spared the rigors of purgatory. Early in his army career, a sergeant entered Popieluszko's barracks and spotted the chain around his neck.

"What's that damned thing around your neck?" The sergeant grabbed the chain and pulled Popieluszko toward him. Breathing heavily into his face, he saw the image of the Virgin.

"It is the Blessed Mother," Popieluszko explained quietly, "Mary, Queen of Poland."

"Don't give me that crap. Take it off now. Wearing jewelry in the army is forbidden."

"Sergeant, with all respect, this is not a pendant."

The sergeant was flushed. Other conscripts were watching the exchange with interest. If the sergeant let the conversation continue much longer, he would lose face. There was no scope for compromise on religious symbols. In one swift movement, the sergeant pushed Popieluszko back and wrenched at the chain. It stayed around his neck.

"Get out of here immediately, Popieluszko." Together the recruit and the sergeant marched out, Popieluszko in bare feet. He was ordered to stand in the rain until countermanded. The order did not come for several hours.

The next day he was given a similar choice: the medal or the rain.

A second incident revealed a certain playfulness in Popieluszko that had not been seen before. Having defied an order from a superior officer, Popieluszko was a marked man for the rest of his military career and must have known it.

Shortly after he returned from leave, he was bawled out for failing to be in bed by 11 PM. The sergeant favored rhetorical questions as a method of grilling and repeatedly asked: "Do you know what the rules say? Do you?" Popieluszko moved his lips as if trying to recall the wording. The sergeant came closer and demanded to know what the teenager was mouthing. He leaned still closer and heard: "Hail Mary full of grace . . . ." Popieluszko was reciting the rosary. The beads were hidden in his pocket.

Popieluszko summed up his tribulations in one sentence of a letter to a seminary instructor: "How sweet it is to suffer when you know that you suffer for Christ."

The sweetness of suffering would be Popieluszko's destiny. His physical health was showing signs of strain under the army's punishing routine. He returned to the seminary in 1968 even weaker than when he had first appeared three years earlier, physically drained but psychologically invigorated and more determined. He was, it seemed to his teachers, still marching—not to the cadence of drill instructors but to the tick of some inner clock, counting off each hour with concern that he might not make the most of it. He attacked his studies with enthusiasm stored up during his two years of army life. His one goal appeared to be the acquisition of his Roman collar as quickly as possible. And he showed in his performance in the classroom that, if not mentally inspired, he was spiritually so. He completed the two years of missed studies in half that time.

It was strength—physical stamina—that the army had taken from him. In 1971 Popieluszko experienced dizzy spells but resisted suggestions that he see a doctor. He deteriorated noticeably, and toward the end of his penultimate year in the seminary he was admitted reluctantly to the public hospital on Warsaw's Plocka Street and diagnosed as having hyperthyroidism. By the time his condition was discovered his thyroid gland was dangerously enlarged. Part of it was removed in an operation, and the young man was told—erroneously—that he need not worry about the dizziness recurring. The operation gave him the physical reserves he needed to pass his final examinations and the day of his ordination, May 28, 1972, dawned sunny and full of promise. It was a day of ambition realized, work rewarded. The thirty men gathered in the sacristy of St. John's Cathedral eyed each other, looking for some visible proof that they were different on this day from what they had been twenty-four hours earlier. Bogdan Liniewski, who would later become one of Popieluszko's best friends and a vocal Solidarity supporter, Jan Gorny, who would quietly become priest of a Warsaw parish, Tadeusz Gensic, at twenty-three the youngest graduate of the class of '72. Thirteen of Popieluszko's classmates were his elders, seven younger than he, nine born in the same year. Among them he looked unremarkable: a man with the bemused pride of all graduates, hands folded in concentration. Each of the thirty new priests felt the tradition of the thousand-year-old Polish Church as he walked in procession down the center aisle toward Cardinal Wyszynski. The primate knew their inadequacies, their ambitions, their potential. And he knew something else: their first assignments as soldiers of his army. Robed in red, crowned with a mitre, Wyszynski looked even more imposing than usual. He could look simultaneously to the future and the past, remembering his discussions with each of these men during their seminary training and at the same time projecting their careers. And it was of these challenges that he spoke. They were only beginning their work, he said. Unshaped vessels was a favorite expression of his, and he used it now to describe them. Roused, chastened, charged, the thirty men, prostrate throughout Wyszynski's sermon, rose one at a time as the primate stopped before them to administer the laying on of hands.

Alfons Popieluszko, son of a farmer whose family had planted crops in Okopy for two hundred years, was the twenty-second priest created that day in St. John's Cathedral. His father and mother watched from the back of the church. He took—as was his right—a new name that day: Jerzy Alexander Popieluszko. That night, at an ordination dinner attended by the new priests, their seminary teachers, and their parents, a classmate later recalled that Popieluszko was subdued and looked unwell. But on that night it was not his erratic health that was his concern. It was the news that he had been assigned to a parish not in Warsaw but in the industrial suburb of Zabki, ten miles east of the capital. Holy Trinity parish was set among car repair shops and a brick factory. It was hardly an ideal assignment, but it was, the classmate assured Popieluszko, only a first job. Popieluszko was not easily comforted. It seemed to him that he had been abandoned to the wastelands, shunted aside from the action and excitement of Warsaw. Popieluszko did not tell his parents where he would be working, and they did not ask. Marianna Popieluszko fought back tears in describing the first encounter with her son after his ordination.

"Mother," said Jerzy, wearing his new Roman collar. She looked at him and replied, "Congratulations, Father."

Holy Trinity in Zabki was under the strong guidance of Father Tadeusz Karolak, a man who felt his career would have benefited from a move into the capital. Karolak could be rough on new young Trinity men, especially if he thought they saw their time in Zabki as training for more important jobs. Karolak was the focus of a local legend in which he stood in the back of his church while a recently arrived priest delivered his Sunday sermon, then strode down the aisle, mounted the pulpit, and preached his own, improved version of it. Karolak's crusty realism was in violent contrast to Popieluszko's youthful idealism. There was little doubt that Karolak would endure, but would his young assistant?

It says something about his intense drive to succeed that Popieluszko was soon winning praise from his priest. And it was certainly typical that his was praise not for his inquiring mind or his brilliance in theological theory but for his hard work. In a village like Zabki, parishioners found it easy to believe that the Church and its personnel were there exclusively for their benefit. Women with drinking or philandering husbands came to the rectory to pour out their woes. Individuals seeking character references almost always turned to their clergyman. The sick, the dying, and the recovering felt they had earned a slice of the young priest's time. The children of the parish were also entrusted to this newest arrival for their religious education. Popieluszko, himself only eight years removed from his schooldays, could hardly have forgotten the impact of his religious training. He made a special effort to pass this on to the next generation. He conducted between twenty and thirty hours a week of catechism, in addition to celebrating daily masses, hearing confessions, preparing young couples for marriage, burying the dead, and comforting the bereaved. And these were merely "collar duties"—the highly visible tasks for which a priest's physical presence was needed. Within his first year, Popieluszko had also formed an early evening rosary session for teenagers. Word quickly spread that Popieluszko mixed prayer with no-nonsense discussions about life in Poland.

Not everything went so smoothly. Popieluszko and Karolak had clashes about the younger priest's cultivation of the Zabki artists' circle. He met and befriended painters, writers, actors, and sculptors who found the village atmosphere congenial and conducive to creativity. Popieluszko was less interested in admiring their crafts than in learning how they might be exploited for his own purposes. He tried, without success, to persuade Karolak to institute a weekly mass in which writers might read from their works, artists exhibit their latest canvases, musicians contribute their talents. But the priest said no, and the idea of "artist's masses" had to be postponed.

Novice priests, like army recruits, cannot establish roots. They are moved when and where they are needed and are seldom consulted in advance. In the summer of 1975 Popieluszko was told that he had been transferred to Mother of God, Queen of Poland in Anin, seven miles east of Warsaw. This was, in professional terms, a step neither up nor down. But psychologically it revealed a complex relationship between the state of Popieluszko's health and his attitude toward his superiors. Przekazinski, working at a parish in the Warsaw suburb of Piaseczno, concluded: "Jerzy was not an easy young priest to get along with. I observed in him something that can be called 'an escape into illness.' I think he couldn't find himself (at the Anin parish), and this must have hurt him very much, because he found contact there only with a narrow group of people. And this hurt him so much that he started to feel bad and began to undergo examinations and treatment."

In May 1978, he received a welcome transfer to the Infant Jesus parish. Not only did it mean that he would be leaving Anin, which he later told acquaintances he had come to dislike intensely, but the new church was in some ways a promotion. The Infant Jesus parish was within the city limits of Warsaw, a northern part known as Zoliborz.

The move into the city proper was significant, a coming of age for Popieluszko, who by now had six years of priesthood behind him. But if anything, his third parish assignment was less enjoyable than the second. From the first day of his new assignment Popieluszko gave hints that he was less than enamored with the priest, Father Jan Szymborski. After less than a year

and several conflicts with Szymborski, Popieluszko collapsed
on the altar while celebrating mass. Again he went into the hospital and was diagnosed as being anemic and having a generally
weak constitution. He obtained a rapid transfer from parish
work at Infant Jesus to a post in which it was deemed he would
be under less stress. This was the parish of St. Anna, which spe-
cialized in the needs of students in Warsaw regardless of their
hometown. Since St. Anna's was classified as an academic
church, Popieluszko was relieved of some of the parish work
which had been a source of conflict between him and his superiors at Anin and Infant Jesus. The job entailed also looking after
medical staff. Since his first hospitalization for the thyroid
gland operation Popieluszko had felt himself comfortable with
people in the medical profession, especially the nurses, order-
lies, and assistants who in Poland are collectively called the
"middle-level medical milieu." Popieluszko found that he was
entering into a realm of spiritual medicine. The priest he was
replacing warned him the position called for more effort than he
might think. "Only a small group of people attend the [church]
meetings and they are mostly older." When Popieluszko was
introduced to the medical corps, "the nurses looked at him with
incredulity, wondering how such a frail man could cope with
the work." But he overwhelmed them with his hope and his de-
cisiveness. In less than a month, Popieluszko transformed the
church into a gathering place for young people. The church was
filled.

Within the first weeks of 1979, Popieluszko was thrown into a
responsibility that would forever alter and shape his life: he was
selected to organize first aid preparations for the June visit of
Pope John Paul II, the former Karol Wojtyla of Krakow, the
Polish Pope, who was returning to his homeland less than a year
after his election.

Popieluszko was entrusted with the early negotiations with
the Ministry of Health, his first direct contact with the Polish
government. The matters to be discussed were straightforward
enough: how many first aid stations, how many nurses, ambu-
lances on standby, plans for emergency evacuation in case of
fire, of thunderstorm. There were also discussions between Popieluszko and representatives of the ministry on how to deal

with the contingency of an assassination attempt, or a terrorist attack. Popieluszko had visited America for the first time in 1978 and had seen the climate there. He knew that the possibility of insane violence existed. No one had said this role, clearly a mark of honor, of favor by Wyszynski, would be entirely pleasurable. This was the dark side of the papal visit.

There were no madmen, no terrorist attacks, no detonated bombs, no spray of gunfire. Popieluszko's gravest concern during the first papal visit was the lamentable tendency of devout, aged ladies to wilt under a hot sun. More importantly, he made contact with members of the papal entourage and impressed them as a priest intelligent enough to negotiate with officials. He insisted on some things, conceded others, and came away with the goals he had been sent out to achieve. For Popieluszko, no doubt, merely seeing the Pope's trip go without hitch in his own sphere of responsibility was satisfying. To the members of the Polish Pope's inner circle, it was an intriguing first look at a young, unknown priest. Popieluszko had made friends in the Vatican.

4
.
Whose Church
Is It
Anyway?

FOR A FEW HOURS in June 1979 Victory Square, the center of Warsaw, the hub of socialist Poland, had a cross. Not a makeshift, portable pilgrim's cross but a huge sturdy construction that towered over the square casting its shadow on the black marketeers and loose cafe girls of the nearby luxury hotels. It was a cross that had been built with the assistance of the authorities: a reminder for the Western film crews accompanying the Pope that although Poland was a Communist state, it was still a country of Catholics. Pope John Paul, standing under the cross, wove its symbolic appeal into his sermon to the hundreds of thousands of Poles squeezed into the historic square. The crowd understood and chanted an extraordinary demand: "We want God, we want God with us. God in our families, in our books, and in our schools, God in our government, we want God. . . . "

As the last of the young believers, giddy with faith, trickled out of the square and the sun sank behind the opera house, a convoy of grimy trucks churned through the trampled carnations and the limp yellow and white papal bunting, the debris of a pavement mass. Two priests, two friends, Father Andrzej Przekazinski and Father Jerzy Popieluszko, watched, first with curiosity, then with dismay, as platoons of men in battle fatigues jumped out of the vehicles and gathered around the platform. "We were stunned," recalled Przekazinski, who was in charge of organizing the Victory Square mass. "They had come to take away the cross. It was incredible. After all the chicanery and dithering of the authorities before the mass—suddenly changing seating plans for 'security reasons'—they were showing themselves to be super-efficient at taking apart the Christian symbol." By the next day, Victory Square was back to normal. Staff cars came and went outside the military headquarters on the east side of the square, soldiers goosestepped in routine guard duty outside the Tomb of the Unknown Soldier, and at the hundred-dollar-a-night Hotel Victoria, overlooking the bald space where the cross had once stood, the girls were back, shimmering in lurex, trawling for the papal press entourage.

The operation was characteristic of Party leader Edward Gierek, demonstrating an iron law of pragmatic Communism: that which disappears overnight never existed. The first response to the Vatican's proposals for a visit had been to put up tripwires. But in the end the Gierek leadership realized that to refuse the Pope access to his homeland would be more damaging than a carefully controlled tour. The authorities were beginning to understand that Poland was on the verge of economic collapse. Western governments had to be kept sweet, persuaded that their loans and credits were generating a more open style of Communist rule, that detente was worth the dollars. Gierek sold the idea to a skeptical Moscow that was running out of patience with the Silesian miner in his kipper ties. As Poland's debts grew deeper, the Kremlin became increasingly alarmed. How much leverage was Gierek giving to the West? What if the papal visit backfired and, rather then notching up public relations points, sparked an anti-Communist crusade?

The Pope came to Poland not in May as originally planned but in the summer of 1979, a furiously hot June that brought millions of young Poles on to the streets and dusty lanes of rural Poland, plucking guitars, singing religious anthems, and sleeping under hedgerows as they made their way to Krakow, to the shrine of the Black Madonna icon at Czestechowa, and to Auschwitz. In a Communist state, the movement of so many people, openly stating their faith in Christ, planted the seeds of a social revolution. The Poles frequently describe the first papal trip to Poland as a gift from God to a tired nation. For many the teachings of the Pope took second place to a kind of exalted hero-worship, a personality cult. Photographs of the Pope blossomed on windowsills and, unlike the Victory Square cross, did not disappear. The Pope was not just a Pole who had made good, but a good Pole. His life showed that it was possible, even imperative, to live with honesty and dignity in a country that was being governed dishonestly and whose atheistic ideology was destroying the dignity of belief. The Pope had given the Poles a sense of political cohesion. Acting together, they realized their faith could move mountains or, at the very least, governments.

For Father Popieluszko and his generation, the Pope's trip brought a more specific message, smuggled between the lines of the pontiff's homilies and in his personal meetings with bishops. The Pope was telling the priesthood that they could be the catalysts of this social revolution. The Pope had spoken diplomatically but also with candor of the need for governments to respect civil rights, of the dignity of work and of the need to organize work in such a way that it could bring satisfaction to workers, of the possibilities offered by the independence and strength of the Catholic faith. The revolution begun by the Pope was a revolution of the heart. He gave Poles courage, the vocabulary of change.

That was the main effect on the Popieluszko generation of priests, a generation who had swabbed the wounds of fellow students beaten by police during the riots of 1968 and stumbled into a political awareness during the worker unrest of December 1970, when Party leader Wladyslaw Gomulka, deposed soon afterward by Gierek, had ordered security forces to fire on demonstrators. This generation was only in its late twenties at the time of the Pope's first visit, but it was already a radicalized group. Outside the clergy, it included scores of intellectuals, hundreds of workers who were to be the leaders, advisers, and spiritual guides of Solidarity.

Inside the clergy the most decisive change had come with the Second Vatican Council. Priests like Popieluszko, who were shaped by the council's message that the Church must be closer to the people, had developed a social commitment to the needs of Polish workers so equally they had no trouble identifying with the intellectuals calling for change in the system.

The Pope's 1979 visit gave meaning and purpose to the budding generation of activist priests. For Popieluszko, the Holy Father had made it plain: Those in government had certain inescapable moral responsibilities to the governed. The basic expectations for a freer life, for uncensored opinion, for a reasonable standard of living, had to be met by any government with pretensions to legitimacy. Citizens also bore an important responsibility, to speak the truth, and to live principled lives. Father Popieluszko read, listened, and tried to understand how the Pole's natural bent for romantic struggle could gain a realistic dimension from the teachings of the Polish Pope.

Captain Grzegorz Piotrowski also read, also listened. He was a young secret agent whose lazy mouth and casual shoulder shrugs disguised a competitive nature and sharp political instincts. He had grown up in an atheist household, which, even in the Communist state of Poland, was an oddity. The other children at his grammar school in Lodz, Poland's second largest city, had dutifully gone through the motions of entering the Church. To most of them, being Catholic meant little more than a new suit of clothes for First Communion and jumping to their feet when a priest or nun entered the room. Young Piotrowski was not interested in the rites and rhythms of an institution from which his family had long since departed. Years later, a lawyer would point at Piotrowski and exclaim: "How little this man understands about the essential nature of the Church."

It was true. Grzegorz was not a dullard, according to those who knew him in his youth. Nor was he wild or misbehaving. Once, he was lured by some shouted taunts into a preteen schoolyard scuffle. The memory remained with him through his adult life, because it was so out of character for him to engage in violence or destruction. He was popular with a small clique of boys from the better families of Lodz. They were youths who, in the words of one of them, "took ourselves rather seriously." They felt they had responsibilities to their families.

Piotrowski excelled at mathematics. Its cool formulae, used

properly, yielded answers. It provided the comfort of bedrock, in deep contrast to the Church's mysterious hints of eventual judgment, of salvation or damnation. Years later, Piotrowski would tell a courtroom: "I am a student of logic. And I know that in a series all components have to be true, if the final conclusion is also to be true."

After high school, he entered the University of Lodz, majoring in mathematics. It was more a duty than a challenge. Money was always a problem, and in his last year Grzegorz found it necessary to work part time. And faced with that reality, he reached the first major watershed of his life. His decision foreshadowed others he would make.

Piotrowski's father, Wladyslaw, was a secret police agent in Lodz. His mother, Irina, also worked at the local Interior Ministry, as a secretary. Under such circumstances, it was impossible to separate completely home and professional lives. The parents had schooled themselves not to gossip about office matters at the dinner table, but Grzegorz, by the time he was a young man, had a good idea of how the country's police system worked.

It was in that year, 1968, when he was in need of employment, that his father one night began a rambling, ponderous monologue that ended with the possibility of putting in several hours a week as a filing clerk at the ministry. The suggestion was not an off-handed one. The elder Piotrowski had first submitted his son's name to a superior, along with his school records. It seemed like a sure thing: the unblemished son of two police employees, no Church connections. Word came back: young Grzegorz should stop by.

The son hesitated. He knew that if he took the job he was making a moral commitment from which there was no turning back. In 1968, students across Poland were staging demonstrations against government efforts to control the subjects they studied and the appointment of professors. Grzegorz of course had taken no part in the protests. That was enough of an indication of where his loyalties lay. Did he actually want to help compile police dossiers of those who did? There was a period of inner struggle, and then he made his decision to take his place in the family dynasty.

He graduated from university the next year and, because he was already listed as an Interior Ministry employee, served an abbreviated hitch of one year in the army. There was no trauma, no assault on Piotrowski's conscience, no jagged clash with authorities. Unlike Popieluszko, the young man from Lodz had already learned how to conform, even when he disagreed with others. He knew how to dissemble, how to emerge a survivor. By the time he was twenty, he had the equivalent of a bachelor's degree in mathematics, certification as a teacher, and an army rank of lieutenant, junior grade.

He tried one more time to loose himself from the tugging gravity of his heritage. Instead of returning directly to the ministry, he took a job as a mathematics teacher at a local college specializing in economics. But his horizons had been broadened by the work at his father's office and the year of army life. The world of academics was underpaid and seemed to him a refuge for dead-enders. His military service would allow him to rejoin the Interior Ministry at an equivalent rank. The pay was better. And it seemed, somehow, fitting, to be carrying on the tradition into which he had been born.

The election of Cardinal Wojtyla to the Throne of St. Peter was for Piotrowski and his colleagues in the secret police a source of great consternation. The question repeatedly asked in the Polish Interior Ministry was how far and how quickly the Pope would try to interfere in Polish affairs. How to ensure that the Vatican would not try to build a bridge to dissident groups? Since 1976, when riots protesting price rises were brutally suppressed by the police, opposition groups had begun to flower. There was the Committee for Workers' Defense (KOR), which later helped steer Solidarity. The Flying University offered clandestine lectures giving the non-Communist view of Polish history, economics, and literature. A harvest of dissident intellectual journals appeared, including the influential *Zapis*, a large circulation underground paper called *Robotnik* (Worker) and an illegal publishing house, Nowa, which laid the foundations of a true alternative culture. Secret policemen had much to occupy them as the Gierek era staggered toward collapse.

The danger was that the Church, enthused by the election of

a Polish Pope and perhaps guided by him, would spread its wings to protect the dissidents. Even the socialist dissidents were overcoming their prejudices about the Church. A leading dissident, Adam Michnik, although an atheist, praised the Catholic clergy for standing up for human rights throughout the twists and turns of postwar history. And the founding statutes of every new opposition group contained a commitment to help those repressed for their beliefs.

Were priests about to become more militant? What kind of social malaise would enter the body socialist? The first reaction of the secret police was to expand its Church monitoring arm, known simply as Department Four. No longer a poor cousin of the anti-opposition department, it received funds, a larger staff, and the prestige that comes with having a general as head of department. Throughout the 1970s, the budget of the Interior Ministry had ballooned. By the time of the Pope's first visit, official state allocations to the ministry—and therefore to the police—were larger than the combined budgets of the Health, Education and Culture ministries. There was plenty of money available for growth, and the young Piotrowski found his career in the Church Monitoring Department. For a while, the department was happy enough to draw up memoranda for the interior minister and the Council for Religious Affairs, which technically handles the day-to-day running of Church-state relations. The secret police prepared profiles of the Polish staff selected by the new Pope. Secret police agents in Krakow were instructed to keep a close watch on the journalists of the Catholic weekly *Tygodnik Powszechny*, which was known to have close links with the pontiff.

Piotrowski, who in 1979 was still working in Lodz, became involved in the planning of the papal trip. That meant checking for bombs, trying to foil assassination plots, and vetting the helicopter pilots who ferried the Pope around Poland. It also required regular contacts with Church officials, with the Vatican security men, with BOR, the Polish elite bodyguard service. There were also consultations with the KGB, the Soviet secret police, and with other departments of the Polish police to coordinate antidissident operations. Hostile priests had to be trailed and tapped. For a young officer, it was an extraordinary experience. He found himself plunged into the very heart of Church–state relations, seeing reports of ministerial conversations, reading intimate details of the private lives of clerics, and sometimes reporting personally to the head of the SB, as the Polish secret police is known. Piotrowski's zeal caught the eye of a deputy interior minister, Miroslaw Milewski. The word on Piotrowski was that he was impatient of bureaucracy, worked best alone or in small units where the hierarchy of command was blurred.

The Gierek leadership, self-deluding to the last, believed that the Pope's visit had not damaged its ideological credibility. But Moscow was far from happy with the papal expedition, which had received blanket coverage in the West, in contrast to the Soviet bloc. Some Western analysts believe that the Soviet Politburo under Leonid Brezhnev decided that summer to distance itself from Gierek, to encourage his rivals within the hierarchy. For the Polish secret police, which picked up the signals of discontent, it was a time of political opportunity. If Gierek was on the way out, then the possible successors could include Mieczyslaw Moczar, a hardline Politburo member with links to the security apparatus, or his protégé, Miroslaw Milewski.

Piotrowski's acquaintances insist that the young agent did not take part in the political scheming. The papal trip convinced him that there was something rotten at the core of Polish socialism. Piotrowski kept quiet, tending his career conscientiously, concentrating on his young daughter and trying, with occasional outings, to make up to his wife for the evenings on duty that had preceded the Pope's trip. For Piotrowski it was time of waiting rather than the sharpening of knives.

To the secret police, Popieluszko had not yet become a threat. After the Pope's visit he started to feel weak and dizzy, and though he enjoyed his work with nurses and medical students at St. Anna's, he found that the work was sapping him. He wanted time to collect his thoughts about the papal trip. Instead, life was a race with physical exhaustion. The normal routine labor of a Polish priest, arduous but tolerable for his healthier contemporaries, brought Popieluszko to the brink of collapse. His doctor, Barbara Jarmuszynska, diagnosed Addison's disease, a strain of anemia that kills red blood cells. She injected Popieluszko regularly with vitamin B12 and put him on a strict non-fat diet, but the fundamental problem was stress. "Sometimes," she said, "we had to put him into hospital for his own good, to protect him from his own lifestyle, and to limit his visiting hours. It was never easy. We had to fight to keep him in."

For the sake of his health the Warsaw curia decided to move Popieluszko to St. Stanislaw Kostka in Warsaw's northern district of Zoliborz. Popieluszko knew Zoliborz from his time at the Infant Jesus parish, and his job was undemanding, a post normally given to a priest on the brink of retirement. It proved an inspired choice. It was May 1980, only months away from the Solidarity explosion, and the parish seemed like a melting pot of Polish society. At the Sunday masses the workers, squeezed into blue synthetic suits, would travel the eight bus stops from the highrise buildings near the Huta Warszawa steelworks to hear the flush-faced, irascible priest Teofil Bogucki. At the same time, many intellectuals living in the more comfortable tree-lined streets of Zoliborz would also make their way to the Sunday services. Under the influence of the Pope's trip, many filmmakers, writers, journalists were moving closer to the Catholic faith, and St. Stanislaw Kostka was benefiting. When Popieluszko arrived in Zoliborz he brought with him the medical workers and students who had been his closest friends in St. Anna's. Actors who had known Popieluszko in Anin started to make Kostka their church. St. Stanislaw Kostka, with its twin spires, its white-washed, well-scrubbed look, was once before World War II an important parish attracting widespread attention with its own magazine and masses for the fatherland. After the war, the traditions lapsed, the parish boundaries receded, but within months of his arrival Popieluszko was making St. Stanislaw Kostka into a meeting point for social groups, fusing workers and intellectuals in a way that presaged Solidarity.

The months after the Pope's visit were a form of gestation. On television screens and in newspapers, Poland was ticking over, trumpeting meaningless successes. To steal from G. K.

Chesterton, the crisis was so big that it had become invisible. Popieluszko had applied for a passport to visit his aunt in Pittsburgh again that summer, and within a few weeks of arriving at St. Stanislaw Kostka, he was told that he could go abroad. He was apologetic to Bogucki and his parishioners, but his summer plans had been laid well in advance.

The mood in Poland when he left was somber. The government, straining under economic pressure, decided to push up meat prices and cut subsidies on food production. For fear of the prospect of street protests, it was decided to announce the rises by stealth rather than with candor, in a quiet, embarrassed communiqué at the beginning of July, a time when schools and universities were breaking up and energies were concentrated in queuing for holiday tickets.

Nobody was fooled. The Huta Warszawa steel plant and the Ursus tractor factory in Warsaw immediately stopped work and only started the machines again when their managers had guaranteed substantial wage increases. Throughout Poland factories followed suit, and the authorities responded with the political equivalent of fire extinguishers: extra meat supplies and the promise of better wages. There was no money to honor the promises, but the government thought that it had time on its side. Then, in the middle of July, railway workers in Lublin blocked the main rail artery to the Soviet Union, responding to rumors that meat was being shipped to Moscow for the Olympic Games. The first Russian invasion scare began. The giant eastern neighbor was restless.

The Church leadership took the reports seriously. The primate, Cardinal Wyszynski, had a natural sympathy with the strikers, a natural skepticism about Gierek and his ministers. But to declare open support for the strikers would thrust the Church into the political crossfire and probably aggravate the crisis to the point that Gierek would again feel the need to use violence against workers. Church advisers were already channeling information from one end of the country to another, urging caution and compromise.

Cardinal Wyszynski's approach was finely balanced, taking into account the historic mission of the Church in Poland and his own experience with Communist governments. Poles knew that the temporary silence of the primate was not a sign of indifference but rather reflected confidence that the Church would act in their ultimate interest.

Poland has always been easier to swallow than to digest. In the nineteenth century, Poland ceased to exist as a state; it was, in effect, a stateless nation divided between the three conservative pillars of the Holy Alliance: Russia, Austria, and Prussia. But though it disappeared from the map of Europe, Poland still considered itself a nation, feeding on a romantic patriotism. During this and other periods of struggle—the Nazi occupation, for example—it was the Catholic Church that maintained ideals and shaped dreams. It was in church that one heard of brave Poles who had defied kings and won. The Christian faith had been rooted in Polish culture since 966 AD and had outlived leaders, hereditary and elected, military governors, and the Gestapo.

The thousand-year-old Church was not intimidated by the forty-year-old Communist system. But, in August 1980, neither was it going to rush into the embrace of a week-old strikers' organization in Gdansk that called itself Solidarity.

The strikers had twenty-one demands. The Church was pleased that the shopping list included a legal right to have holy mass broadcast on state radio every Sunday. The infant trade union was in the words of one of the strikers "making eyes" at the Church, but it was more than a political flirtation. The making of common cause with the Church was both a matter of elementary self-defense and the genuine wish of the workers. Formally the union declared that it "identified itself with no ideology and no religion . . . it is not politically related to the Church nor does it consider the Catholic social doctrine to be its program." But in practice the primate's senior lay adviser started to attend sessions of the union's national leadership.

Poland was already a country of shrines. Every village, every few miles of roadside had its stone, flower-bedecked tribute to the Virgin Mary. Now, as a result of the Solidarity movement, no provincial governor dared to refuse a building permit for a new church.

Before he became Pope John Paul II, Karol Wojtyla wrote a

poem, much admired and quoted by Popieluszko, who other-
wise had very little time for literature. It was entitled "The Car
Factory Worker" and asked the question: "What makes you
think that man can tip the balance on the scales of the world?"
To Popieluszko's generation, Solidarity supplied the answer.
Man can alter the shape of the world if he is spiritually guided.
And that was an ideal worth fighting for.

5
·
Solidarity

IN AUGUST 1980, different government ministers were dispatched to the Lenin yards to negotiate with leaders of the upstart union. Each met a brick wall of resistance from the angry, buoyant Solidarity leadership. The union was being guided by Lech Walesa, an electrician who had been fired from the shipyard for persistently campaigning for workers' rights. Walesa's reinstatement had been one of the initial demands of the strikers, who were inspired by his courage and enjoyed his earthy populism. Walesa could afford to take a tough stand against a government whose credibility was crumbling by the day. The ministers who faced him across a table threatened, promised, implored, and lied.

By August 24, the eleventh day of the strike, Gierek, who had been on a summer holiday in the Crimea, returned home to take personal charge of the crisis. His personal broadcast to the nation was the usual recipe of sympathy with the underprivileged, an appeal to patriotism, a promise of change, and a hint of repression. He began to find scapegoats. Out went the prime minister, Edward Babiuch, the old trade union chief, Jan Szydlak, and the propaganda controller, Jerzy Lukaszewicz. In came hardliners like Stefan Olszowski and Tadeusz Grabski, both of them in favor of the Soviet Union's tough line and critics of Gierek's free-spending economic policies. But this attempt to broaden his Party support did little to quash the rumors of Russian troop movements. Moscow had decided that the Gierek leadership had given away too much too quickly. Instead of buying social calm and then picking off the troublemakers one by one, the government appeared to be cowering before workers inspired by anti-Soviet advisers and backed by the Catholic Church. That backing became manifest on August 25. Together with the primate, Poland's bishops drafted a statement that at last declared their sympathies. The inalienable rights of the nation, said the communiqué, should be obvious to all. These included the right to truth, the right to worship, the right to bread and a reasonable standard of living, the right to private property, in farming, the right to work with dignity, the right to a fair wage, and the right to unions. That was as close as the Church could come to full support of the principles underpinning Solidarity and the strikers' demands. The following day, Cardinal Wyszynski met Stanislaw Kania, the podgy Politburo man in charge of both internal security matters and relations with the Church. Kania talked of the dangers if the workers became overexcited, of the need to preserve order in the country, and of the useful contribution that the Church could make in soothing the Poles.

For Father Popieluszko, the time of being a mesmerized spectator passed on August 31. Throughout Poland, factories were staging their own occupation strikes to give muscle to the Gdansk shipyard negotiators. The most important sympathy strike was in the Silesian coal mines, but Warsaw too was making its mark with a protest at the very heart of socialist heavy industry—the Warsaw steelworks, known as Huta Warszawa.

Father Popieluszko had returned from his holiday in the United States on July 30. He had spent most of the holiday with his aunt in Pittsburgh, and though it was a good time—a time of physical recovery and frank, open fascination with American fast food and hi tech—he was nagged by the lack of news from Poland. Something important was happening, and it irked him to be so far from his new parish. There was a grave risk that

Gierek would call out the troops or the riot police and start to break up strikes with force. On his return, Popieluszko saw the situation differently, perhaps because he was enthused still from his American visit. Much had changed in Poland since December 1970, when Baltic coast workers were shot down. "Perhaps," he told a friend, "we should look at what is possible, how far the possibilities can be stretched, rather than at the impossible."

As the strikes gathered pace and the Gierek leadership began to buckle, so Popieluszko became more and more certain that Poland was on the brink of radical changes, not just another round of musical chairs in the Politburo. From the beginning of Solidarity, Popieluszko exhibited none of the caution of Cardinal Wyszynski, none of the calculated distance of the Church elders. He acted, by most accounts, like a man in love. "I believe," said Father Przekazinski, "that Solidarity helped Jerzy find those people who made him feel needed, who accepted him and his ideas, and who became his greatest friends. Even today we can see how those people loved him. It was a genuine friendship and love for him. He and they were attracted to each other. Jerzy was not just a passive member of Solidarity, he was one of the spiritual founders of the movement."

It was at the striking steelworks in Warsaw that Father Popieluszko seized his chance to take a active role in Solidarity's struggle. By the third day of the strike the workers were tired. There were some ten thousand on the site of the sprawling plant, and they had been catnapping in their departments in sleeping bags next to the foundries. The strike committee had decided there was a risk of "provocation"—the possibility, for example, of a secret policeman creeping in, sabotaging machinery, and then using this as an excuse for bringing in the specially trained riot police, the ZOMO.

The foundry men missed their wives. They were nervous about the next day, a Sunday, and the workers wanted to hear mass. Two weeks before, Father Henryk Jankowski had celebrated mass with the shipyard workers in Gdansk and had strengthened their resolve just as they seemed about to waver. The strikers in Warsaw thought an appearance by a local priest might similarly restore their spirits. A dozen foundrymen came to the office of the strike committee that Sunday morning and asked the main organizer, a gaunt, energetic man named Karol Szadurski, whether they could leave the plant in search of a priest. He agreed. That decision was a turning point. It would be the first time that a priest would enter the territory of the steelworks. In all Communist countries, heavy industry is the bastion of socialism. Most of the steelworks, the shipyards, the truck factories, the smelters, and the foundries were built and developed during the postwar Stalinist years, put together swiftly and often at great sacrifice. The political representatives of the works are often among the most dogmatic of Marxists, opposed to decentralizing reforms that would challenge their power base. In Polish, hardline Communists are called "concretes" not only because of the reputed thickness of their skulls but also because their authority is all too often bedded in the foundations of one plant or another. For a priest to be admitted to terrain consecrated by the blood and tears of the Stalinist era was unthinkable before that August.

The workers split into two groups. One scoured the neighborhood for churches with likely priests. The second made its way to the primate's palace in Miodowa Street to ask Cardinal Wyszynski to assign them a priest. "In the parishes nearest to the Huta," Szadurski recalled, "the priests refused to come. A strike was something very uncommon and they were scared. But after working their way through the neighboring churches, they arrived at Kostka, and there they met Father Jerzy." Meanwhile the second group had passed its message to the primate, who instructed his secretary to find a suitable priest. The secretary's nominee was Popieluszko. And so it was that both the workers and the Church chose Popieluszko to be Solidarity's priest.

Popieluszko recalled his arrival at the foundry.

I was quaking. The situation was absolutely new. What would I discover there? How would the workers receive me? Would there be a place appropriate for celebrating mass? Who would do the readings and who would sing the hymns? All those questions which today sound naive, then troubled my heart. And then, as I approached the gate, I was astonished. The crowds smiling and crying and clapping. At first I thought there was somebody important right behind me. But they were clapping for me—the first priest in the history of this plant to enter through the main gate. But it seemed to me that this applause was for the Church, which has been knocking at the gates of industrial plants over the past thirty years.

It was to be a memorable mass. The main courtyard just inside the gates was converted into an open air church. An impromptu altar was erected together with a wooden cross, which was to stay long after the mass was over. From the spikes of the fence hung safety helmets. Bundles of flowers and large pictures of the Pope, ripped out of magazines, were glued to the railings. Only a few hundred of the workers could attend that first mass—most had to stand guard in the departments—but Szadurski recalled how the mood of the strike changed. "Their spirits were lifted, they were very cheerful, their faces alight, they had overcome their fear." The makeshift church was in that strip of factory land that separates the special sentry hut for the factory security guards from the approach road that leads into the heart of the plant. Popieluszko knelt in one corner, and the workers stood in a large semi-circle facing him. One by one they knelt next to him on the jagged asphalt to deliver their confession. Then the news came from Gdansk: the government had given in to the demands of the strikers. A Communist leadership had agreed to the establishment of a free, independent trade union. To the men in the Warsaw steelworks, the victory seemed to belong as much to the shy young priest as to Lech Walesa.

The chimneys of Huta Warszawa can be seen two miles away, spewing out tufts of smoke the color of nicotine. The drive there transects the northern fringe of Warsaw, a prematurely old and flaking urban wasteland of high-rise apartments, rusty cars, and littered playgrounds. Where the tram tracks end, the Huta begins. On the right side of the gate, half in, half out of the factory, there is the main administrative block, sheltering the managers, the head of the factory guards, the Party committee, and the SB industrial security agents. The workers, as they stream out of the 2 PM shift change, hardly cast a glance at the building.

The block, with its bosses and its agents, is not popular with workers. Once among the elite of Polish industrial facilities, the Huta, and indeed the whole steel sector, had lost its foothold. By the time of the 1980 strikes, the Huta's sheen had disappeared and the quality of its managers had dropped accordingly. Orders came from the ministry: productivity had to be increased. But there were no funds for new machines and few spare parts. Instead, more stress was piled on the workforce. Like their brothers in Gdansk, by the summer of 1980 the workers had been stretched to breaking point.

That was the plant which welcomed Father Popieluszko and gave him his political education. When he arrived to say the first mass at Huta, he already knew something of the workers' problems. Through the confessional, through less formal but even more candid encounters in the cramped room which served as his study, a picture emerged of a fragmented, demoralized community. Wives complained that arbitrarily imposed shifts were destroying their marriages: What should they do? Husbands thought they had discovered police informers in their department: What should they do? Daughters were pregnant, the factory doctor had recommended abortion: What should they do? "Going into the Huta opened up new problems—Jerzy saw how much he was needed," Father Przekazinski said. "The workers at the Huta had come to Warsaw mainly in the 1950s. They were people without local roots. Their family and communal ties had been severed and their social problems were becoming more and more obvious. Don't forget: the harsh working conditions, the shift work, the difficulty of maintaining a religious life. The task for him as a priest was how to reach these people with religion and how to instruct them in the social teachings of the Church."

A few weeks after the August strike, Popieluszko entered the Huta again—"incognito, without my collar, guided through the gate by a friendly worker"; and formally made contact with the Factory Commission of Solidarity. He was invited to sit in on Solidarity meetings and became a regular observer, though he always stopped short of joining in the decision making. "He mostly listened," Szadurski explained. "He didn't participate so much as watch us, saw how people would come to us with their worries." The priest swiftly drew up a plan of action. The first step would be to hold regular mass in St. Stanislaw Kostka at ten o'clock on Sunday mornings, specifically for steelworkers. The idea was to create a Catholic cell within the Communist steelworks, a religious community that would grow and at the same time march in step with the Solidarity movement.

Popieluszko was not overburdened with parish duties. For all his physical frailty, he needed to be stretched and challenged, needed, as he later described it, "a constituency of souls."

"Father Jerzy had an instinctive feeling about Solidarity," said one senior union activist. "It crystalized for him every thought, half-thought, and observation of the previous five years. The union had its roots in the teachings of the Pope, it drew courage from Popieluszko's great mentor, Wyszynski, it created a romantic ideal of a noble, pure, just Poland—something close to his heart—and simultaneously presented him with the practical task of evangelizing a working class that had been battered and driven to vodka by decades of depressing, soul-destroying, atheistic Marxist ideology."

Solidarity may have answered some inner call of Popieluszko's, but in those early days, the autumn of 1980, the union was itself rather confused, nervous, unsure of the limits of what was later to be heralded as the "self-limiting revolution." Poles were flocking to the Solidarity standard, and not just workers: students, actors, bandsmen, farmers, were setting up their own "self-governing" independent associations and unions. The Communist Party, which in every Soviet bloc country demands a controlling role in every interest group, was pushed into a corner and, frequently, mocked in the manner of a displaced monarch. There was a feverishness about the movement, a sense that everything had to be changed within days, or weeks, before the gates slammed shut. The paralysis of government that allowed the people to get away with so much so quickly would not last for long. The only chance for Solidarity was to build as much as possible, and to gain some kind of legally recognized position. The union prodded, threatening a strike in October because the authorities were dragging their feet on raising wages. It organized, rented rooms, printed T-shirts and posters, created, in an astonishing spurt, the infrastructure of a mass movement. And, as more priests joined Popieluszko in forging links between the union and the Church, Solidarity felt easier with itself.

By November 1980, Solidarity had been officially registered and was a legal entity. The step was as usual accompanied by some fast footwork on the part of the authorities. The government wanted to build a formal commitment to the leading position of the Communist Party into the statutes of the supposedly independent union. After strike threats, loud words, anxious glances eastward, the proviso was put in the appendix.

At the Huta, workers, partly under the intelligent guidance of Szadurski, were gaining confidence day by day. It was now no longer a question of how to enthuse the steelmen but of how to restrain them. The Warsaw industrial complex, embracing the Ursus tractor factory, the FSO car plant, the Roza Luksemburg lightbulb works, and the Huta, was now a rival in radicalism to the Baltic seacoast. The power of Solidarity was not so much the ability to bring workers out on strike but the authority to bring them back to work. Only that gave Solidarity a negotiating base with the government. It came close to a crisis when in November, soon after the registration of Solidarity, Huta stayed on strike in protest at the Narozniak affair. Jan Narozniak was a printer who had received a confidential prosecutor's office document—little more than a background report on the opposition—and who intended to help the Warsaw Solidarity chapter publish it to reveal the perfidy of the authorities. Police raided Solidarity offices in Warsaw, the document was found, and Narozniak was arrested. The Warsaw region of Solidarity called a regional strike. Days of tension, sweat, and deals followed. By November 17, Narozniak and the man who had supplied him with the document were freed. The strike was called off, but Huta refused to comply. The steelworkers wanted more: a reduction, for example, in the budgets of the secret and uniformed police and a parliamentary investigation into the activities of the security police. Walesa flew down from Gdansk to try to put out the fire—he knew than that this was the first sign of future danger, of the revolution running ahead of its leaders. Jacek Kuron, a cofounder of the Workers Defense Committee, delivered what would become a standard text: the need for strikers, and for Solidarity, to take into account "geo-political realities." This meant simply that the Soviet Union remained Poland's eastern neighbor, there was an unsympathetic Czechoslovakia to the south and a vehemently hostile East Germany to the west. The message was historical: remember the great power partitions of Poland, remember the Warsaw Pact invasion of Czechoslovakia in 1968, remember that every strike, every demand that touched on defense and security issues brought a silent partner, Moscow, into the negotiations with the government. Go easy.

Huta relented. It came close to a strike again in March 1981, when police stormed a sit-in by a group of private farmers pressing for the recognition of an independent farmers' union. The police beat strikers, and pictures of the local Bydgoszcz Solidarity leader Jan Rulewski, blood trickling down his face, brought the national movement to a frenzy. Huta was put on strike alert, like factories throughout Poland. Outside the fence of the steelworks, the Hutniks hung a huge red and white banner: "We condemn the bestial beating of the Solidarity Committee by the MO and the SB." MO stood for Citizens Militia, but most Solidarity members seemed convinced that the beating was specially carried out by secret police dirty tricks squad, disguised as ordinary coppers, who were trying to push Solidarity into open war with the authorities.

During these troubled days, large parts of the security *apparat* felt that the policy of conciliation with Solidarity had been discredited. The initial logic in dealing with strikers in August 1980 was to buy social peace, but it was not supposed to establish a new "social contract" or anything of the kind. When the strikers, in Huta and elsewhere, began to bare their teeth, the secret police began to act. In February, General Wojciech Jaruzelski became prime minister and showed signs of wanting to install his own men in the police leadership. Was the violent police action in Bydgoszcz an attempt to forestall a purge by Jaruzelski? Or was it intended to force the general to declare a state of emergency? The police had been driven underground by Solidarity; now there was impatience, a longing for air. A state of emergency would put the effective exercise of Party rule into the hands of the police. And *that* was a goal worth fighting for.

The high politics were barely noticed by the Hutniks—the steelworkers—and their priest. For them Bydgoszcz demonstrated certain truths: that the Communists were still able and willing to play dirty, that one had to be correspondingly wary of making deals with the authorities, and that Solidarity was still strong enough to press the government into agreement on many issues. Of course it was a perilous game, but after a decade of detente the risk of tanks rolling in as they did in Prague in 1968 did not seem high; possible yes, but not likely. The statistics seemed to give some credibility to their sunny confidence: nine and a half million Poles were members of Solidarity, some two million were Communist Party members, and one-fifth of those were also in the new trade union.

Popieluszko could lean on his own statistics: about thirty-four out of thirty-six million Poles were self-proclaimed Catholic believers. At the Huta he was beginning to sense some of the spiritual reserves hidden by those figures. In the early days of Solidarity he had established, in mountaineering terms, base camps in the Huta. By April 1981, he was within sight of the summit.

Early that year, the Solidarity chapter at Huta had asked him to find a designer for a Solidarity standard, an ornate banner to be displayed at every major plant in the country, that would symbolize the permanence of the union. The end result was simple enough. The Polish eagle with a long tapering tongue and generous plumage, odd prehistoric features, more of a pterodactyl than the noble protector of the nation. But unlike the eagle that serves as the socialist emblem, this bird had a crown firmly on its head. Alongside the wings the initials NSZZ—independent self-governing trade union—and under the claws in the bold script: Solidarnosc. At the foot of the banner: 1980 HUTA WARSZAWA. To demonstrate the alliance between Church and Solidarity (and between Solidarity and Poland), Popieluszko decided that the banner should be consecrated in a special ceremony, devised and choreographed by himself. Word spread throughout the Solidarity chapters, and on an April Sunday a group of steelworkers in their ceremonial headgear gathered on the balcony of the Church of St. Stanislaw Kostka that overlooks a small park. Behind them, the large inscription, which remains to the day, BOG I OJCZYZNA—God and fatherland—and in front of them, spread out among the trees and bushes, some twenty thousand Solidarity supporters, many carrying their own union flags. The service was in many ways a debut for Popieluszko as a church innovator: he adapted the normal mass into a form of patriotic theater, a performance with changes in tempo, pauses for applause, scope for audience participation, readings of nationalist poetry. It did not have much to do with the routine masses celebrated by many of his fellow priests, and many of his Church superiors disapproved. The idea was to make the believers, but, above all, workers who might not otherwise attend mass, think about the nation in a religious way and apply Christian values to national problems. That meant departing from normal Church liturgy and giving parishioners a more active say in the service. As the believers left in a triumphant motorcade—horns honking and lights flashing—there was little doubt that the idea had been enthusiastically supported by Solidarity. "The priests were becoming democratized too, that's what we thought. It was a sign for us really," remembered a union activist, "the way that Father Jerzy was able to delegate and involve us, without actually losing his authority as a priest." The lessons learned from that April mass were to be carried into his masses for the fatherland and, as the congregations swelled, the sharp-eyed secret police who monitored the Church began to take an interest.

A week after the consecration Popieluszko managed to get permission for the first visit by a bishop to Huta: a first not only for Huta but for the whole of heavy industry. The bishop was Zbigniew Kraszewski, a sharp-witted, red-faced man with a rough tongue. "The workers treated this event as something unbelievable," said Szadurski, "and it really was." Popieluszko was nervous: the workers were a tough bunch. Would they start to curse and swear at the government in the bishop's presence? That would be more than embarrassing; it would also bring a bludgeoning from the government and perhaps permanently set back attempts to build a bridge between the Church and the

Solidarity chapters in the factories. Kraszewski, accompanied by Popieluszko and his friend Father Przekazinski and a third priest, toured the departments, expressed amazement at the difficulty of the work, the squalor of the conditions. In the suffocating heat of the foundry, Kraszewski, wearing a safety helmet in place of his mitre, called on the workers to pray. There, among the clanking of machines, the workers got down on their knees and listened to his blessing. After the change of shift the workers crowded into a hall to talk to Kraszewski; most of them had only seen Church dignitaries at an altar, unapproachable in purple. "I was taken aback by the maturity of the workers' questions," Przekazinski said. "They asked quite remarkably sophisticated questions about the Church's position on a wide range of issues, not just Solidarity." There was no speechifying, only, as Przekazinski remembered it, "a remarkable curiosity about the Church and what the Pope said about this or that."

Those were the salad days of Solidarity, a time when Poles relaxed a little and began to enjoy the spring. The shops were still in chronic short supply, the queues often measured in days rather than yards, but the political relaxation was such that every day life gained in exhilaration, as if ozone had been pumped into the system. May 3 had been declared a holiday by Solidarity. It was the anniversary of the 1791 liberal constitution, the basis of Poland's claim to a great democratic tradition. The workers of Huta decided that they wanted a mass held in a large recreation center in the Bielany woods outside Warsaw. It was a weekend, and coming so soon after the May Day holiday, the workers were in carnival mood. The Bielany recreation ground is a patchwork of playing fields and tennis courts, and, on that weekend, the sun beat down. The workers played soccer, stripped to the waist, handkerchiefs knotted on their heads. Some lounged in the grass soaking up the sunshine. Some drank beer, but neither Popieluszko nor Przekazinski was going to enforce strict sobriety. The priests had agreed that Przekazinski would deliver a sermon on the meaning of Constitution Day for Solidarity's Poland, while Popieluszko would celebrate mass. The loudspeakers called the workers to an open space in front of a tennis practice wall, and Przekazinski started to preach to the Solidarity men the need for Poles to understand their own history. "I talked about the May 3 constitution and I said that it was of course destroyed by the partitioning by the great powers (Russia, Prussia, Austria)—but that it was also destroyed to a great extent by the Poles themselves. From this fact I moved on to Solidarity." Poles should not let things drift, he argued, but rather become positively involved, take tighter control of their own destiny. It was an intelligent sermon that ran counter to the mood of the times, certainly to the mood of the day.

Popieluszko approached his friend. "That was a very pessimistic speech, Andrzej." Przekazinski was a little hurt by Popieluszko's criticism. "By saying these things," Popieluszko went on, "you are making it sound as if disaster is inevitable. That's not the way it is." The unspoken thought was that Solidarity needed courage, not Cassandra-style warnings.

The exchange revealed something of Popieluszko's complicated relationship with Solidarity. His friends insist that he was not uncritical of the union. "It always surprised me when I heard him express his own views, I had become used to the idea that he and Solidarity were one, but that was not quite the way of matters," a close friend said. "He saw Solidarity very directly, blemishes too, the commonsense vision of a country boy, but also that of a priest." The fact was that Popieluszko was a "patriotic" priest, rather than the "political" priest label assigned to him by an irritated Jaruzelski government. Popieluszko was drawn to the Solidarity movement because it was articulating the accumulation of a nation's woes. As a priest it was his task to look after people in distress and encourage their protectors. His own energetic nature pushed him further.

Popieluszko was to refer increasingly to the "solidarity of the nation," rather than the actual trade union. He wanted to show that Solidarity was more than a sectional lobby for organized labor, rather it was an idea that embraced intellectuals, farmers, housewives, and, yes, priests. When martial law, imposed in December 1981, first suspended then destroyed Solidarity as a union, "solidarity of the nation" became the only kind of solidarity. It meant a shared memory of the abuses of the authorities in the student demonstrations in 1968, the shooting of workers in 1970, the beating of protestors in 1976. It meant a shared confidence, a sense of togetherness that had nothing to do with the "fraternal" or "collective" togetherness inspired from above. "The truth is that solidarity of the nation grew out of the tears, the injustices suffered, and the blood shed by workers," he told his congregation in August 1983. When the government was forced to negotiate and make concessions to strikers in the stormy August of 1980, they did so with Solidarity, not with the formal trade union but with the national movement. Solidarity was not something that could be removed with a stroke of a pen or a swipe of a baton, it simply existed as the expression of a nation's sufferings. In one sermon, he recalled the story of a famine-stricken African country whose ruler forbade the use of the word "hunger" on the grounds that when the word disappeared, so would the problem. "In our country the problem exists and will continue to do so, for solidarity is the hope of appeasing that hunger of the human heart for love, justice, and truth."

Popieluszko was always bemused when he was accused of being a political priest. In his own eyes he was simply doing his duty as a Pole.

Yet there was something more. His own energetic nature pushed him further. Marek Miecznikowski, a Solidarity organizer from the FSO car factory, believed that Popieluszko, though never a paid-up member of the union, was intimately involved in the movement. "He passed on information. He was a sort of courier between Warsaw and Gdansk and gathered all kinds of materials. He helped to arrange for a small printing press with some other priests who had the facilities.

"He helped to keep the materials flowing. His place was always full of the stuff. A kind of contact point, distribution center between the [Solidarity] regions. It was open activity in those days, not a conspiracy." He was, Miecznikowski said, a man willing to take on his share of the Solidarity work. "After the strike at Huta Warszawa, he thought it was worthwhile to get involved, to help. He saw the sense in our freedom, he didn't separate himself as a man wearing a cassock." There was nothing very sinister in this work. By Western standards, it seems almost laughably irrelevant, but in a country where the telephones cannot be trusted as a means of communication, where the authorities interfere with mail, where the public transport network is haphazard, a man willing to run errands in his own car has value. Miecznikowski gives a concrete example. "He brought me stuff from Gdansk about PKS [the transport company], stuff that I needed for union work. I asked him to do it and he did it in three days. He managed to find all the right people."

The result was that Popieluszko was one of the best-informed priests about Solidarity in the Warsaw region. This reputation added to his attraction. People started to come to his services because they thought that they could find out something about the situation but also because they felt that this was a priest with authority, the authority of his contacts. The board of the Warsaw Solidarity region was truly a powerful body in the sixteen months of the union's official existence, and Popieluszko was in contact with several members. The other effect was to stir up interest in the Rakowiecka Street headquarters of the secret police.

6

•

Martial Law

SINCE MARCH 1981, detailed plans for a state of emergency—or martial law—had been under preparation. It was a joint operation planned by a crisis team of Polish army officers, militia and secret police commanders, and advisers in the Soviet embassy. A list had been drawn up of some five thousand potential enemies of the state who were to be interned as soon as the guillotine fell on Solidarity. After the ceremony to consecrate the Solidarity banner, Popieluszko's name was added to the list.

At first, Popieluszko did not feel like a marked man. He was certainly under observation, but as his friend, the dissident Jacek Kuron once remarked, "It is a brand of freedom to know that the secret police exists and is watching, and yet to behave as if it is not." Popieluszko began to feel uneasy about Poland: perhaps it was the wild talk at the Solidarity congress in Gdansk about leaving the Warsaw Pact and the message of support to workers in other Communist countries in their own struggle for independent unions.

The winter of 1981–82, he knew, would be hard, and crucial for the future of Solidarity. The infrastructure of the country—the water services, social welfare, gasoline supply, energy reserves, the hospitals—was beginning to crack from the strain

83

of over a decade of inadequate investment. Anyone as closely connected with the health service as Popieluszko could see the problems of a nation encapsulated in the everyday difficulties of a Polish hospital. In the autumn of 1981 there were acute shortages not only of drugs and medicine but also of detergent to wash floors and equipment, shortages of syringes. Western-supplied one-use-only syringes were used perhaps thirty or forty times, and the cross-infection was rampant. The Warsaw provincial hospital had managed to secure funds to install double-glazing in two of the wards ahead of the winter, but to do so the wards had to be closed. The result, as Popieluszko witnessed on a visit to a doctor, was a traffic jam of patients in the damp, ill-lit corridors. Popieluszko supported Solidarity's drugs committee, which was supposed to reassure Western donors that their medicines were being fairly distributed and not siphoned off on to the black market. But Solidarity alone could not solve the problems; it was reaching the limit of its powers to help people.

When the medical academies went on strike in Warsaw it was natural that Popieluszko would join them. The strike was not about the state of the health service but about the implementation of a higher education bill drafted on Solidarity advice to promote greater democracy in universities and colleges.

Students were worried that the government would try to claw back some of its promises, that it would suddenly ban the independent students union, or install its own trustees as university heads. For a while, students were again in the revolutionary vanguard, almost every college building in the country could boast its banners: NZS OCCUPATION STRIKE, written in the red, blotchy, Solidarity script. For Popieluszko, it was enough to stroll among the strikers and let them know a priest was present. Karol Szadurski explained why this symbolic presence was important for strikers. "During a strike everybody carries some fear in him because nobody knows how it will end. But when one finds out that a priest has come—as I found out that he had arrived in the Huta—then one sees that one has nothing to fear, that one is on a higher moral plane."

Popieluszko's participation in the medical students' protest led to a friendship with Seweryn Jaworski, a gray-bearded physicist and Solidarity organizer. Jaworski approached the priest and asked him to take part in a sit-in at the Firemen's Academy, whose students were also protesting restrictive education laws. Jaworski argued: "Remember the time may come when these and other young people will be encouraged to shoot at us. These boys here were simply refusing to be in a militarized school whose cadets were used in the past to fight workers' demonstrations. Can we not draw the right conclusions: that everything is and was being done to subordinate this school to the military and Interior Ministry educational systems."

Acting on orders from the new interior minister, General Czeslaw Kiszczak, several hundred ZOMO riot troopers surrounded the academy. Although the unit was familiar enough to most Poles, it was the first time in the Solidarity era that so many of them had been seen on the street with their perspex shields, long batons, and shock absorbent helmets—headgear that earned them the mocking description of "cosmonauts."

Popieluszko moved easily among the chaos of students slumped in sleeping bags, singing songs, talking away their fears. A reporter who recognized the priest among the besieged students asked him why he was in civilian dress.

"Well, I am not here exactly as a private citizen, I have my white collar in my pocket. I needed it to smuggle myself into the school, through the gate which is so carefully guarded. On the first day of the strike they wouldn't let me in, but I simply waited until the policemen's shift changed and then the gentlemen were more relaxed."

It was characteristic of Popieluszko to slip his collar on and off according to strategic need. But Popieluszko became more closely involved in the dispute because the trainee foremen were threatened by the ZOMO outside the gate.

When a group of academics failed to persuade General Kiszczak to call off the ZOMO, Popieluszko embarked on a peace mission of his own. Slipping out of the academy he made his way to the primate's palace in Miodowa Street. In May of that year Cardinal Wyszynski had died, and Popieluszko had felt the blow as bitterly as any of his contemporaries in the priesthood. It seemed cruel that at the very time Solidarity's revolution needed a strong support from the Church, the re-

vered Primate of the Millenium should die. He had been suc-
ceeded in July by his former secretary, a wily canon lawyer
named Jozef Glemp. As Popieluszko made his way to Miodowa
Street, Glemp was still an unknown quantity: What were his
real feelings about Solidarity? How powerful was his support in
the episcopate? Glemp had met Walesa and Jaruzelski on November 4 to try to find a way out of the crisis. Jaruzelski, however, was not prepared to give any ground. There were already
critics of Glemp, but they were muted. Popieluszko thought
any attempt to stave off a national breakdown was worthwhile,
providing it kept Solidarity alive and answered the people's demand for a more pluralistic society.

The priest, looking tired and creased, was ushered up the
red-carpeted staircase to Glemp's study. Glemp, a small,
paunchy man, sprang from his chair and greeted him. At one
side sat Archbishop Bronislaw Dabrowski, secretary of the
episcopate and one of the best Church negotiators with the
Communist authorities.

"Greetings Father Jerzy," said the elderly Dabrowski, un-
folding himself from his plush eighteenth-century chair.
"Please tell the primate what is happening inside the academy.
What is the mood of the students?"

Popieluszko, flattered, gave a comprehensive account of the
strike from the first day: the issues involved, his view on how
the students would react if the ZOMO came in, the importance
of a peaceful outcome. Dabrowski nodded encouragingly,
Glemp stayed impassive, stroking the cuffs of his cassock. After
twenty minutes of exposition, punctuated by questions from
Dabrowski, Popieluszko stammered to a close. He was not
comfortable, the meeting had the air of an exam. After an awk-
ward pause, Glemp rose again and stretched out his hand. "Get
some sleep now so that you can be useful for those boys." It was
Glemp's longest remark in the whole interchange, and it proved
to be his warmest statement to Popieluszko in their troubled relationship.

Popieluszko felt a vague dissatisfaction with the meeting. He
needed response in his contacts with others. But he became enthusiastic when next morning the primate gave him a letter to
the staff and students of the academy. It was a reply to an appeal

sent by the strikers to the Church leadership. It clearly bore the marks of Dabrowski's drafting, and it contained little apart from an admonition to stay true to God and to work toward peaceful solutions. But even so, it was a message from the head of the Polish Church.

But Popieluszko never delivered the letter. The security forces, under the orders of General Kiszczak, had decided to close in on the strikers. The ZOMO troopers drew the net tight around the academy. The students had grown accustomed to the clattering of police helicopters overhead; this was a standard part of the repertoire in such crises, partly intimidation, partly an attempt to monitor the nearby streets to ensure that no demonstration built up outside the school. But on December 2 the mechanical howling was stronger than ever before, louder and louder. "Keep away from the windows," shouted the ZOMO megaphones, but enough of the strikers had leaned out to determine the facts: commando units had landed on the roof. Down below, the ZOMO smashed down the academy gate and double-marched, shields raised above their heads.

The students and professors ran to the auditorium and awaited their fate, fearing another Bydgoszcz. But Kiszczak's orders were evidently not to use personal violence against the strikers. A major appeared in the auditorium, assured the students that nothing was going to happen, and then had them escorted, class by class, to buses in which they were taken and dumped, like parcels, at two Warsaw railway stations. There was relief in the Church: it could have been worse. But the academic community and the Solidarity leadership were outraged. One student remarked: "We should organize a new, better school in which the head wouldn't bring out guns against his students." Popieluszko found it absurd: commandos, helicopters, riot police to end a harmless sit-in. Was the Jaruzelski leadership going mad?

The Fireman's Academy raid had been a dress rehearsal, testing the ability of militia and army to act together, illustrating what could be achieved by a show of force. At the time of the raid, it appeared as if the authorities were giving a more specific warning: don't stray onto Interior Ministry territory or we will come down hard on you. By the weekend of December

12-13, it was plain that this was not a shot across the bow. It was an important move in the government's end game, the countdown to martial law.

The ZOMO's actions inflamed a Solidarity meeting in Radom, and strong words were spoken. Walesa came under attack. The authorities later claimed to have tape-recorded the session and together with other "evidence" discovered in raids on Solidarity offices decided that they could show that the union was planning to overthrow the Communist system by force. Martial law, declared on December 13, was a last-minute decision to save Poland from disaster, ran the government argument. Mieczyslaw Rakowski, the deputy prime minister whose chameleonlike political skills had made him first champion then critic of various Party leaders, described the decision to announce martial law with typical self-dramatization in an interview. Jaruzelski called Rakowski into his office on Friday, December 11, at the time of day when bureaucrats are usually clearing up their desks for the weekend. "Jaruzelski looked very serious, more serious than ever. He raised his eyes and said, 'The day has come, it's for the day after tomorrow, the 13th.' I answered, 'I understand.' There was nothing to add."

Andrzej Przekazinski, handsome, alert, with smooth, coordinated movements and an authoritative manner, is the very model of a modern churchman, though as an art lover and museum curator he would thank no one for the label. Zipped into a flyer's jacket, a turtleneck sweater tugged over his clerical collar, tossing the keys of his Polski Fiat from hand to hand, he strode through the snow of the Kostka courtyard to the priest's house. He had promised Jerzy Popieluszko that he would deliver the sermon at ten o'clock mass and hadn early overslept. Outside the priest's house it was minus 12° Celsius. Inside the temperature was lower.

"My dear friends, why so grim?" he announced cheerily to Fathers Popieluszko and Bogucki, searching at the same time for his vestments.

His friends were thunderstruck. "How did you get here?"

Popieluszko and the other priest spluttered the question simultaneously.

"Normally. What's up?"

"They've declared a state of war, haven't you heard?" said Popieluszko, pale but calm, in control of his emotions. "Jaruzelski has been on TV, everything's forbidden, everything's in a vacuum. There are soldiers everywhere, didn't you see them?"

Przekazinski recalled that there were a lot of troops on the Vistula bank highway, armored cars, soldiers on the bridge huddled around the braziers. He hadn't thought much about it, just that they've gone crazy again. He sat down. The mass seemed less urgent now. "So," he said after a while, "Who are we fighting?"

A few minutes later, in front of the congregation, Przekazinski expressed some of the confusion of that first encounter, the confusion of a nation that has been seized by its own army. "We have a war," he told the congregation. "But we don't know with whom. One should assume that a war has been declared on Solidarity and on the nation."

It was a safe assumption. Although more sophisticated explanations were to emerge, Jaruzelski had suspended Solidarity, had interned most of the union leadership and a large number of advisers and sympathetic intellectuals. Telephones were cut, the airport closed, there was a dusk-to-dawn curfew. The country was being run by a closed group of officers known as the Military Council for National Salvation—a title that made Popieluszko wince with displeasure—and trusted Jaruzelski appointees in the state rather than Communist Party machine. Later, apologists for martial law argued that Jaruzelski had to take drastic steps to "restore order" in order to buy time to purge the Party, to weed out those who were opposed to his economic and limited political reforms. Jaruzelski himself spoke in a television broadcast to the nation that cold thirteenth, of Poland being on the brink of an abyss. Poles were supposed to understand this as a coded reference to the prospect of a Russian invasion. Martial law, said Jaruzelski, his advisers, spokesmen, and eventually even the Church leadership, was the lesser evil.

Popieluszko, Solidarity's priest, saw a different world, a different Poland. He knew that it was the authorities and not Solidarity who would cause the shedding of blood. It was the Jaruzelski leadership and not the people of Poland who had to be restrained. He understood that respect for human life and the quest for compromise were Christian virtues. But there were other values too: to suffer for one's faith, to resist betrayal, to speak truth, to press for a change in society that would accommodate God and God-given human rights. These too were Christian goals. The primate, in his appeal to the nation, had not mentioned any of these aspects of Christian existence. Was there nothing worth fighting for?

After the Sunday mass on the thirteenth, four men arrived at the church looking for Popieluszko. They were of a certain type: leather jackets, mustachioed, trim haircuts, small identification badges under their lapels. In short, the secret police. When they asked they were told nobody had seen Popieluszko that day. Neither the duty nun, nor the parishioners, nor the various odd job men and housekeepers could remember. Perhaps, they said, Father Popieluszko had gone away for a trip, a short trip, a long one, who knows? The policemen went away empty-handed, and Popieluszko spent the rest of the day escorted by a burly guard from the steelworks. The plainclothes men gave up with surprising ease; by the time they had reported back to secret police headquarters in Rakowiecka Street the order had filtered down that no priest should be interned or arrested. General Jaruzelski needed the cooperation of the Church.

Popieluszko was not regarded as the most dangerous of the "radical" priests. Some sections of the Church monitoring department were even a little mystified. Who was this country boy-turned-priest who seemed to be so close to the Warsaw Solidarity leadership? Father Stanislaw Malkowski, summoned for questioning on the night of December 13, found his interrogators asking why he had not been present at the Firemen's Academy strike.

"There was no need," Malkowski replied. "The students were well taken care of by Father Popieluszko."

"Popieluszko, who's he?" the agent asked.

"Shortly after this interchange," Malkowski recalls, "in the early days of martial law, I found out, much to my surprise, that Father Jerzy had become even more hated than me. If one were to compare the contents of his sermons and the length of time of his involvement with the opposition, then I should have been subjected to greater aggression. The SB studied not only the contents of one's speeches but also the overall role, the degree of engagement."

While his many friends in the Solidarity movement were still in a state of shock, Popieluszko was already organizing assistance for the crippled union. The families of the interned had to be cared for, given money and clothes. Solidarity at its peak was employing forty thousand full-time workers, but the union's funds had been confiscated and there was a cold winter ahead. There were two main priorities: to gather as much Western aid as possible, and to build up an information network that would identify who had been detained and the names and addresses of their relatives. The main work was carried out by the parish of St. Martin's in Warsaw's Old Town district; there, lay Catholics, actors, writers, and doctors built up an information clearinghouse. A map pinned to the wall identified the main camps, probable numbers, names of the inmates. Even today it is unclear how many were arrested without trial; perhaps fifty thousand at the initial swoop, though many were freed within weeks, and the government was soon claiming that the number never exceeded five thousand at any one time. In a long vault, children's clothes and food supplies were stacked box upon box awaiting distribution.

Popieluszko could not compete with that degree of organization, but he nonetheless wanted to keep open a separate line of supply to his parishioners, especially those steelworkers and medical students who were his specific charge. His wide, intricate contacts with actors and doctors allowed him to create his own welfare system. Polish actors were boycotting television in protest at martial law, denying themselves important sources of income but at the same time also giving them time to take a very active part in helping political prisoners. "In some ways," remembers a leading character actor, "we felt guilty that we hadn't been interned with our friends, the writers, the workers.

Perhaps somebody was sheltering us, somebody in government I mean. Anyway we pulled together and showed the regime exactly what we thought. It was, I suppose, our greatest performance."

Solidarity had infiltrated almost every niche of society, including the police, where a group of rapidly arrested militiamen had tried to form an independent union in the force. Popieluszko knew where to look. Joanna Sokol was in the Solidarity chapter at the Warsaw courthouse, and, as more and more activists were slapped in front of summary courts and swiftly sent down for a year or two, she became a useful conduit for the priest.

"He wanted to have firsthand information," Sokol said, Popieluszko's dog trotting around her feet, "so he could be present at the court sessions. He wanted to see for himself what was going on there, see the people, see the evidence. That was what he was interested in ... he gathered some of the information himself. He acted a lot on his own and mobilized people into work. It wasn't just information that he was interested in, he wanted to do something straight away. Lists of political prisoners were made, their homes were visited so aid could be given, and the priest himself distributed parcels."

The first weeks after martial law were dark days, and information was power. The authorities were rigidly censoring all reports of unrest, of resistance in the heavy industrial fortresses of the Gdansk shipyards, the Silesian mines, Huta Warszawa, and other steelworks. When the government conceded that ZOMO troopers had shot down nine striking miners at Wujek, the response was: If they are admitting that, what savagery are they concealing? It will probably never be known how many were the victims of martial law; Solidarity put the list of fatalities well over a hundred. But the state of war was relatively bloodless, not because of astonishing self-control by the ZOMO, whose indiscriminate beatings led many Poles to think that they were on drugs, but because Solidarity was never really equipped for armed revolution. If only a fraction of the official propaganda had been true about Solidarity's plans to seize power, the streets would have been crimson.

Popieluszko's priestly duty was to mix with the victims, and in so doing he brushed with Solidarity fugitives who were to set up an "underground" opposition. Those men on the run in a Communist police state need material assistance. They had to change apartments every night, had to be clothed, fed, given access to printing machines. Some of this help came from priests and seminarians; their contacts, their relative immunity from arrest, helped to buy time for the establishment of the underground. There was fanciful speculation that Zbigniew Bujak, head of Warsaw Solidarity who, until his arrest in 1986, became leader of the underground, was hiding in a church or a monastery, that the surprisingly moderate tones coming from his smuggled tape-recorded speeches and his mimeographed texts indicated that the Church was controlling the temperamental worker.

When police shot and killed striking miners in the first week of martial law, Popieluszko began to ask himself whether he should not himself join the underground resistance. It was his natural inclination, not because he was a guerrilla leader in a cassock but because he understood that there were historical moments, such as the 1863 uprising against the Russians, when priests had, as part of their priestly function, to stand at the barricades with their flock. He had come close to that during the sixteen months of Solidarity's legal existence, but to do so now would be to act in defiance of law and against the explicit instructions of the Church elders. Father Przekazinski, probably his closest friend, commented: "I think that Jerzy must have gone through the stage of resisting the temptation to organize resistance to what was happening—that is only a very human reaction to violence. But as priests we have different tasks and maybe history will judge us negatively for that. In the religious sense we are supposed to fulfill different roles. But if we talk about political involvement on our part, we can only speak about one thing: that we prevented the Solidarity people from collapsing."

7
•
God
Who Watches
Over Poland

FATHER POPIELUSZKO made his choice. He would try and make the Catholic Church a bridge between the underground and the overground. His own church would be a meeting place of patriots: Poles who wanted to restore a sovereign, democratic nation. The parish priest of St. Stanislaw Kostka, Father Bogucki, had revived the tradition of masses for the fatherland in October 1981, and his rough tongue and brassy phrasing had found an interested congregation. The tradition was not unique to St. Stanislaw Kostka; in 1861 Joseph Conrad's father had been picked up by the tsarist police for organizing patriotic masses in a Warsaw church. It was in the nature of fatherland masses, with their traditional emphasis on national independence, that they should have an anti-Russian flavor.

When Popieluszko took over the masses after martial law, a slightly different concept emerged. His first sermons were bald, without charm, as if to say: we all feel the same about the situation, let's not waste words on anything so despicable. On the last Sunday of January 1982, his sermon was confined to a single sentence: "As freedom of speech has been taken away from us by martial law, the state of war, let us, listening to the voice of our heart and conscience, remember those brothers and sisters who have been deprived of their freedom."

The masses, celebrated on the final Sunday of the month at seven in the evening, grew in sophistication. When the secret police began to interrogate acquaintances of Popieluszko, a persistent question was, Who wrote the sermons? Had they bothered to ask the priest, he would probably have replied that there were two ghostwriters: Pope John Paul II and Cardinal Stefan Wyszynski. The late primate's prison diaries, written while undergoing two years of house arrest in the Stalinist 1950s, were a constant source of inspiration. And there was an obvious political maturity about using the Pope's words to analyze the current situation; it was difficult, though not impossible, given the imaginative resources of the Church monitoring department, to throw somebody in jail for quoting the Polish Pope.

In April 1982, Popieluszko started to recite special prayers for the victims of martial law in his fatherland mass sermons. That meant not only the interned Solidarity leadership and Lech Walesa, those jailed for trying to resist the ZOMO in the first days of the crisis, but all those suffering daily humiliations for their political beliefs. "The trials of democratically elected worker representatives do not assist reconciliation [between governors and governed]. Shattered families do not help reconciliation, nor do children who long for their imprisoned parents, wives awaiting their husband, mothers their sons and daughters. Rounding up people returning home peacefully from church services does not assist reconciliation, nor does a show of force"—this with a slight hand gesture toward the water cannon nearby—"near churches where people pray . . . reconciliation is not served either by documents which state that if a Solidarity activist agrees to set up a new [progovernment] trade union in his factory he will have his salary doubled, but if he chooses to stay faithful to his conscience, he will be demoted and transferred to a factory on the other side of Warsaw."

The sermons at the masses for the fatherland were a catalog of wrongs, a naming of names. The congregation swelled. People stood on parked cars the length and breadth of Felikskiego Street, which adjoins the church boundaries. A typical fatherland Sunday saw young workers, earnest bearded men holding high their tape-recorders ("for the underground" whispers a neighbor), out-of-town priests (the ultimate compliment, for few stray into other parishes on a Sunday) taking notes. There were old women, Home Army partisans, schoolboys wearing plastic lapel badges of the Black Madonna of Czestechowa or Solidarity badges. The steelworker ushers, with armbands, were officious. Their task was to prevent any provocations that would allow the lurking ZOMO units to intervene. Everybody was alert for agents and provocateurs. When the thousands knelt to receive benediction, there were sidelong glances to see who remained standing. When the trademark hymn of the fatherland mass, "God Who Watches Over Poland," was sung, hands shot up in V-for-victory salutes. Those with crossed arms were suspect. Popieluszko's voice came clearly through the loudspeakers. Outside the church it seemed as if he were speaking at normal conversational pitch. It was good Polish, educated, grammatical, and rehearsed. The congregation loved it and responded generously when the collection basket was passed on behalf of political prisoners.

Popieluszko enjoyed it too. He was proud that anything spontaneous could still flourish in the desert of martial law. In his first private diary entry on November 13, 1982, he recorded his feelings about the masses for the fatherland.

Eleven months of tormenting the nation under the dictatorship of the military regime. Glory be to those who suffer for the fatherland, those who do not break down under the pressure of UB [secret police] methods. I don't really know why I picked up the pen today to write down my thoughts. Recent days were very interesting for me so it would be a pity if they were forgotten. Our authorities—not the Church authorities of course—cannot forgive us for these masses for the fatherland which I celebrate on every last Sunday of the month. They say they are the biggest meetings held during martial law. On November 11 I was at the cathedral. I had a chance to compare the atmosphere of the Holy Mass there and at our church. There maybe it could be called a rally, not a dangerous one, but a rally.

There was shouting and clapping. [At Kostka] there is
dignity of prayer, of patriotic feelings. People live in dignity and concentration.

In Warsaw's Rakowiecka Street, seat of the secret police, nobody was interested in the dignity of prayer. Popieluszko had
made the transition in that first year of martial law from being a
mild irritant to a first-order problem. The Warsaw militia were
complaining. Popieluszko was a crowd-control problem forcing
the police to deploy month after month heavy concentrations of
riot troopers. To the average ZOMO trooper Popieluszko was
the best-known priest in Poland not because of his sermons but
because he cost them their free Sundays. "Whole work rotas
were written and rewritten," one policeman confided, "to accommodate this priest." The message meanwhile reaching Department Four, the Church monitoring department, was that
Popieluszko was a political stumbling-block.

General Jaruzelski was satisfied that Poland had not taken to
the barricades after his crackdown. There were, it was true, big
street demonstrations on August 31, the anniversary of the
signing of the Gdansk agreement, but as long as the factories
were not paralyzed by strikes, he could tell Moscow and the
other Warsaw Pact neighbors that the situation was under control. Whether Moscow, or the general's hardline critics in the
Polish Communist Party Politburo, believed him was a constant
worry.

Jaruzelski was also under pressure from Western banks and
governments, which had loaned Poland twenty-seven billion
dollars. They had reacted with alarm to martial law and were
insisting loudly that there would be no more cash until the situation eased. To calm Western creditors, Jaruzelski needed to
make concessions, to begin to dismantle the apparatus of martial
law. The West wanted the freedom of Walesa? Very well, he
would free the Solidarity leader providing that he humbled
himself sufficiently to request his own release. Pope John Paul
was willing to come to Poland for a second time even while
martial law was still in force, but he wanted a gift. He suggested
the end to internment without trial and the freeing of Walesa.

Jaruzelski believed that a second papal trip would signal the end of Poland's diplomatic purdah and guarantee Church cooperation in the medium future. It was a carrot to be held before the nation: behave or your beloved Pontiff will be forced to stay outside the country.

The price of this deal, negotiated in the summer of 1982, was simply this: the Church should keep its distance from Solidarity. The government fear was that if all the internees were to be released in one swoop they would cluster round the Church and pick up their opposition activities. Popieluszko's following showed that this was a realistic danger. The word was thus passed down from above. Popieluszko and other "radical" priests had to be stopped. A parallel strategy was devised. The Council for Religious Affairs, headed by a lawyer, Adam Lopatka, would put pressure on the Church leadership to silence its priests. This was the gentlemen's club approach: We are all men of reason, we know what is good for Poland, that the nation craves the Pope. It would be a tragedy if the words and deeds of a few, a mere handful of hot-blooded priests, jeopardized such an important breakthrough. And were not these priests actually violating the Pope's explicit instructions in meddling with politics?

The second line of attack was handled by Department Four. Its job was to make life unpleasant for the radical priests. They were to be stopped for documents checks. If they met with Solidarity notables their tires were to be punctured or the metalwork of the cars scratched and daubed. They were to be followed ostentatiously, their telephones bugged, their contacts scrupulously monitored. The accumulated information was handed over to Lopatka's deputy, Alexander Merker. The Council for Religious Affairs would draft letters of protest to be delivered with a theatrical display of anger at joint meetings of the episcopate and the government.

There was no great subtlety to this approach. It was one of the standard Communist devices to destroy the Church. The Church was divided into sober, reasonable men like Primate Glemp and a handful of extremists, like Popieluszko. Logic dictated that, eventually, the Church would eat itself.

However, handling extremist priests was proving a complicated task for the SB. In the beginning of 1982 it appeared to the analysts in Rakowiecka Street that Church monitoring operations could be concentrated on three main areas: Warsaw, Krakow and Gdansk, the main focus in the Baltic seaport being Lech Walesa's confessor, Father Henryk Jankowski. But it soon became plain that the problem was nationwide. The tenuous thesis that Popieluszko was an isolated case looked shaky. Striking against one of these priests was a calculated risk. In some cases it could bring about the desired effect of a bishop reprimanding and reining in young outspoken priests. But it could just as easily bring about closing of ranks, healing rather than opening the natural gulf between a bishop and his priests.

What degree of pressure and harassment on Popieluszko would have positive rather than negative effects? That was the calculation that had to be made in Rakowiecka Street by ambitious, frustrated men. The first part of 1982 was spent in preparation. For the initial pressure on the Church leaders to have any chance of success, SB harassment would have to be carefully paced.

The Council for Religious Affairs had two official complaints about Popieluszko in 1982. Typical of the written protests was a letter sent by Minister Lopatka to the church leadership in August 1982. "Father Popieluszko's attitude, as well as the atmosphere he created, changed a religious gathering into a political demonstration, threatening law and order in the capital." This, said the minister, contributed "toward increasing alarm among the public and excited rowdy individuals." Unless the Church acted against Popieluszko and priests like him, it would be regarded as sharing responsibility for the collapse of public order.

The bombast of the letter was matched by the carping, menacing tones heard in the private meetings in the Warsaw Curia. Two bishops were drawn repeatedly into the crossfire between the authorities and Father Popieluszko. They were his former instructor Wladyslaw Miziolek and Zbigniew Kraszewski, who had visited the Warsaw steelworks with Popieluszko. "He did not involve himself in politics at all," said Kraszewski.

"He worked with the workers from Huta Warszawa, but not in a political sense."

This was the kind of response that the bishops gave to the authorities. There was evidence that the primate was unhappy with Popieluszko, but to the outside world the Church presented a solid wall: Popieluszko was a man of the Church, he was not playing in politics, there was no reason to discipline him.

In November 1982, the government stopped relying solely on letters of complaint about Popieluszko and authorized the secret police to begin a cruder form of harassment. Popieluszko's diary entry for November 13 records:

> Last night "unknown perpetrators" sprayed Father Henryk's car with white oil paint. They confused the cars—I don't doubt that the paint was prepared for my car. Old methods—the same as that used on actors [who boycotted television]. My car is only a little smeared. I won't wash it. . . . On November 11 I went to the Curia in the morning. The chancellor informed me that the Council for Religious Affairs is not happy with the form of my masses for the fatherland. Minister Lopatka is supposed to have told Bishop [Jerzy] Dabrowski that they have to arrest in the near future three priests—[Leon] Kantorski, [Boleslaw] Prus, [Stanislaw] Malkowski—and that I will be the first one to be interned.

That evening, Popieluszko saw Bishop Miziolek. He had just returned from Czestechowa, where he attended a plenary session of bishops. In the corridors of the monastery, the talk had been of Popieluszko and the gathering storm clouds.

"Father Jerzy, you are still walking around free?" the elderly bishop exclaimed. His tone was bantering, half-ironic, half-worried that one of his favorite pupils should be stumbling, as a mutual friend put it, "into the jaws of the crocodile."

Popieluszko was shocked. It was one thing to pick up another reprimand from the Council for Religious Affairs, quite another to have one's imminent arrest treated as a foregone conclusion. On November 10, a Monday, General Jaruzelski had met the primate, a meeting that coincided with the announcement of the Pope's visit. But the two men had also discussed Popieluszko, Miziolek now confided.

"You are one of three priests to be arrested, that is what Jaruzelski told the primate," said Miziolek. Later Popieluszko wrote in his diary, "I am aware that they can intern me, arrest me, fabricate a scandal, but I can't stop my activity which is a service to the Church and to the fatherland."

Popieluszko was never deflected from his mission by the needling policies of the authorities, but he became dog-tired. Small signs showed that the police and its informer network were drawing their web closer around him. His brother was interrogated after his car had been seen outside the priest's house. A former colleague on an anti-abortion program had denounced Popieluszko as a traitor to the state during a Party meeting. And on November 18, Popieluszko was told at the Curia that a formal complaint had been registered against him by the main Warsaw militia office. He noted in his diary: "I was told that they had given me many, many warnings and that if my behavior did not change then they would act according to the martial law decrees. But how can my behavior change? I can't stop serving the people?"

Popieluszko had become a dossier in the files of the secret police. The authorities knew that pushing the Curia was no real solution. The threat to invoke the full force of martial law was a bluff since Jaruzelski was already preparing to suspend the "state of war."

The police could silence Popieluszko either directly by building up criminal charges against the priest, or by stealth, by demonstrating that the priest was in so much personal danger the Church should transfer him. Perhaps to Rome, perhaps to the countryside, far away from workers, from intellectuals, and from Solidarity.

Before the November fatherland mass, Bishop Kraszewski drove to Kostka and tried to persuade Popieluszko not to give his sermon. The Curia had heard that there was a warrant for his arrest to be issued as soon as the mass was over. Popieluszko was bitterly disappointed; there was so much that he wanted to say, about the promised papal trip, about the freeing of Walesa, about the prisoners still in jail. Were the authorities still bluffing? Would they ever dare put a priest like Popieluszko on trial for his sermons? Bogucki decided that Popieluszko should not take the risk and delivered the sermon instead. Outside the priest's house his car was daubed with white paint again.

8
•
Bomb
Through
the Window

POPIELUSZKO WAS wrapping Christmas presents on December 13, 1982, the first anniversary of martial law. Spread out in the chaos of his room were small gifts to be distributed to the families of political prisoners. The apartment was no more than a single room divided by a stained wooden bookcase. Adjoining the bedroom section there was a cubbyhole that served as a kitchen, the washing up left for days. The walls were plastered with Solidarity posters, and from the night of December 13 there was a large improvised map of internment centers and political prisoners. Even his closest friends said that the room was a small temple of Kitsch: needlework tapestries with "Solidarnosc" emblazoned on it, a chunk of carved coal from Silesian Solidarity, pictures of Walesa, and gaudy symbols of protest. He was too nice to refuse gifts from workers. Popieluszko, humming to himself, suddenly heard the bell ringing downstairs at the main door. Then came the sound of breaking glass and, as he opened the door of his room, the muffled sound of an explosion. Somebody had thrown a miniature bomb strapped to a brick into the building with the aim of injuring Popieluszko. Police agents were out to get this meddlesome priest.

When the Huta steelworkers heard of the incident the next

morning they promptly set up their own round-the-clock guard. Burly young men in the main but also middle-aged, roughened, sinewed characters such as Tadeusz, who came to be the principal minder. The priest's house thus became something of a fortress. The screen of workers, who sometimes irritated fellow protesters or spontaneous visitors, headed off unwelcome guests and, as the priest's schedule grew more crowded and more dangerous, bought time for Popieluszko. The next day a man who was clearly a police agent was seen interfering with Popieluszko's car and chased to the safety of a vehicle with a militia registration.

Excluded by the worker guard from the actual territory of the church and the priest's house, the SB units tried different tactics.

"Last night," recorded Popieluszko in his December 28 diary entry, "was difficult. They are trying psychological harassment. Between 1 AM and 4 AM they drove like crazy around the house." Honking, revving their engines, braking, shouting, they just wanted Popieluszko to know that they were always there. The effect was of Apaches encircling a wagon train. The worker guards rushed out and took some twenty pictures of the policemen because, as one of the workers later put it, secret policemen are "allergic to bright light."

The primate was informed of the police games, but Popieluszko received no message of support. Solidarity and Popieluszko were upset with Glemp. The word was out: the primate was "Comrade Glemp." The Polish language had a new verb, *glempic,* meaning to talk like marshmallow. Cartoons in the underground press showed Glemp, his ears sticking out like the handles of a sports trophy face to face with government spokesman Jerzy Urban, whose ears were also disproportionately large. The primate knew about the jokes and he was deeply upset.

Glemp had wanted to restore some of the balance between the bishops and the primate. His predecessor, Cardinal Wyszynski, had inflated the role of the primate into a kind of superman figure whose authority was beyond question. Glemp, a canon lawyer but also a devout churchman, thought that the bishops could be given more muscle without sapping the power of the primate. The government thought otherwise. The passing of Wyszynski was a unique opportunity to drive a wedge between Glemp and ordinary priests. By the time the bomb was thrown through Popieluszko's window, in December 1982, discontent with Glemp had already reached a head. No priests who openly supported Solidarity could expect the enthusiastic backing of the primate. Under pressure from the discontented priests in Warsaw, Glemp agreed to a public meeting with some three hundred clerics. Popieluszko attended, curious to see whether the primate would change his line. The atmosphere was tense.

Glemp was at his most insensitive. "I do not see any chances for the political victory of Solidarity," he said, tugging at his sleeves, sitting squatly at the head of the table. "Moreover after the military victory of the authorities, one should expect an attack on the Church. It is therefore the duty of priests to prepare for this assault by concentrating on religious work, strengthening the faith, and completing the various matters important for the Church. Priests should stay clear from politics."

One priest burst out: "Is that any reason to do a deal with Jaruzelski over the Pope's visit at the expense of Solidarity?"

The air grew thick with ill-considered words. Glemp, said one cleric, was playing the role of orderly in a "giant concentration camp." The primate hit back: "Some priests are behaving like journalists"—a particularly virulent insult in Church terms—"and they are juggling slogans." The Church should not behave as if it is on the political rostrum, he said, nor should it break the law by sheltering the Solidarity underground.

The Church, Glemp said, was in a particularly exposed position, vulnerable to the sharp bite of the Communists. The authorities had been giving the Church everything it asked for—building permits and licenses for new churches and much else besides—in the hope that it would make the Church appear like a privileged institution and, eventually, discredit it in the eyes of Poles. "This is a deliberate policy," said Glemp into the bemused gaze of the priests. "The authorities know that the public is critical of the consumer lifestyle adopted by some priests." To Popieluszko and his friends, it appeared as if the primate was an ambassador from another planet. There were indeed high-living priests, priests with fast Western cars, but they were not many. In any case, the only way to protect the Church was to ensure that it carried out its God-given duties to the full, and that meant protecting persecuted groups.

Popieluszko stayed silent, his fears confirmed. He knew then that Church pragmatism would always leave priests like himself on the cusp of opposition.

Captain Piotrowski and his colleagues were encouraged by the friction in the Church. It offered an opening that they could exploit against Father Popieluszko. By naming secret police informers in his sermons, he had crossed an invisible line from being an irritant to being a direct threat. As soon as anyone directly attacks the practices of the secret police, or tries to embarrass agents, he risks the full force of institutional vengeance.

Popieluszko had begun leading prayers for the special agents hiding in the congregation. "This is for you, brothers," he declared. "Let this Lent be a time of reflection so that violence does not win." The police were a part of everyday life in Poland, and Popieluszko had no intention of excluding them from his texts. More, as his diary shows, they were so much a part of his own life that he was becoming obsessed. The entry for February 7, 1983, narrates an incident that suggests that the police were preparing to take action against him.

On Feb 3 at 6 AM I left Warsaw taking Krzysiek O. and Malgosia Z. We were going to the mountains for ten days. The others were supposed to join us there eventually. Right after leaving Warsaw a Fiat 125 caught up with us— I stress that it caught up with us because they didn't stop and check anybody else, I pulled over. "Documents. What is this—an illegal group? Prepare the engine number and the chassis for inspection." There wasn't the slightest doubt that this was a prepared provocation. He [the policeman] took all the documents and went to his car. He phoned somebody. After a long time he returned with the documents. "I'm sorry but I had to write everything down." Later: we could see the cars that were "following us." Fifteen Kilometres before Kielce there was a roughlooking bulldog in a brown Fiat 125. My car started to jerk, the engine seemed to be cutting out, so Malgosia suggested tea at her parents', and afterward we drove on. Now it turned out that there was a militiaman with a radio telephone and transmitter, but without a cap, in that [brown] car. We wanted to lose him in the small streets of the suburbs. It was really a game. When he started to get lost another car came to help him out. I stopped five meters after turning right so that he had to stop at the intersection and Malgosia went to ask for Grojecka Street—there is no such street. He told her: "Stop playing games and return to your vehicle." He was very nervous. He stayed with us, parked in front of Malgosia's parents. They switched cars throughout the day.

Popieluszko's diaries are full of such mundane clashes. There is menace in them, some gamesmanship too, but mainly menace. All of those brown Fiats, anonymous drivers with radio telephones and interchangeable number plates, seemed to be saying: We'll get you in the end.

Most of the action against Popieluszko was under the supervision of the Warsaw Internal Affairs Office. This was the name given to the center controlling the capital's uniformed and secret units. Every regional headquarters of the secret police has a degree of autonomy from Rakowiecka Street, the main nerve center. Daubing Popieluszko's car, following him, checking his engine number, throwing bricks through his windows were all low-level dirty tricks carried out by the regional police based in the Mostowsky Palace, the sugar merchant's sprawling mansion. Rakowiecka Street did not have to issue detailed instructions. It was enough for the man in charge of the operation, Lieutenant Colonel Leszek Wolski, to tell Department Four in Rakowiecka Street: "We are continuing the Zoliborz action." But there had to be some kind of coordination. How else would the Gdansk agents know when to intercept Popieluszko? The overall planning for the "curtailment of priest Popieluszko's nonreligious activities" was in the hands of Department Four and specifically the subgroup headed by Captain Grzegorz Piotrowski. His section was responsible for the day-to-day harassment of radical priests. Sometimes Piotrowski's group worked in tandem with Wolski's men, at other times it conducted operations on its own.

Popieluszko's diaries chronicled in increasing detail this constant surveillance, the barrage of legal summonses and complaints, and the monthly presence of ZOMO battalions, camped like armies at rest, on the fringes of his masses for the fatherland.

Everything undertaken against Popieluszko between 1982 and early 1984 was authorized from the top. That meant the operations were cleared by either the head of Department Four, General Zenon Platek, his boss, the secret police chief, General Wladyslaw Ciaston, or sometimes the overall head of police operations in Poland, Interior Minister General Czeslaw Kiszczak.

If there was any argument within the police about Popieluszko, it was not about the rights and wrongs of persecuting him but rather on the speed with which they should be proceeding against him. By the spring of 1983, Colonel Wolski was reaching the limit of what he could do against Father Popieluszko. Like any executive, Wolski had a budget. Huge resources were being used to persecute Popieluszko. The cars that followed him, the agents that worked overtime shadowing his movements—all these cost money. And yet, no legal charges had been filed against the priest.

Piotrowski was openly contemptuous of the penny-pinching colonel. "Wolski has legs of jelly," Piotrowski once told a friend. "He sees nothing but his own shadow, and that frightens him." Piotrowski wanted a systematic operation against the priest. Evidence had to be gathered and presented in such a way that Popieluszko could not possibly escape punishment in court. Once convicted, Popieluszko would lose the support of the Church leadership, and this in turn would destroy him.

9.

Return
of a Hero

THE PETTY BETRAYALS, the interrogation of friends, the tailing
and the threatening had become as much a part of Popieluszko's
life as the priestly routine of mass vespers. He was bewildered
by the persecution. So much effort, so much energy was being
poured into making his life unpleasant. Why me? he would ask
in letters to friends. The most painful stab came as preparations
were underway for the Pope's visit. Priests from the Curia were
swishing in and out of the Miodowa Palace clutching clipboards
like army quartermasters. The visit was on: that was the word
from Rome and the whisper from Warsaw. There would be no
last-minute cancellations, no whistle-blowing from over the
border. But the government wanted to play it safe; only "good"
priests would handle the trip lest the whole pilgrimage erupt
into a Solidarity jamboree. Glemp had made it clear that the
state authorities would not be allowed to vet the organizers of
the trip, but he had accepted the need for consultation with the
government. Already, by April, it was obvious that the authorities would not let the Pope visit the north of Poland, specifically the Baltic seaport of Gdansk. The very thought of the
Pope in the Lenin shipyards made the authorities blanch. In the
last stages, many concessions were made to Jaruzelski. Nobody

in the episcopate wanted to jeopardize the visit at the last minute, and the more Machiavellian advisers knew that the general needed to present Moscow with the image of a compliant Church.

In April the Council for Religious Affairs sent the Curia a letter stating that Popieluszko should not be included on the organizing committee for the Pope's visit. His involvement, said the letter, would be regarded as provocative. But the bishops— mainly Popieluszko's staunchest defenders, Bishop Miziolek and Bishop Kraszewski—insisted that the priest should be allowed to arrange the medical care during the Pope's stay in Warsaw. He had done so successfully in 1979, they argued. Popieluszko was pleased that the bishops had stood firm, but he knew that the worst was not yet over. The Pope was scheduled to visit the Franciscan monastery at Niepokalanow outside Warsaw as a mark of respect for Maximilian Kolbe, the first Pole to be beatified in Pope John Paul's reign. The priest decided to drive to the monastery to check on medical care and to collect a number of crosses to be used to mark first aid tents. As usual he was tailed. "The SB followed me to the monastery," he recorded, "to check what I was picking up. Then after I had left they burst in to see the prior and claimed that I was printing something there. How primitive! Why should I jeopardize the monastery if I have so many other opportunities?"

But the government refused to accept Popieluszko as a medical organizer. "The authorities simply don't want to talk to me—they say I am an extreme extremist." The authorities had persuaded a former colleague in the pro-life movement to denounce the priest's sermons as treacherous and deployed this against him. The authorities made two last attempts to persuade the Church leadership to withdraw Popieluszko from the planning of the papal trip. The first bordered on farce. The mayor of Warsaw, General Mieczyslaw Debicki, sent a catalog of political sins to the Warsaw bishops: on May 13, he pronounced, Popieluszko celebrated a mass at the Holy Cross Church "where texts were spoken which abused the spirit of a holy place." There was indeed a mass on that day, actors had indeed recited patriotic verses and the congregation had raised their arms in the familiar V salute. All this was true. But Popieluszko was not in that church at the time; he was at St. Stanislaw Kostka's hearing confessions. The SB's Church monitoring department had slipped up.

By this time General Kiszczak, the interior minister, had decided to intervene himself. He shared the anxiety of his secret agents about Popieluszko. The priest was a "radical," a "troublemaker," a "revolutionary hiding behind a cassock," a "professional union organizer"—to use just some of the choice epithets in circulation at Rakowiecka Street. The general, who had in the past year become central to Church–state relations in Poland, waved the text of a Popieluszko sermon and demanded an explanation from Bishop Miziolek. Why was the Church not acting against this kind of subversive speech? Did the Church not understand that a prerequisite for the Pope's visit was that clergymen stayed clean, kept away from politics and rabble-rousing? Miziolek studied the text in silence; Kiszczak tapped the desk impatiently.

"Well?"

"I see nothing controversial in this sermon. I see that it calls for national agreement conciliation. The government stands against these aims?" That was the problem. Hardly any of Popieluszko's accusers ever read his sermons in their entirety. Fragments were extracted by the eavesdropping agents, underlined, and overinterpreted. If the authorities were not able to freeze Popieluszko out of the papal trip, then they were at least allowed one final act of spite. Popieluszko would be prevented from meeting the Pope, his protector, champion, and inspiration. The closest he came to John Paul was at the airport, where, in the midst of bobbing bishops, he could smile distantly at the head of the Catholic Church.

And there too, on the tarmac, introduced to the Vatican entourage as "Mr. Piotrowski from the ministry," stood the eager young captain. Only yards divided them, the hunter and the victim.

For a chronicler of social comedy, for a Communist Trollope, Okecie Airport on June 16 would have provided a rich harvest. Some of the welcoming officials, moving quicker than the camera shutter, ducked, almost curtsied, kissed the ring of the Pontiff. Suddenly, there were no Communists left in Poland.

At the head of the line of ambassadors, waiting like chocolate soldiers, was the Bulgarian envoy, doyen that year of the diplomatic corps in Warsaw. In May 1981, the Pope had survived an attempt to kill him in Saint Peter's Square. The gunman, an unhinged Turk named Mehmet Ali Agca, claimed he had Bulgarian support. Since then, the Polish aides around the Pope had tried to shield him from official contacts with Bulgarians. But on Warsaw airport tarmac it was unavoidable: a quick grip, the sliver of a smile.

Other Soviet bloc ambassadors had discovered pressing engagements that day. The absence of the Soviet and Czechoslovak envoys was particularly glaring; both countries had resisted the Pontiff's second trip. The Jaruzelski government had tried in the negotiations with the Church to anticipate the most obvious criticisms from their neighbors. The Pope would not hold a public meeting with Lech Walesa. The Pope's sermons should not stir up the old battle cries of Solidarity.

Two government agencies were crucial to the Jaruzelski game plan. The first was the propanganda machine. This was now firmly in the hands of Jaruzelski supporters, and the more controversial of the Pope's sermons could be filleted for public consumption. The main point was to keep control of the presentation of the visit, but not in the heavy-handed manner of Gierek's censors in 1979.

The other vital arm was security. This was to be shared out among the specialist bodyguard unit known as BOR, the Vatican security police, and three departments of the SB, the Polish secret police. The militia and voluntary police reservists were to be in charge of crowd control. The ZOMO riot police units were on alert especially in the Krakow region, where the Pope was due to give most of his sermons. The military anti-aircraft battalions were put on twenty-four-hour duty to protect Polish air space. The military police intensified their patrols in the capital in the days before the Pope's arrival to discourage "provocations," that all-purpose Polish term for politically inspired incident.

The Vatican saw the logic of this arrangement. Nobody wanted another assassination attempt. But it gave an important, politically dangerous role to Department Four, in charge of watching the Church. The whole security operation was being supervised by the interior minister, General Czeslaw Kiszczak, who entrusted most of the broad execution to three of his deputy ministers, one of whom, General Wladyslaw Ciaston, was head of the SB.

The anti-opposition department of the secret police ensured that as many potential Solidarity sympathizers as possible were put under protective arrest. Clandestine printers were raided. The industrial wing of the SB told local managers that factory buses and vehicles could not be put at the disposal of pilgrims and canceled leave for anyone with even mildly expressed Solidarity sympathies. The counterespionage department of the SB, one of the largest and most powerful, barred entry to Poland to known Solidarity supporters in the West. Overall coordination was in the hands of Department Four, the Church affairs specialists.

Piotrowski did not shake hands with the Pontiff, nor did he stand in the first and second ranks—that was left to the top brass. But he was there, alert, on duty.

The speeches from the rostrum had words for both the priest and the policeman. The Polish head of state, Professor Henryk Jablonski, reminded the nation that he was the figurehead of a Marxist state. The Pope was welcome, he said, blinking through heavy spectacles, but "we will not abandon the road of socialist reforms, nor shall we cease striving to make our socialist state organism strong and efficient." Piotrowski approved.

The Pope immediately set the tone for the eight-day pilgrimage. He would be trying to heal the wounds opened up by martial law but would not forget the Church's duty to side with the victims. "The kiss placed on the soil of Poland has a special meaning for me, it is like the kiss placed on the hands of a mother . . . a mother who has suffered much and who suffers anew." Sensing that he could not fulfill all the nation's high expectations from the visit, the Pope spoke directly to the victims. "I myself am not able to visit all the sick, the imprisoned, the suffering, but I ask them to be close to me in spirit." As he spoke the word "imprisoned," a ripple of approval passed through the audience of priests. Father Popieluszko was reassured: the Pope was not going to be silent about political prisoners.

"The Holy Father must show us the way," he told a friend a few weeks earlier. "He is the only one who can speak straight into the hearts of Poland. We must bypass ears and insert the message straight into the hearts."

"A complicated piece of surgery," his friend replied.

"No more so than the raising of Lazarus. We need somebody to tell us, in the name of Christ, Pick up your bed and walk!"

The priest and the policeman were busy that week, a week of alternating heat and unseasonable driving rain. The priest used his organizational talents to good effect. "Jerzy's skill was to create an organization solely on the basis of personal relations," said Father Przekazinski. "He knew every one of the nurses and doctors—they were his parishioners or former parishioners from St. Anna's Church. Just as he mobilized the medical community to help provide a practical solution to the problem of unmarried mothers, so he deployed Christians for the Pope." The nuns and lay Catholic assistants set up, dismantled tents, liaised with the state ambulance service, cajoled doctors into finding syringes, cotton wool, antiseptics. "We worked like galley slaves that week," recalled one nurse. "To rescue even one swooning girl in the middle of half a million people was a major piece of logistics."

That week a ragamuffin army was on the march. The Pope traveled to Wroclaw, to Poznan, to Czestechowa, to Krakow, and at every stop his audience was rarely less than half a million. They trekked from the north, from the Baltic ports that had been left out of the itinerary, and they slept under hedgerows, in cinemas, in abandoned buses, sometimes, it seemed, in trees. Father Popieluszko's expectations of the visit changed as the papal caravan progressed. By the third day, it was evident that the Pope was not proposing a political escape route for the young pilgrims who clutched at his words. But, undeterred, they managed to convert any congregation into a Solidarity carnival.

From the weathered battlements of Czestechowa's Jasna Gora monastery, the Pope's baritone echoed over their heads.

"We do not—we do not—want a Poland—a Poland—that costs us nothing—costs us nothing," came his voice duplicated by the loudspeakers. Dozens of Solidarity banners sprouted in the crowd in response to trigger words: workers, two mentions of solidarity with a small "s," any reference to truth or oppression or human rights.

The sharp-eyed Captain Piotrowski, glaring from the ramparts, could have unraveled most of the country's underground opposition simply by pinpointing the banners: "Ursus [tractor factory] Solidarity greets the Pope," "Warsaw Polytechnic Solidarity Is with You." But a million people shoehorned into the meadow surrounding the ancient monastery would have defeated even the most vigilant secret agent. Piotrowski had flown down to Czestechowa in a security helicopter accompanying the papal chopper. Protecting a famous visitor and harassing an outspoken priest were woven into the same rudimentary code, the defense of People's Poland.

For the police, the trip was a three-tier operation. First, in all regions to be visited by the Pope, Solidarity organizers had to be put under preventive arrest, or given "warning talks." That applied especially to those who were active in the gray zone, where it was no longer quite possible to distinguish between Church and Solidarity work. That meant lay Catholic clubs, Church aid centers for political prisioners, journalists on Church newspapers. Radical priests like Popieluszko had to be "put on ice," to use the agent argot. Stage two was the security planning of the trip, the eight days divided into high-risk and medium-risk blocks. Where was the Party headquarters in relation to the papal mass? Might workers unable to reach the mass vent their anger on the militia station? Stage three was a subtler operation: how to ensure that the Church and Solidarity did not cement their links, how to prevent the Pope's trip from launching an anti-Communist crusade.

Even before the Pope arrived, Piotrowski had a sober view of the probable consequences for Church–state relations. After the Pope left, things could only get worse between the Church and the authorities.

But even armed with that foreknowledge, Piotrowski could not find much reassurance in the panorama from the Pauline monastery. "I simply had this feeling," he explained later to a friend from Lodz, "a feeling that said—and these are Poles? These are my countrymen? All that talk about dignity—there was no dignity during the visit, not in Czestechowa or anywhere else."

But they were Poles, rowdy and proud. It was difficult to know whether the Pope gave the Poles what they wanted. The bellowing applause, almost frightening when voiced by so many people in such a confined space, was a poor measure. Sometimes the young pilgrims seemed to be applauding their own misery. The Virgin Mary, Queen of Poland, the Pope declared, "knows your sufferings, your difficult youth, your sense of injustice and humiliation, the lack of prospects for the future . . . perhaps the temptations to flee to some other world." That earned the loudest applause on Saturday night for it showed that the Pope understood both those who fought through the Solidarity era and the post-Solidarity generation.

"Today when we are fighting for the future form of social life, remember that this form depends on what people will be like," the Pope declared. It was a difficult message for the young listeners—but not for Father Popieluszko. He had seen the link between fighting for a free Poland and adherence to traditional Catholic tenets. No sex outside marriage, no artificial contraception, no abortion, no divorce, no woman priests, no abuse of alcohol. When a member of his parish strayed he treated him sensitively but with a firmness about what was right and wrong. He was, in every way, the Pope's man.

On that June Saturday in Czestechowa the Pope's most pressing problem was how to hold a dialogue with a million people. When he rose from his throne on the ramparts of the monastery, the crowd chanted in deafening unison, "Long live the Pope," making it impossible for him to speak. After a few minutes, he said with mock humility: "I would like to ask if a man who comes to Poland from Rome has the right to speak."

"*Bardzo prosimy*"—please go ahead—sang the pilgrims. But: "Come closer!" The Pope, to the confusion of the BOR bodyguards, walked to the very edge of the ramparts; a simple revolver could have picked him off, a pellet, a stone. "Any other requests?"

"Stay here forever!" came the reply.

The Pope did not stay, but he left behind the hope of a new beginning for Poland. A private meeting with Lech Walesa had underlined his support for the ideals of Solidarity. The Pope's two rounds of talks with General Jaruzelski provided grounds for speculation: Would the government now give way to pressure from the Church and Solidarity for a freer, more open society? At the top of everyone's list was the question of the hundreds of political prisoners still in jail.

If Popieluszko expected Polish prison gates to clank open, then he was disappointed. Warsaw began to hear loud grumbling from Moscow. The Kremlin wanted East–West relations to be free of the millstone of Poland. There was real business to be transacted between the superpowers. It had accepted the Pope's visit as the price of Poland's rehabilitation. But if this unleashed a new wave of antistate preaching, then the price was too high.

Seven weeks after the Pope had departed, Leonid Zamyatin, chief of the Soviet Central Committee International Information Department, arrived in Warsaw to convey the warnings in person. Apparently, not all the Polish comrades fully understood the concern of the allies; they were ignoring the very serious signals that Moscow was trying to pass on. Priests were acting as if the papal visit had given them immunity from socialist law. They were sheltering counterrevolutionaries (read: Solidarity activists), letting antisocialist culture thrive in the country's ten and a half thousand churches.

Zamyatin did Jaruzelski a favor. The general was never able to meet the expectations aroused by the Pope's visit. If there was to be liberalization, it would have to be gradual, not under pressure. Potential rivals in the Party had to be neutralized, the economy put into some kind of shape, and Solidarity destroyed as an underground opposition. Then, only then, he could go some way toward honoring the spirit of the papal visit. In the meantime, the country would have to be content with sham "dialogue," patriotic front organizations that would try to make Communist decisions palatable to the non-Communist country. Moscow, the general could claim with justice, was leaning on him to muzzle political priests. Popieluszko's name was mentioned prominently. Unless the Church put its own house in order there could be no social breakthroughs, no amnesties for political prisoners. If the government seemed sluggish, it was solely because the Church's own internal discipline problem was holding up progress on real issues.

The last major joint operation against Popieluszko between the Warsaw SB of Colonel Wolski and Department Four was drafted soon after Zamyatin's visit and had the personal approval of Interior Minister General Kiszczak. The minister and the Party leadership knew that despite the limitations for maneuver imposed by Moscow, some form of political amnesty would have to mark the lifting of martial law and Poland's return to the community of nations. The Pope's trip had made this inescapable. The form of the amnesty was still in doubt in the late summer of 1983, but it was plain that if Popieluszko were to be jailed, he would not be in for long.

Piotrowski saw the situation differently. He sensed that the Party was now serious about setting up firm demarcation lines between Church and state and that there would be no high-level objections to teaching Popieluszko a lesson. It would show if Jaruzelski was willing to bring formal legal charges against the priest.

Popieluszko, at ease after his summer holidays, saw nothing of this. His diary and his letters chart as usual the daily harassment but do not reveal any great awareness of a secret police plot against him. On August 30 he tried to drive with his bodyguard Waldemar Chrostowski to Gdynia to deliver a sermon to celebrate the third anniversary of the Gdansk agreement between the shipyard strikers and the government. It was an important occasion, and Popieluszko has prepared a lengthy sermon about the Christian duty to defend Solidarity. Before they got very far, three militia cars and two secret police vehicles forced him to draw up at curbside. Chrostowski was jailed for forty-eight hours—the maximum allowed without presenting charges—and Popieluszko for eight hours. There was only the most perfunctory questioning; the idea was simply to prevent Popieluszko arriving at his destination. The SB commander eventually contacted the Warsaw Curia, and after giving the usual protest, a priest was sent to the police station to sign for the release of Popieluszko. The next day police cars surrounded St. Stanislaw Kostka to make sure that Popieluszko did not stray northward.

To Popieluszko and his friends this was "anniversary behavior": the police were on alert for trouble and had, the churchmen assumed, been instructed to hem in the movements of anyone who might stir up unrest. After the Pope's visit, it was imperative that the security *apparat* demonstrate its control.

But soon the situation began to look more threatening. On September 26 the Central Committee Information Department sent one of its regular telexed news bulletins to Communist Party cells in Warsaw. Father Jerzy Popieluszko of St. Stanislaw Kostka, it said, was the subject of a formal criminal investigation. He was to be charged with abuse of religious freedom. The penalty was up to ten years in jail.

The Party had signaled that the time of tolerance for outspoken priests had passed. But while the Party had decided that Popieluszko's offense was political preaching, Piotrowski wanted to create a more serious crime: illegal possession of weapons. Piotrowski assigned one of his deputies, Lieutenant Leszek Pekala, to coordinate the operation with Wolski. They were to keep Popieluszko's modest apartment in Chlodna Street under observation for a week using one of the ubiquitous communications vans. Intended to rush around town conveying technicians to repair telephones, they were sometimes used as camouflage by the security services. Pekala was to make a reconnaisance visit to the apartment using a duplicate key supplied by Wolski's unit. Then, under his supervision, the agents would distribute enough incriminating material to press serious charges.

The plan seemed attractive in Rakowiecka Street. First, there was a general propaganda point to make. Popieluszko was not only an "extremist priest" but also aligned with the "extremist" wing of Solidarity; by harboring weapons and explosives in his apartment, the priest would be shown to the public as terrorist, a proponent of violent confrontation. Of course this stood the facts on their head: Popieluszko's exhortation, at the end of his fatherland masses to "go in peace, pay no heed to the shouts of provocateurs," was well known.

Meanwhile, the case against Popieluszko for political preaching was moving ahead. Twice during November the authorities tried to deliver the summons on Popieluszko but were met by the pleasant, holy obstructiveness of the tall, creamy-complexioned nun who runs the priest's house. Father Jerzy was not at home. No, his whereabouts were a bit of a mystery. No, she could not let the gentlemen into the house because everyone was busy, and anyway they would probably need a search warrant, would they not? And this piece of paper—a crinkled look of distaste—did not appear to say anything about forceably entering Church territory.

On December 2, the police tried again. Popieluszko celebrated the seven o'clock morning mass. It was thinly attended—the steelworkers at the Huta were already on morning shift—but at the back of the church there were some distinctly odd-looking men. After the mass, Popieluszko recorded in his diary, "I entered my room and then suddenly the doorbell began to ring insistently. I saw about twelve gentlemen standing at the door. Outside, parked near the church, there were militia and SB cars filled with people. They had a prosecutor's order to bring me immediately for an investigation."

It worked out differently. Popieluszko called the Warsaw Curia, who told the priest not to leave his house. Father Bogucki, in the short, grunted sentences which he invariably used to express contempt, said that he could not accept the summons on Popieluszko's behalf. Popieluszko was on attachment to the parish, not a formal member of the hierarchy. His superior was a bishop. Meanwhile news had escaped of the attempt to bring in Popieluszko. The militia jeeps and the Polski Fiats crammed with alert, fit young men were evidence enough. First the congregation from the mass, then people from Zoliborz, then Solidarity members from further afield arrived in the courtyard of the church. Led by three particularly raucous middle-aged women, specialists in aggressive prayer, they began to chant patriotic anthems and call on God to protect their priest from evil. A police car screeched its way through the crowd to the Curia, but the rest of the police remained, growing more embarrassed by the minute. At the Curia, Bishop Miziolek kept the police commander waiting; he had no intention of handing over his former seminary pupil without a fight. Eventually the officer was ushered into Miziolek's study, which blends a few elegant sticks of furniture with the functional g-plan of the working cleric. Pope John Paul smiled down from the wall.

"Please be seated," said the bishop, ignoring the rank of the visitor. For a while, a long while, the bishop studied the warrant as if it were a particularly rare piece of Medieval parchment. Then, handing it back with equal delicacy, Miziolek announced, "This appears to have only historical value, young man. The priest in question was due to appear before your prosecuting authorities at nine o'clock this morning. Now it is noon. Nine o'clock has therefore passed. We seem to be wasting each other's time."

Improbably, the SB seemed unsure over whether the summons was valid when it was served personally to a priest or to his superiors and, who, in the case of Popieluszko, was formally his superior. This legal inadequacy allowed Popieluszko to gain time and pushed back Piotrowski's plans to pin terrorism charges on the priest.

Popieluszko knew he was being pursued. The only comfort was the warmth and concern of his parishioners. After a service marking the miner's holiday, he noted in his diary: "I had to leave the house several times to show myself to the people. They were chanting *Szczesc Boze* [God give you luck—the traditional miner's greeting] for me."

But he concludes the entry on a dark note: "People were saying it was our small victory, but Satan is getting even angrier."

10
•
Negotiating
with
the Devil

THE FULL FORCES of the militia, the secret police, and the prosecutor's office eventually managed to enmesh him; it was unrealistic to expect otherwise. On December 9 the postwoman brought another summons when Popieluszko was out. Popieluszko went the post office and found that there was no trace of the summons. The prosecutor had given the summons directly to the postwoman to avoid delay. The religious affairs minister, Adam Lopatka, telephoned Archbishop Dabrowski at the episcopate and promised that the police would free Popieluszko after no more than two hours of interrogation. The Church agreed. The date was set: December 12, a day before the second anniversary of martial law.

"Well, the date wasn't good for me [before the thirteenth]," Popieluszko wrote, "but I had no choice. And it happened. One should never negotiate with the Devil."

At nine o'clock on December 12, friends drove Popieluszko from St. Stanislaw Kostka to the Mostowsky Palace, a former sugar baron's residence and now the principal militia headquarters in Warsaw. The Church had engaged the two best human rights defense counsel in Poland—Edward Wende, a tall, ruddy advocate who was already close to the priest, and Tadeusz de

Virion, whose record of acquittals was second to none. The priest, looking like a gawky schoolboy next to Wende and his wife, entered the police headquarters surrounded by a gaggle of well-wishers clutching red and white carnations. Upstairs in one of the reception rooms, the questioning proceeded as expected: the laborious checking of personal details, age, career, address, that were already meticulously documented in the priest's dossier. The questions and answers went on until noon—an hour longer than promised by Lopatka. Popieluszko was anxious to get back to St. Stanislaw Kostka and work out the final details of how he should commemorate December 13. On the desk in front of him was some of the "evidence" deployed against him: tape-recordings of his services, television tape confiscated from an American network, and photographs. To the defense lawyers these looked like unconvincing theater props.

At one o'clock a uniformed officer entered. "We have a warrant to search your apartment in Chlodna Street. You may take your lawyers or a witness. Please give me the keys." Popieluszko did not have the keys with him; he used the Chlodna flat barely more than once a week, to have a bath, to nap undisturbed by telephones, to prepare a sermon. Only close friends would ever accompany him there, and they saw a different Popieluszko. Not a self-assured priest who thought nothing of giving interviews to Western film crews, or of posing, head cradled in fists, for photographers. The Chlodna Popieluszko was shy, private, and self-doubting. At St. Stanislaw Kostka he was required to give everything of himself to the parishioners, to worried steelworkers and their families, to charity and organizational work. In his apartment, bought legally in 1978 with dollars transferred by his aunt in Pittsburgh, he could again look into himself. Sometimes he would be accompanied by a woman friend, but despite the immediate suspicion of the SB that she was his mistress, the young teacher simply listened and talked to Popieluszko. She was a discreet, understanding person outside Popieluszko's milieu: not a priest, not an actor, not a doctor, not a steelworker, not a policeman. Popieluszko had come to cherish his oasis in Chlodna, though his visits there were rare.

The lawyers refused to go. The summons had been for an interrogation, but this "invitation" smacked already of dirty tricks. If the authorities were planning something, it was tactically better for the lawyers not to be drawn into a separate case as witnesses, which could exclude them from acting as defense counsel. Popieluszko, flanked by two uniformed policemen, was taken to a patrol car. An SB car accompanied them on the drive to the apartment. Popieluszko was puzzled but not worried. "I went there calm," he noted in his diary, "because I did not even keep a premartial law (Solidarity) leaflet there." Even so, as the car bumped through the high-rise estate that now occupies the territory of the Warsaw ghetto, he quietly prayed for strength.

Popieluszko unlocked the flat. Waldemar Chrostowski, his loyal driver and bodyguard, had collected the keys at police behest. And while the commander of the operation Lieutenant Chylkiewicz from Wolski's unit, stayed with him, the others fanned out with astonishing familiarity. Three of the officers started to go through his books, skimming the leaves of a Bible. Books are a common hiding place in Polish households for money and confidential papers. But a fourth officer, a short wiry man with hair cut *en brosse*, went straight to the sofa bed. It was Lieutenant Leszek Pekala, assigned by Department Four to make sure that the mission was not spoiled by the blundering of Wolski's men. The catch-spring on Popieluszko's sofa bed did not function properly, and it was necessary to jerk it to one side before lifting open the bed. Pekala had obviously done this before. There was no hesitation, no pause for thought before throwing open the bed. And there, instead of the usual stored bed linen, was the planted booty. A simulated gasp of astonishment from Pekala, a grim nodding of the head from Chylkiewicz. The other officers joined Pekala, and slowly they unloaded the bed, like dutiful longshoremen.

Chylkiewicz started to draw up an inventory: fifteen thousand Solidarity leaflets; a message smuggled from the Solidarity leadership in Rakowiecka Street prison, translated into French; sixty copies of a report drafted by Father Malkowski describing his angry encounters with the primate; a letter from an antigovernment exile in Paris; four tubes of printers' ink; some caricatures of Glemp. Then came the crucial find: thirty-six-machine-gun bullets, dynamite with wire and detonators, four tear gas containers.

Popieluszko, at first pale and unsteady on his feet, had regained his composure. The "discovery" of the dynamite had tapped the essential farce of the occasion. As Bishop Kraszewski said afterward: "After all Father Jerzy had been in the army. He knew about these things. He knew that you don't sleep on explosives." Popieluszko laughed. "I think you have rather exaggerated, gentlemen." The priest denied having anything to do with the material in his apartment. The police commander asked him to sign the inventory. "I will confirm that these things were found in my apartment, that they do not belong to me, that I have never seen them before, and most of all I wish to point out that one of the officers headed toward the spot where the materials were hidden immediately after we entered the apartment—as if he knew they were there all the time."

If there was any doubt that the whole incident was carefully staged, it was dispelled when a Polish television team arrived. It was the same team that films Westerners caught in compromising situations, a unit that has what colleagues describe as a "good working relationship" with the Interior Ministry. "They opened all the chests," wrote Popieluszko in the blue copy book that served as his diary, "and the fridge too to film its contents."

By eight o'clock that evening he was back in the Mostowsky Palace in cell number 6. It was clear that the police wanted to humiliate him. He was ordered to strip, an unusual measure even for hardened criminals. A police sergeant stood propped against the door while a young militia man, hardly more than twenty years old, carried out the search. The young policeman was nervous, his hands fluttering, barely touching the priest's body.

"I'm sorry I have to do this," he whispered. "I never thought I would have to do something like this in my lifetime. I had no choice, honest to God."

Popieluszko was impressed by the courage of the policeman. His superior was standing within earshot, yet the boy felt ashamed enough to risk punishment.

"Don't worry," Popieluszko told him, "Calm down. This is

not your decision. If you hadn't been ordered to do it then somebody else would have. That's the way they wanted it." The priest was moved. He was seized with the idea that the police who had been pursuing him with such intensity could also be victims.

The priest was led to the investigation cells through a long, grim corridor. "Do you know what it's like?" asked a political prisoner. "It's like being a bullet in the barrel of a gun. You sit there in this long, narrow container and you wait for someone to pull the trigger." Popieluszko was the sixth inhabitant of cell number 23. There was a man accused of murdering his wife and throwing her into the Vistula, a man accused of killing four people while driving a locomotive, a confidence trickster, an informer, and as the priest recorded in his diary, "a nice rat which came to the cell through a small window to pick up some bread." "Politicals" are not treated differently from common criminals. They are packed together indiscriminately like passengers on the Tokyo underground. At the same time as Popieluszko was sharing a cell with murderers, the Solidarity leadership was cooped up in Rakowiecka Street jail with drug smugglers from Sri Lanka.

But the prisoners knew the difference. From the moment that Popieluszko arrived with his mattress and two blankets, the cell inmates treated him like a visiting statesman. The warders—also embarrassed by the presence of a priest—gave Popieluszko soup with the best bits of meat. The priest was grateful for the small kindness, but he had decided to fast during his arrest. He passed the food on to his cellmates. They in turn did all of Popieluszko's orderly duties, emptying the latrine bucket, swabbing the floor, even making up his bed for him.

That night he hardly slept. He prayed and thought about the weekend exactly two years before when martial law was declared and his life changed.

By the following morning, Archbishop Dabrowski had been on the telephone to the religious affairs minister, Adam Lopatka, and had made contact with General Kiszczak at the Interior Ministry. It was essential for the future development of Church–state relations that Popieluszko be released, Dabrowski told them. But the authorities let Popieluszko sweat. A long morning passed. Popieluszko heard the confession of one of the inmates and listened to the animated talk of the accused murderer and one of the warders, whose brother was a priest. Shortly before six in the evening he was taken to the police photographer, put against a curtained background, and photographed in profile and full face. The authorities were going to carry on treating him as a criminal. After the photo session he was brought to the main conference hall in the palace. A long table, a couple of dozen chairs tucked neatly away and at the far end, the prosecutor, two SB officers and Edward Wende, and Wende's wife, who nodded encouragingly to the priest. The prosecutor began to read: "Taking into account the serious and dangerous nature of the material discovered in Priest Popieluszko's apartment and the lack of a satisfactory explanation for it, the Warsaw prosecutor has decided to extend the terms of the investigation against the accused to include articles 143, 282, and 286 of the Penal Code for the Polish People's Republic." The charges were as close as one can come under Polish law to branding someone as a terrorist. Total possible jail term: twenty-one years. Popieluszko, glancing briefly at his lawyer for reassurance, said he refused to comment on the charges, but: "I consider the whole incident is aimed at stirring up public unrest because for some time now I have been more than just a private citizen."

Popieluszko was still unaware that the Church had secured his freedom. When Wende's wife brought him some cigarettes, he smiled his gratitude. A heavy smoker, he could measure out his day with the tobacco, ease the boredom and tension by filling his lungs. He had only been in prison for a day and a night, but already he was beginning to calculate like a prisoner.

Back in the cell, the murderer wanted to know how things had gone. "Bad," Popieluszko replied. At nine o'clock, when the lights began to flicker in the cell, the warder unlocked the door.

"Collect your things, father."

"Why? Where am I going?"

"I expect they want to move you somewhere else. Maybe Rakowiecka Street, maybe"—he looked distastefully at the other inmates—"somewhere with more congenial company."

Everything moved quickly. First to the police doctor, then to the room where he had been interrogated. Then, a bustling, officious entry. "It was two lawyers and the prosecutor," Popieluszko noted, "and the latter said the authorities had decided to release me but that further action against me would depend on my attitude." As he left the room and made his way through the main reception area, he bumped into one of his two police guards. "Pray for us, father," said one. The younger of the two moved slightly to one side and spoke in a quick undertone: "Father, I know this is perhaps not the right moment, but, well, my wife is expecting a baby next month and it would be nice, I mean an honor, if you could come to the baptism."

"At a quarter to ten," the diary reports, "I was free. Free?"

There was a great deal of relief that Popieluszko was free, not only at Kostka—where parishioners had constructed a huge V-for-victory sign to greet their priest—but also among other priests close to Solidarity. Did this not show that the primate would give full backing to clerics exposed to harassment by the authorities? It did not. The price of Popieluszko's freedom was high, and he was to learn soon enough that Glemp had resented paying it. The Church leadership and Jaruzelski had been edging their way toward a summit meeting, the first significant encounter since the Pope's visit. Glemp wanted to press the government into honoring the promises made during the Pope's visit. Half a year had passed, and the hints that had been so loud then—that the authorities would permit a Church fund to help private farmers, would allow the Church legal status in Poland, would move toward freeing political prisoners—were little more than whispers. As far as political goals were concerned, the government was suggesting that the Church had a role to play in persuading the Solidarity leadership, the union's main thinkers and organizers awaiting trial in Rakowiecka Street prison, to leave the country or give up their political ambitions. If they did so the government would be able to release the several hundred jailed Solidarity members. The Church was a reluctant actor, but it was at least worth talking about. On the Church's legal status, the government had no objections in principle, but it wanted to ensure that legislation did not just give the Church rights—to publications, to theological colleges, to all the ground captured during the Solidarity years—but also duties. A joint declaration of principle would make clear that the Church accepted the legitimacy of Communist rule and the limitations bound up with being a strong Church in a Communist state. If agreement could be reached on these points, said the authorities, then normal diplomatic relations could be established between Poland and the Holy See.

For Glemp, these were big prizes, and the summit with Jaruzelski, fixed for January 6, beckoned like a lighthouse. At last the investment of the papal trip would start to pay dividends.

But the *quid pro quo* was the depoliticization of the Catholic Church in Poland. The primate, the bishops, the Pope all understood this, though Glemp supported the idea most zealously. More than almost anybody else in the Church's leadership, Glemp was convinced that Jaruzelski had to be given flanking support against Moscow. According to the primate's analysis, Zamyatin's visit to Warsaw and other Soviet signals since the papal visit were indications of the delicacy of Jaruzelski's position. One did not have to compromise with Communism to recognize that the Church would make it easier for Jaruzelski. Restraint rather than confrontation would in the long run be of greater benefit to the Polish people.

That was the high-level political calculation, and Popieluszko, whose directness was so disturbing to the authorities, had stumbled into the crossfire. After Popieluszko's arrest, Glemp had to send a letter to General Jaruzelski. It would be difficult for them to meet, the letter said, as long as such a well-known priest was in jail. The letter was written reluctantly. The Church had precious few bargaining chips before the Glemp–Jaruzelski meeting, and the last thing the primate wanted to do was ask for favors.

On December 18, the priests at St. Stanislaw Kostka read out a statement prepared by Popieluszko, reassuring his parishioners that his apartment on Chlodna Street had been bought legally and that the Church knew of it, contrary to the information in the official press. It also said the explosives were "a provocation." Bogucki added his voice to the statement. It was important to preempt any propaganda barrage against Popieluszko. It was too easy for small specks of mud to stick, and the charges were still hanging over him.

Popieluszko drew strength from his contacts with his parishioners, from Bogucki, his parish priest, from friends like Przekazinski. He began to realize the depth of his isolation, the fear of loneliness. In his diary, he was cautious, censoring emotion like a boy shamed out of tears by his strong mother.

But some pain was so powerful that it could not be contained. On the Monday after his explanation was read aloud at St. Stanislaw Kostka during every mass, Popieluszko drove to Miodowa to thank Archbishop Dabrowski for securing his release. He clutched a huge bouquet of flowers and had some hope that the primate, too, would receive him. Dabrowski was gentle and kind, touched by the evident relief and gratitude on the face of the young priest. The primate was not in, but Popieluszko could see the primate if he went to the Warsaw seminary where Glemp was visiting. Popieluszko paused only to buy more flowers and arrived just in time to meet the primate at the gate.

Had Popieluszko a better feel for Church politics, he would not have been surprised by what happened. That week the primate had released the text of his Christmas message to the Poles. Its warning to Popieluszko and his fellow Solidarity priests was unmistakable:

> The un-Christian slogan "The worse it goes, the better it is," leads to suicide. We understand that the word "reconciliation" which has lost its meaning offers no program. All the same, Poland must be saved. The scanty garment which covers the nakedness of the fatherland must not be torn to shreds. . . . At this time, the Church wishes to do its duty with humility. In accordance with the Holy See's regulations, the bishops will warn the clergy against engaging in politics.

It was an uncharacteristically clear statement. First, the primate stressed, contrary to popular belief, he had no great confidence in the Jaruzelski leadership. But it was the Church's task to prevent the destruction of the nation, either at the hands of Russian invaders or from internal paralysis.

That was Glemp's position, and Popieluszko knew it well enough. But as he went with the primate back into the seminary to a small study, he had no plans other than to offer the warmth of gratitude and receive in return the warmth of a superior who cared about the freedom of his clerics.

Instead, he came in for a cold, blunt chain of reprimands, talk appropriate for a headmaster. The hurt shone through in the Popieluszko diary entry:

> What I subsequently heard was worse than anything I could have expected. It was true that he had a reason to be nervous because he had put so much effort into the letter he sent to Jaruzelski about me. But his charges against me completely knocked me off balance. Even the SB during the interrogation showed me more respect. It was painful, but I consider it was God's grace for it will help me to purify and increase the fruit of my labors. What hurt me most was the accusation that I have ruined the services for the employees of the medical service corps, the very thing I've been so devoted to over the past five years. . . . God, what grave experiences you are sending me, while at the same time giving me so much strength and human friendship.

The primate attacked Popieluszko for neglecting his official function as chaplain to nurses and doctors in order to build up the masses for the fatherland. Glemp was also unhappy about the use of Solidarity emblems at Popieluszko's services, the use of actors to read nationalist verse, and his contacts with Solidarity activists. He wanted once and for all to scare Popieluszko away from politics, partly for his own good, and partly because the priest had become inconvenient in the grand Church–state strategy. As Popieluszko left the seminary shaking with tension, he suddenly burst into tears, tears of incomprehension.

11

•

Amnesty

"GROWN MEN CRIED," Piotrowski the police captain would say
later, "when they heard that Popieluszko had been freed." It
was an improbable vision: hardened secret agents allowing salt
tears of frustration to course down their cheeks. But Piotrowski
was exaggerating only slightly. Such was the mood in Rakowiecka Street or at least that part of the Interior Ministry
which was still peopled by police professionals. The release of
Popieluszko highlighted a deep division within the ranks of the
secret police; the division between the newcomers, the pragmatic army men like General Kiszczak, who had been installed
at the top, and the long-term secret agents who had joined the
ministry much as they would join a family firm.

The history of secret police control is like a page out of the
research notebooks of Margaret Mead. Competing tribes fight
around the totem of power, make blood sacrifices, deflower political virgins, and marry off their daughters to end family ri-
valries. Department Four, like many other parts of the secret
police, was based on an elaborate old-boy network. The deputy
director, Colonel Adam Pietruszka, was in charge of recruiting
new blood during the department's rapid expansion. New, energetic agents who could be trusted were needed to combat the

132

growing confidence of priests, since the election of the Polish Pope. A former colleague in the UB—the forerunner of the SB—Zenon Chmielewski rang up Pietruszka and together they had a snatched lunch at one of the grubby cafes near Rakowiecka Street. "I have a young son who does not know what to do with himself," Chmielewski declared. This son was intelligent, a good worker, and just finishing the higher officer militia school at Szczytno. He did not want to be sent to the provinces. Could Adam, for old times' sake, find a place for the boy? The old comrade obliged.

Waldemar Chmielewski had drifted from a job in the foreign trade bank into military service with the ZOMO riot units. He was tough enough and, as aptitude tests showed, much brighter than the average police officer. But he was a tyro at secret police work. His father had only stirring tales of shooting anti-Communist partisans in Poland's near-civil war after the Communist takeover. Times had changed and Chmielewski needed a tutor. He found one in the offspring of another secret police family: Grzegorz Piotrowski.

Piotrowski impressed almost everybody he came in contact with. He had a capacity for clear, logical presentation of arguments, for bureaucratic infighting, and for generating enthusiasm in his subordinates. Chmielewski was overjoyed at having Piotrowski first as deputy section head, then as operational chief. When a rumor swept the halls of Department Four that Piotrowski was about to be transferred, Chmielewski asked the captain to take him along. "He helped me and explained things," said Chmielewski. "It was thanks to him that my work brought good results and I was awarded prizes. I believed him to be a man of strong personality, capable of dealing with any situation."

Piotrowski came from a secret police dynasty in Lodz. Since the rise of Mieczyslaw Moczar, the power-hungry former secret policeman who was a challenger for the Party leadership, Lodz had become a kind of Eton for agents. Piotrowski senior knew Moczar well, Moczar in turn had influence that stretched deep inside the secret police. Even after he was pushed to the outer orbit of power, he could fix appointments in the police with a telephone call from his Senacka Street apartment. Piotrowski moved to Warsaw in 1981. He was thirty years old and eager to make an impression on the ministry. He had been a deputy section head in Lodz and was appointed to the same level in Rakowiecka Street, a captain's position, but there was never any doubt that this was a promotion. Rakowiecka Street was the central clearinghouse for all secret police activity; it throbbed with rumor and classified information. Even a lowly captain would know by the end of Monday evening what had happened—what had really happened—in the Politburo session that morning. His Lodz apartment had been larger, but the three rooms in Bernadynska Street were good by Warsaw standards. Most people on the block had bought their apartments for dollars, so there was a fair sprinkling, among his neighbors, of retired (or semi-retired) prostitutes and businessmen, even other security men who had somehow managed to enrich themselves. It was his wife, the daughter of another secret policeman, in any case, who had most contact with the neighbors, especially the woman next door, who would later be required to put up an alibi for the captain—because every spare moment he spent in the ministry or in the cafes nearby. Piotrowski was a blend of flawed idealism and opportunism. Within the first year of his new assignment, Piotrowski was approached by Aleksandr Wolowicz, who at the time worked in the Council for Religious Affairs. The contact itself was hardly unusual, since Piotrowski's branch of the Interior Ministry existed to serve the needs of the government in its dealings with the Church. Wolowicz's request was strange: Would Piotrowski please ensure that a certain family applying for passports receive them? Calculating and cynical, Piotrowski was not the sort of new recruit to ask too many questions. He was on the inside of the police network, and too much introspection was a sign of bad faith. He would do what he could. Passports were not an easy matter to arrange in Poland, especially after martial law. Poles, once among Europe's most active travelers, now had to justify their need to leave the country. Piotrowski was not at all pleased to learn that the family requesting passports included a Jewish dissident who wanted to go to Israel. However, he overcame his ethical scruples. Helping Wolowicz would win him an influential debtor, while failing to help would make him a powerful enemy. Within a few weeks, his contact with the passport office provided another opportunity to be of service, this time to himself. An automobile repair man, Grzegorz Suski, turned up in Piotrowski's office to ask about the Audi sedan parked outside. Suski mentioned that it was in need of extensive repairs. Piotrowski had bought the car in Lodz, and it had given him nothing but trouble since then. Suski commiserated. Then he got round to the reason for his visit. He wanted a passport to go to West Germany. A few weeks later, Suski was in Frankfurt. Piotrowski, glad to be of service, was driving an overhauled Audi. Later when these sideline services were mentioned in a courtroom, Piotrowski was furious. "I helped and intervened in passport matters many times, which was not rare in our department. Others did it, and I myself arranged hundreds of urgent passport matters. I simply fulfilled the requests of an institution with which we had permanent cooperation, and all I did was in the line of duty."

The policeman could justify most of his activities, however corrupt, in the name of duty. Piotrowski carried little moral baggage. He did his job in such a way as to win maximum benefits. On a parallel track, he was helping to build the kind of Poland in which men like himself would flourish.

General Czeslaw Kiszczak arrived at Rakowiecka Street more or less simultaneously with Piotrowski, but he did not have the advantages of his young subordinate. He was an outsider with distinctly unpopular ideas about how intelligence should be gathered and used. He was a deer hunter, a specifically military and higher Party recreation. None of the Old Guard policemen disappeared into the countryside for the weekend; if they hunted, it was for girls or bargain cars. If they strayed into nature, it was to go fishing with old SB chums in the provinces. Hunting is one of the best-established methods of extracurricular decision making for the Party elite in Czechoslovakia, East Germany, Hungary, and Poland. After the deer is slung on to the trucks, business can be transacted over vodka between members of the general staff, regional party chiefs, propaganda specialists. The hunting mafia is one of the basic ingredients of a reshuffle, an informal, untapped, noncommital way of communicating outside the official channels. On one hunting expedition, the Hungarian leader Janos Kadar decided to fire his television chief because he had expressed a wish to be interior minister. "Anyone who wants to be police minister should not be allowed to do it," he said, allowing the bon mot to circulate in Budapest. It was a message Kiszczak understood. He did not really want to be in Rakowiecka Street, but it was his soldier's duty to be there. Kiszczak read books—"I know your works," he would tell poets writing for the clandestine press, summoned into his presence after being released from internment or applying for a passport—and he played bridge. A slightly above-average player, he would go to great lengths to persuade top players to sit at his table. Above all, Kiszczak was a self-improver; an army officer, yes, a dabbler in espionage, but also someone who wanted to scent the air outside the barracks.

It did not take him long to deduce that police professionals like Piotrowski's protectors were opposed to his appointment. The Interior Ministry is not simply a synonym for the secret police. It covers a huge range of activities that employs six deputy ministers. Kiszczak's predecessor, Miroslaw Milewski, had given the deputies considerable breathing space. The only way to run the ministry was to ensure that intelligence operations had a degree of autonomy. Kiszczak found himself a victim of this system. The powers of discretion granted not only to deputy ministers but also to department heads meant that almost none of the detail of police activity was reaching him. Milewski had been kicked upstairs, appointed Politburo member in charge of Communist Party control over the police. There were rumors, and later evidence, that old secret police hands were going directly to Milewski, bypassing Kiszczak.

Trying to break out of the clogged machinery of Rakowiecka Street, General Kiszczak brought in his own men. It was rather as if the U.S. Defense Intelligence Agency had decided that the FBI was not trustworthy enough and sent its own officers into the field. Kiszczak had spent most of his army career in military counterintelligence, directing it from 1972 to 1979, and then for two years heading the WSW, the Army Internal Service, which embraces both counterintelligence and the military police. With Jaruzelski's encouragement, Kiszczak had started to expand army intelligence activities into the civilian area. That gave the WSW *carte blanche.*

The idea of giving the military greater powers was to block any attempt by Moczar to seize power. The nationalist, anti-Semitic campaigner had consistently used the secret police lobby in his attempts to destabilize the governments of his rivals. Jaruzelski wanted to depoliticize the secret police, and the only way he knew was to install the army.

But the presence of the army officers chafed men like Piotrowski and Pietruszka. It was like a replay of the traditional sporting rivalry between Gwardia, the Interior Ministry sporting club, and Legia, the army club. Every meeting could be measured like a soccer score: Gwardia 2, Legia 1. The main problem was that police operations, which had developed their own impetus, were passed eagerly up the ladder for approval and were then scotched when they reached Kiszczak's desk. The minister would simply scrawl "No," or "Not yet" on top of the draft and send it back into a filing cabinet.

So it had been with Popieluszko. Piotrowski had penned a memorandum outlining four courses of possible action against the priest:

1. Disclosure and counteraction against the influence of Western centers of ideological subversion, reconnaissance of subject's [Popieluszko's] contacts with Western embassies, and methods of exerting NATO special service influence on him.
2. Disclosure and counteraction against creating an underground network training cadres for future social upheaval.
3. Monitoring of trips. Subject's travel itinerary throughout Poland is not accidental.
4. Evidence of the subject breaking existing laws in the Polish People's Republic.

Connoisseurs of the art of office memoranda will recognize that the document is as much an interdepartmental power play as a declaration of war against Popieluszko. Point one would require the counterespionage department in Rakowiecka Street, perhaps the most influential in secret police headquarters, to supply regular sightings and information to Piotrowski. The monitoring of trips, if approved, would give Piotrowski even greater freedom to get out of the office and undertake his own observation of Popieluszko. And point two was to connect Piotrowski's section very closely with the anti-opposition and union-watching departments of the SB.

But nothing had come of the memo.

At the beginning of 1984 there was still some hope that Father Popieluszko could be caught in a web of legal articles so comprehensive that even the Church leadership would not be able to save him. It was a slender hope. Kiszczak's release of the priest simply in the interests of the Glemp–Jaruzelski summit did not augur well. "Popieluszko should have sweated it out [in jail] over Christmas," one agent said. "Instead, what happens? The priest was treated like a returning hero who outwitted the police. Glemp may have chewed him out a bit, but he still celebrated mass with him." Glemp did indeed break the Christmas wafer with Popieluszko in honor of the medical community. There was a huge congregation, the largest gathering of doctors and nurses that anyone could remember; but the primate did not comment. The atmosphere was still subzero, the young priest still smarting, the primate contemplating higher politics. "Cain and Abel," said a Krakow priest, "showed more fraternal solidarity than Father Jozef and Father Jerzy." The intentions of Department Four toward Popieluszko were plain enough: the accumulation of pressure on the priest so that the episcopate would have to intervene either to avoid the scandal of a trial or the breakdown of the priest's health. The donkey work was left to Wolski and the prosecutor's office, but Piotrowski's unit gathered extraneous information about his private life and the state of Popieluszko's health. This intelligence was not shared with Wolski. By this stage, there was little interchange between Rakowiecka Street and the Warsaw Internal Affairs Office. At what point, Piotrowski must have wondered, would Popieluszko break? When would he be overwhelmed by the sheer weight of persecution and give in?

The summit between Glemp and Jaruzelski on January 6 encouraged the authorities—not just the police—to believe that the Church would soon exercise tighter internal controls on its clergy. They issued a bland statement of anxiety about the arms race, but the two men, the stumpy primate and the arthritically stiff soldier, had actually discussed the stages for putting relations between Church and state on an orderly basis. Both men liked calendars of action. The skeptical bodies to which they would both later have to report—the Polish conference of bishops and the Communist Party Central Committee—preferred bad news in easily digestible lumps. The idea was that there should first be a joint declaration of principle by the state and the episcopate—an "understanding"—in which the Church and the priesthood would be granted a legitimate permanent role in the Communist state. A second document would spell out in detail the legal basis for Church publications and Church activities on dioceses, parishes, seminaries, theological colleges. Finally, a protocol could then be initialled in which normal, though low-level, diplomatic relations between the Vatican and the Polish Communist state were established.

The first "understanding" however, would state explicitly that priests had no political ambitions and specify the duties of the clergy. While the primate thought that would give some stability to the Church's special status and the nagging fears that a neo-Stalinist might someday roll back Catholic influence, the government believed the drafts would destroy the immunity of the Church; it could be treated like any other Polish organization. The primate, believing that the legislation was more than a distant dream, acted as if the laws were already binding. Three days after the summit with Jaruzelski, the primate's secretary summoned a friend of Popieluszko's, Father Mieczyslaw Nowak.

Nowak had been using his parish in the Warsaw suburb of Ursus to hold special masses for workers. His sermons were fiercely nationalistic and peppered with criticism of the government. The Ursus district is built around a tractor factory that was once a Solidarity stronghold, a natural rallying nave for a field of banners, the final benediction a signal for protest marches. The authorities resented the fact that Nowak was holding—as was Popieluszko in St. Stanislaw Kostka—a series of worker education classes in the basement and thus keeping alive the relationship between shop-floor activists and intellectuals, sowing the seeds of opposition.

The primate told Nowak to "calm things down." The Warsaw Curia had received formal complaints from the police about the content of his sermons. The legal action against Popieluszko, said the primate, should be taken seriously by other priests. "It is in the nature of our mission," the primate told Nowak, using rotund, formal Polish, "to protect not only lay believers subjected to measures by the authorities but also to protect the Mother Church." It was important to avoid giving the police an excuse to fight the Church: not a question of bravery or integrity, but rather of how best to achieve the Church's main aim of keeping the faith alive and strong in an atheistic system.

Popieluszko was strangely reassured when he heard of Nowak being on the carpet; the primate was not singling him out for criticism. It was a general line which had to be toed by all priests. And the primate could justify it not just by pointing to the needs of higher politics, for spiritual stakes. When, in February, the primate ordered Nowak to take over a country parish in Leki Koscielne—with four thousand parishioners scattered over twenty villages and not a factory worker among them—there was anger in Ursus. But the anger passed, and the protests at Ursus stopped along with the controversial masses.

Department Four was encouraged. Even if Popieluszko was free, the constant barrage of interrogations ensured that the Church hierarchy would watch him closely and made for tougher internal Church discipline. Popieluszko had been due for his first interrogation since his release on January 5, but the Jaruzelski–Glemp summit persuaded the authorities to drop the questioning until January 12. But two days before the scheduled session Lieutenant Chylkiewicz, Wolski's man who had supervised the search of the priest's apartment, came to Kostka, parking his white Polonez in the courtyard and telling Popieluszko to report for questioning.

When Popieluszko went to his apartment on Chlodna Street the following afternoon, he found the reason for the change of appointment. The police had planted new material, ready for a repeat performance of the arrest for explosives. "In the shoe cupboard," noted the priest in his diary, "there were two big envelopes with 200 [Solidarity] leaflets. I put two copies into the counsel's file and watched the rest burnt by the concierge." While he was installing a burglar alarm he found yet more "evidence." "On a shelf under the ceiling we found master copies of leaflets and a typescript entitled 'Report on a meeting with the Primate. Notes made by Father Popieluszko. Text authorized by Father Kantorski.' How devilish they are! They want me to be seen as at loggerheads with the primate. In addition, I found a pile of photos depicting the primate as an internee at Bialoleka [jail] tucked away among my books. I don't even feel angry with them. All I feel is an odd sort of grief. How can such things happen—in the same fatherland? Are they still Poles? Can someone be really so completely bought?"

The leaflets were the idea of Lieutenant Leszek Pekala of Department Four. Piotrowski had ordered Pekala to ensure that the material found in the Chlodna Street apartment included documents attacking the primate. This was in accord with the standard strategy of the department, indeed the whole of the Communist machine, to uncover and exaggerate the splits in the Church and in Solidarity whenever possible. They had deduced that Popieluszko felt wronged by the primate and made the kinetic jump to portraying the young priest as an archconspirator against the Church hierarchy. The lack of subtlety was characteristic of Pekala. He had worked his way up through the ranks. He had none of the family advantages that had accelerated the promotion of Piotrowski or Chmielewski, and he had one large handicap: he was homosexual. Although he and Chmielewski were the same rank, there was never any doubt about who would end up as a department chief and who would have to plod away at the levels of the middle inspectorate. Pekala's skills were those of a dirty tricks operative. Nobody else in Piotrowski's unit knew how to hot-wire a car engine, how to follow unobserved, how to organize an ambush. The Mostowsky police presidium had a roomful of confiscated underground publications loosely classified. Pekala simply filled his car with every document that mentioned or caricatured the primate. What was missing was a piece of paper that directly linked Popieluszko with Glemp or mentioned both their names. This was easily remedied: a matrix, the basic sheet needed to reproduce thousands of leaflets on a printing machine, was made by Pekala's friends, cobbling together fragmented quotations from different Solidarity documents. The result was gibberish, only the title made any kind of sense. It was "evidence" that was never supposed to be read, only quoted.

Pekala, Chmielewski, Piotrowski, and his immediate superior, Colonel Adam Pietruszka, were working together at this stage. Not only was there coordination between the Warsaw Internal Affairs office and Colonel Wolski as well as contacts with the prosecutor's office, the whole propaganda machine was also behind them. It was a centrally controlled operation. On the day after Christmas, the Warsaw evening daily *Ekspres Wieczorny* and then television and radio carried items on "the secret flat of Citizen Popieluszko." The suggestion made by the media and in private talks between the authorities and Archbishop Dabrowski was that Popieluszko had somehow used black market dollars to buy his apartment on Chlodna Street and had kept its existence secret from the Church. The priest toyed with the idea of a libel action but, after talks with friends, decided it would be undignified. Instead, he drafted a statement explaining the circumstances of his buying the apartment and read it from the pulpit at St. Stanislaw Kostka. The teacher, Malgosia Z., who had accompanied Popieluszko on some of his trips around Poland, found herself a target. Her interrogations were an attempt to demonstrate that she was having an affair with Popieluszko. Already before Christmas they had interrogated her and, according to the priest's diaries, "blackmailed her and forced her to collaborate." In fact, she confined herself to answering relatively straightforward questions. After Christmas, the police tried to pick her up outside her house and finally arrested her inside Warsaw University. The television immediately announced that she had been detained and suggested that she was linked in some way with the priest. "She was very brave," Popieluszko recorded. "The previous evening she fell asleep with a rosary in her hand."

Anyone touched by Popieluszko seemed to draw secret police interest. Waldemar Chrostowski, the priest's bodyguard and driver, was interrogated, and a police team searched the apartment of friends from his previous parish in Anin. All the stops were being pulled out to find some real evidence. In his rush to seal the case against Popieluszko, Pekala had gone too far. Nobody, not General Kiszczak, not Jaruzelski, believed that the priest had really harbored an ammunition store in his apartment.

Popieluszko's lawyer, Edward Wende, had already spotted the obvious flaw in the case: if the evidence had been planted, none of the documents or weaponry could possibly bear the priest's fingerprints. Wende told him: "At all costs, Jerzy, do not touch anything they give you." Popieluszko took the advice literally, and the result sometimes approached high comedy. During one session in room 210 at the Mostowsky police presidium, the interrogator laid out a sheaf of documents on his desk, fanning them out like a pack of cards. Popieluszko put his hands in his cassock pockets. This way he would not touch anything by chance. He had to work very hard to control himself. The interrogator, furious, started to throw the papers at Popieluszko, who caught them in his cassock.

Nor did his lips betray him. Popieluszko kept his answers crisp and obstructive. For the first interrogation of 1984, he arrived at 9 AM with Wende.

"Sit down, father," Lieutenant Chylkiewicz said. "How is your state of health? Are you fit for questioning?"

Silence.

"So I shall write, 'As previously described in the files of the prosecutor's office.' Any objections?"

Silence.

"Would you like to say anything about the case against you?"

"Nothing."

"Good, good, well, that is a kind of progress. Do you plead guilty?"

"Absolutely not."

"About this flat in Chlodna Street. Tell me about it. People seem to be talking about it. . . ."

"If they are talking, it's not because of me. I don't see why I should provide an explanation."

Chylkiewicz scribbled in the margin of his notepad after

every answer, though a minute taker, seated at a slight angle to the desk, was writing everything down. Above the interrogator hung a red and white print of the Polish eagle, standard decor for government offices. Popieluszko, glancing at it, thought of the eagle on the Solidarity banner at the Warsaw steelworks. That eagle had a crown on it, the symbol of old, independent Poland. The Communists had taken off the crown.

"What about the civilian guards at Kostka? What are they supposed to do?"

Silence. The priest was praying, reciting the rosary as he had in the army under the hostile gaze of the drill sergeant.

The lieutenant lost his patience. "Just tell me this—are you going to explain anything at all?"

"As a matter of general principle, I should like to use my right to refuse to testify." It was the priest's longest sentence in an hour.

Silence was a gamble. If the interrogations wore on, the strain would begin to tell on him physically and psychologically. An SB officer had warned him on January 16 that there would be a bout of questioning every week until he fully cooperated. It was not an empty threat: the interrogations never abated and their tone grew coarser. Department Four was stepping up pressure, using even Popieluszko's frail health to break him.

His war of attrition with the police drew even larger crowds to his masses for the fatherland. Congregations of twenty-five thousand were commonplace, and every last Sunday, with the predictability of a Swiss railway, the ZOMO riot police parked in the side streets. Nothing could have reassured the crowd more: the police presence was proof that the masses were important and that the authorities had only water cannon for their side of the national "dialogue." But the real source of strength for Popieluszko came from the Pope. The spiritual reserves mobilized in a young priest when the head of the Roman Catholic Church repeatedly signaled that he supported his preaching were inestimable. After Christmas, the editor of the Polish edition of *L'osservatore romano*, the Vatican newspaper, spent long hours with Popieluszko in his room. He often carried messages from the Pope. This time the Pope's advice was simple:

stay strong. In February, Bishop Kraszewski, Popieluszko's old defender, traveled to Rome for a papal audience.

Kraszewski stressed Popieluszko's disappointment that he had been unable to meet the Pontiff in June 1983. John Paul gave Kraszewski a rosary for Popieluszko and the instruction to tell Glemp, "Today it is Popieluszko, tomorrow another priest, and the day after tomorrow, a bishop, and that is how they will deal with the Church." Soon most of the Warsaw Church community knew the facts: the Pope was squarely behind Father Popieluszko. The primate made his peace offering, a book entitled *God's Foreman, Foreman of Human Hearts*, about Cardinal Hlond, the first Polish primate after World War II. The book was supposed to say: Do not judge me too harshly, do not compare me too rigidly with Wyszynski, there have been other primates and other tasks. But there was nothing very warm about the gift. The dedication: "To Father Jerzy with blessings from the primate" was devoid of intimacy. When the rosary and the book were delivered to the priest, he barely looked at the volume but clutched the rosary. Popieluszko said: "The Pope wanted to do this. The primate had to." But when people asked Popieluszko to complain about the primate afterward he told them, "They don't know anything. They do not understand, they might be wrong."

The protracted police interrogations brought the Church leadership closer to Popieluszko, thwarting the whole goal to divide and rule. As the relatively mild Polish winter of 1984 turned into a wet spring, the mood deteriorated in Rakowiecka Street. It was rumored that the Jaruzelski government was planning a full-scale amnesty of political prisoners on July 22, to mark the fortieth birthday of the Polish socialist state. The aim was to send conciliatory signals throughout the world and specifically to persuade America to lift its sanctions against Poland. Perhaps new credits would start flowing into the starved economy. Perhaps Western statesmen would again visit Warsaw and bring Jaruzelski out of the diplomatic cold. It was a great opportunity, said Jaruzelski's advisers. The police had been mopping up opposition groups in factories, universities, even hospitals. But most of those held had been placed only under "temporary arrest." Very few had been brought to trial and the cells were filling up. There was no point in prosecuting before an amnesty. In Rakowiecka Street they were furious at the amnesty. The secret police felt they were working to no point if the "troublemakers and subversives" were to be free within months. Nor was Soviet Ambassador Aleksandr Aksyonov altogether happy. Moscow had to some extent swallowed its own propaganda about the Solidarity revolution, which was that the Polish working class is largely honest, decent, and obedient, but a small group of counterrevolutionaries had not been completely brought under control. Now, so it seemed to Moscow, the Polish leadership was planning to release the political dissidents.

Eleven men sitting in Rakowiecka Street jail were deemed to be the most dangerous. They were four advisers to Solidarity from the Worker's Defense Committee—Jacek Kuron, Adam Michnik, Zbigniew Romaszewski, and Henryk Wujec—and seven regional union leaders: Andrzej Gwiazda, Seweryn Jaworski, Andrzej Rozplochowski, Marian Jurczyk, Jan Rulewski, Grzegorz Palka, and Karol Modzelewski. If the Solidarity leaders could be persuaded to leave Poland, even on a temporary basis, then Solidarity would be a movement without a head. Lech Walesa could be kept under control providing he was isolated from his advisers. Once abroad, the leaders could be stripped of their citizenship if they started to criticize Poland.

Even the most optimistic of General Jaruzelski's team realized that these eleven men, branded as professional agitators, would not consider an offer delivered by the authorities. Only one institution—the Church—would be listened to. Glemp immediately agreed to the negotiations. For him, this was a vindication of his conciliatory policies toward the government. It looked as if the general was finally going to honor one of his promises to Pope John Paul and free Poland's political prisoners.

Piotrowski saw beyond the transitory glee of some of his colleagues. Whenever he encountered police professionals like himself he found his opinions echoed: a Marxist government was using the Catholic Church and a Western organization to persuade a group of Solidarity leaders that they should leave for the West. Quite apart from the ideological absurdity of it all—Piotrowski had become used to what he called "mish-mash socialism"—it was a slap in the face of Department Four. Even so, the department had to be involved in the negotiations. The Council for Religious Affairs, the normal bargaining partner with the Church, was not sufficiently weighty.

But freeing the Solidarity leaders was not easy. The prisoners had very stringent conditions under which they would accept release. The Rakowiecka Street prisoners were in a surly mood when the Church representative visited them on Good Friday. The Solidarity eleven had been living in a cloud of innocence. Locked up since martial law, their information was filtered through unsatisfactory and censored letters and the short intense bursts of conversations with visitors. They knew, however, that the Poles were depressed and searching for solace; that political opposition, even to the underground, was a game of diminishing rewards. But they knew too that they were important and that Pope John Paul had been monitoring the attempts to negotiate their freedom.

"What!" Jan Rulewski exclaimed when he was told by the warders that he was going to meet the authorities, "Do we have a new government?"

No, it was the old government acting in good faith. It wanted the prisoners to renounce any political activities for two and a half years in exchange for freedom. But as Adam Michnik said, prisoners should not be negotiators. Either the government should put the eleven on trial immediately or release them. Michnik refused to leave his cell.

There were genuine ethical and strategic problems. The eleven men wanted to be free, but they agreed they should act only as a group. The advice smuggled into them from the Solidarity underground was that they hold fast, at least until planned demonstrations on May 1 showed how much support the banned union still had.

Meeting on the night of May Day, Polish officials drew two conclusions from the demonstrations. First, and this was to be the official presentation to the outside world, the demonstrations were much smaller than in previous years. Second, Moscow and the hardline critics within the government had to be reassured that an amnesty without the Solidarity eleven would not mean a new surge of public unrest. That was important. Jaruzelski was due to pay his respects to the Soviet leader, Konstantin Chernenko, on May 4, and the Moscow summit had to go smoothly.

On May 2, a United Nations envoy arriving on government invitation was allowed to see the Rakowiecka Street prisoners. In the exercise yard to avoid eavesdropping devices in the visitors' room, the envoy made his proposals to three of the four KOR members (Michnik stayed in his cell). The same message was conveyed to the Solidarity chiefs: prisoners could leave for the Western country of their choice for at least six months, taking their families with them, and the United Nations and the Polish government would guarantee their safe return to Poland. Some of the KOR men could probably study in Rome on a Vatican scholarship. That too would be a kind of guarantee. No need to sign anything.

But the same ethical problems had not disappeared. Whom do we betray by leaving the country? What would happen to political opposition in Poland? What is freedom without political activity? The offer was politely refused. Jaruzelski was not going to be able to discard his political prisoner problem quite so easily.

The discontent in the secret police reached new heights. If ever there was a Nobel Prize for weak government, the Jaruzelski team would win it for its handling of the prisoners. That, at any rate, was how it seemed to the hardliners in the security *apparat.* What appeared to Jaruzelski supporters to be an unusual sensitivity to the entreaties of the Church was, for men like Piotrowski, firm proof that nothing effective could be achieved by a government that was leaning on the silent support of the Church leadership. The frustrations, the echoes of discontent were picked up not by Kiszczak but by Miroslaw Milewski, his predecessor. He was a former member of the Soviet NKVD, the forerunner of the KGB. Wartime circumstances, of course, but there are many Poles who will swear to the truth of Milewski's greatest battlefield achievement: the betrayal to the Russians of an anti-Communist Polish Home Army unit in

Bialystok. Milewski's patron was Mieczyslaw Moczar. He had risen in the ranks of the SB under Moczar and had established, with Moczar's help, a foothold in the once powerful war veterans association. Milewski had friends in Moscow—Chernenko too had earned his political spurs in the NKVD—and friends in Warsaw. Moczar had only skeptical acquaintances in Moscow and an unusually large number of enemies in Poland. Milewski knew that the security police were confused by the amnesty and unhappy with the way that Kiszczak was overriding the internal workings of the ministry. Second, he knew that Chernenko was not as enamored of Jaruzelski's approach as Yuri Andropov had been. Chernenko wanted order, not movement. Jaruzelski seemed to the Soviet Party hierarchy to be proposing movement and neglecting stability. Milewski understood this better than most. At a time then the word "amnesty" was on everybody's lips, Milewski was urging courts to be tougher on all political offenders.

Milewski opposed an amnesty, above all one that would release the Solidarity leadership. But Jaruzelski, following May Day and the rebuff given to the United Nations aide the following day, had decided to take the risk. He would declare a general amnesty, freeing several hundred politicals and tens of thousands of common criminals. There would be a recidivist clause built in; if any Solidarity activist committed a similar offense he would be back in jail immediately and have to serve his old sentence as well as the new one. Even so, it was a gamble and a difficult one to explain to the Kremlin. The Church was happy. Archbishop Bronislaw Dabrowski, who had been dealing directly with Kiszczak on the scope of the amnesty, flew to Rome to inform the Pope. His was a happier mission than the Jaruzelski trip to Moscow on May 4. Chernenko complained about the rise to "clericalism" in Poland and the fear that the Polish Communist Party was losing the souls of the young, post-Solidarity generation. A Soviet observer of May Day would certainly have drawn that conclusion. The demonstrators were often no more than teenagers, and their rallying at churches needed no preparation, no clandestine meetings. Everybody at grammar school or university simply knew that on certain days—May Day, May 3, August 31, November 11—

in certain churches there would be an opportunity to shout aloud the name of the banned trade union. The leader of the union, private citizen Lech Walesa, had done his part on May Day to upset the Russians. He had smuggled himself into the official Communist parade and with a hundred supporters had shouted "Solidarity" and raised their hands in the forked V-for-victory salute as they passed the Party dignitaries. On the rostrum, next to Gdansk Party Chief Stanislaw Bejger, sat the Soviet consul.

Jaruzelski returned from Moscow convinced that Poland would have to explain the background of the amnesty to Soviet officials. The Soviet procurator general's office sent a delegation to Poland, the Polish Ecumenical Council was sent to Moscow to "learn about the religious and social activities of the churches of the USSR." Notes were exchanged, Soviet and Polish propaganda experts conferred. It was decided that not Chernenko but Prime Minister Nikolai Tikhonov (who retired in 1985) would come to Warsaw for the fortieth anniversary of Polish socialism on July 22. It would be a good gesture, thought the planners in Warsaw, for the aging premier to be allowed to address a major factory and see for himself that the Polish economy was not riddled with disillusioned, anti-Communist, fervently Catholic workers. By some remarkable coincidence, the authorities decided that Tikhonov should be made welcome at the Huta Warszawa steelworks, which could safely boast the most disillusioned, anti-Communist, fervently Catholic workforce in the capital. It was also the same plant that Popieluszko had entered, with his clerical collar safely tucked away in his jacket, in the heady August of 1980.

When the amnesty was announced, the government paused expectantly for applause but heard none. The Solidarity leaders made their way out of prison, one by one. Michnik, defiant to the end, had to be carried out of his cell and up two flights of stairs to his apartment. For the Warsaw dissidents, Popieluszko's church seemed a natural haven. Even the avowed atheists, including Jacek Kuron, found themselves swearing *bruederschaft*—a process involving alcohol and a promise to call each other by first names—with Popieluszko. They had been out of touch for almost three years, and when they were jailed in the winter of 1981 most of them were only dimly aware of the priest. But there was never any doubt who had kept the flame of the union alive in their absence, never any doubt that the future of the opposition in Poland lay in churches like St. Stanislaw Kostka.

At a thanksgiving service in Kostka for the freed prisoners, almost every member of the Solidarity eleven attended. The steps of the church looked a little like the Lenin shipyard as one bearded dissident jostled another. The congregation became a crowd, and soon enough it was a demonstration. As each celebrity passed through on the way to the church a cheer went up. It was Solidarity carnival time again. The authorities had freed the union's leaders, and whatever Jaruzelski's motives, it was regarded as a victory by the men and women outside Kostka. Suddenly Popieluszko and Michnik appeared and the call went up, "A-dam, A-dam." Michnik, his back developing a scholar's hunch, was embarrassed. "Go on, Adam," said Popieluszko. "Give them a hare." Obediently, Michnik raised a clenched fist and then split his fingers to resemble the ears of a rabbit. Victory.

For the men in the shadows, there was no longer any doubt: Popieluszko was Public Enemy Number One.

12
•
Preparations

FOR PUBLIC ENEMY Number One it was time to rest. Without his dog collar and cassock, he looked like any sallow Pole in search of a suntan. He blended with the Baltic Sea beach crowd precisely because he was so unremarkable: thin body, eyes squinted against the strong rays, reflexes still set on city speed. Without stirring from his shallow trough in the sand, he heard them approaching, voices shrill as a seagull's screech: "Father Jerzy. Jerzy, where are you?"

He shivered with alarm, but the sensation lasted for only a second. He played dead for a while. Just as two young boys, the sons of his host, roared up beside him, he sprang to his feet and raced the children down to he seashore looking more like an elder brother than a persecuted cleric. He stopped just short of the water. Recently he had developed an irrational aversion to water.

In Debki, with its pine woods and fine-grained beaches, Popieluszko could relax and shrug off the pain of police pursuit. For weeks, it had been unclear whether he would benefit from the amnesty that freed his friends in the Solidarity leadership. It seemed as if the government were waiting until the very last moment before letting him off the hook. Cushioned by his friends, he would forget Poland's political woes. Popieluszko was the guest of Jerzy and Katarzyna Moss, leading figures in the active, fashionable elite of Poland. The family had managed to keep a sizable portion of its fortune after the Communist takeover. By any standards, they lived well. To play host to such a well-known priest was a considerable social coup.

Jerzy Moss worked as a volunteer at St. Stanislaw Kostka's center for the distribution of clothes and medicine to the needy and had invited the hardworking priest to his family's summer beach house. Moss had expected excuses. Instead the priest made immediate plans to become a temporary family member.

But even reclining on the beach, Popieluszko could not entirely escape the national debate. Two unknown young men had joined the group as the sun began to lose its sting and, on being introduced, launched into a critical attack on Solidarity. They blamed the union for Poland's miserable condition. Solidarity had gone too far, too quickly, had provoked the Russians, forced Jaruzelski to declare martial law. They were all familiar arguments. Popieluszko listened silently while his hosts vehemently defended the union. The priest, Solidarity's chaplain, abruptly stood up and strode through the sand to his room. "We all went to find Popieluszko and see what he would say," one member of the group recalled. "He was already in bed. We told him how stupid those people were, saying such things. He replied we should stay calm because they had to mature. They were going through a phase. He started to make excuses for them. Finally, he reached under his bead, got out a bottle of cognac, and shared it with us."

The priest was getting used to critical voices about Solidarity and received his share of hate mail. A letter that he had just received was typical. "You hideous Nazi," it greeted him. "Your cronies should not be surprised if they soon find you with your throat cut open, you whore. Pray, maybe it will help you, you degenerate lousy creature." Usually, Popieluszko laughed off these missives, crumpling them up or handing them, with a smile, to his friends. But he could not ignore the mounting number of threats on his life, nor could he forget the constant police surveillance. He had been followed by a convoy of police vehicles on his way to Debki. And even in the sleepy seaside resort, there was no respite. At six o'clock one morning, he was jolted awake by the sound of scores of scuffling boots and muffled commands. Outside the window, police in battle fatigues were moving in formation from house to house calling on drowsy residents to open their doors. Popieluszko immediately suspected that the police were looking for him. A friend ran into his room to warn him. "I see them," said Popieluszko in a low voice. "I don't want them to find me here." The emphasis was not on the "me" but on "here." He did not want to involve his hosts in any trouble. He reached out the window, grasped a branch, and, tense with concentration, slid out. He wore nothing but bathing trunks. Once he had established a purchase, Popieluszko shinned down the tree and hurried toward the beach.

The reason for the dragnet was never clear. A week earlier, he had made a controversial appearance at a mass in Gdansk also attended by Lech Walesa. Solidarity supporters had crowded around the two men and loaded flowers onto the priest rather than the electrician. The Gdansk police were enraged by this fresh sign, so soon after the political amnesty, of the strong ties between the Warsaw preacher and the leaders of the outlawed union. A detailed report on the incident was sent to the Interior Ministry headquarters, and a copy landed on the desk of Captain Grzegorz Piotrowski.

Within a few days, Piotrowski had roughed out at least three plans for putting an end to the priest's disturbances. He asked for a meeting with his immediate superior, Colonel Adam Pietruszka. Although schooled as a railway engineer, Pietruszka was a long-serving secret agent. His grasp of detail and his links with the upper reaches of the Interior Ministry had ensured his advance. During the long absences of Department Four's director, General Zenon Platek, Pietruszka ran the Church monitoring operation. Also present at the meeting was Colonel Wolski of the Warsaw regional secret police. Wolski had been invited because the discussion involved two Warsaw priests, Father Stanislaw Malkowski and Popieluszko.

It was not an easy meeting. Piotrowski spoke like a man obsessed with the need to strike at the priest. Malkowski, he argued, had important enemies in the Church hierarchy and was therefore more exposed. Popieluszko, on the other hand, was probably the more dangerous, with the built-in forum of the fatherland masses from which he could launch his monthly attacks. Wolski asked how either priest could be silenced. To Piotrowski even to ask such a question smacked of cowardice, and he said as much. The climate between the two men would never improve.

Pietruszka made sure everyone knew who was in charge. Both priests, he said, "carry a cross on their breast and unequivocal hatred in their hearts." There was, however, an important difference. Malkowski, said the colonel, was "a howler," whose words were irritating but forgettable. Popieluszko, on the other hand, presented a real problem. His sermons were being reprinted in the underground press, broadcast back into Poland by the BBC, Voice of America, and Radio Free Europe, quoted by other priests. The priest from Zoliborz, Pietruszka said, "has to feel authentic pressure, a real threat, because he has abused the functions of a priest for politically harmful aims."

Both officers nodded obediently. Each drew his own conclusions as the meeting broke up. For Wolski, accustomed to the bureaucracy of working under the noses of top officials of the ministry, any action required a chain of approval from bottom to top. Wolski was not timid; rather he was concerned, in a way that Piotrowski was not, about the layers of insulation that could form from thin air to protect those above and smother those beneath.

For Piotrowski, the meeting set out the situation in black and white. He was in no doubt that Pietruszka wanted Popieluszko to be dealt with severely. The colonel had said, "Enough of this game playing. We will take decisive action." And then, in words that would later damn him, he commented: "I surely do not have to add, comrades, that this decision comes from the very highest level." He pointed to the ceiling of his office.

Piotrowski knew he needed help for what he had in mind. He needed at least two other men who would understand the seriousness of the mission both for socialist Poland and for their careers. He never considered anyone other than Pekala and Chmielewski. He was also slightly less than forthcoming with

them. Their initial meeting set the pattern for later, less lei-
surely summits. Both men were called to Piotrowski's office. He
spoke of trivial matters for a few minutes, then rose and led
them past his secretary, Barbara Story, and toward Three
Crosses Square, a busy hub for cars, buses, and pedestrians.
They entered the Wilanow Cafe. Here, Piotrowski could be satisfied that they were not being bugged. The captain came to the
point. Did they want to take part in a special operation that
would counteract Popieluszko's antistate activities? As he expected, he had little trouble convincing his two subordinates
that they would be acting under special protection.

For Chmielewski, intelligent and perceptive, this was the
moment of decision. His wife, pregnant with their second child,
could not be expected to raise a growing family on his lieutenant's salary. And Piotrowski, whom Chmielewski admired, was
guaranteeing them immunity. The lieutenant asked only one
question: Popieluszko had a weak heart. What if their action
against him killed him?

Piotrowski remembered the moment well. "I informed my
colleagues that the bosses had taken into consideration the possibility of [Popieluszko's] death." It did not bother him,
though. "I knew at what level such a decision would have to be
taken. For me, it had to be at least a deputy minister."

For Leszek Pekala, there were other motivations. Popieluszko
had already slipped through one trap that Pekala had helped set:
the planted explosives and literature at his apartment. That had
been because the "top" had deemed it expedient to include the
priest in its political amnesty. This time, the same "top" was
ready to give Popieluszko what he deserved. And fate had once
again put Pekala in the skein of events. Besides, a dangerous
mission would silence a lot of his tormenters, the ones whose
wrists went limp when they shook his hand, those whose voices
became falsetto when they called his name.

Piotrowski had his team.

The next meeting in the colonel's office was for Piotrowski a
vindication of all his planning. Pietruszka said he had heard that
the priest had taken a train to Katowice to deliver a sermon.
"How much longer is he going to travel around the country

freely like this?" the colonel stormed. "Couldn't he mysteriously fall off the train?"

Wolski began to reply. He had several ideas which he would develop further after consulting his superiors.

"Don't bother with superiors," Pietruszka chided. "The less they know, the smaller headache they'll have."

Abashed, Wolski said that he would have to put down his proposal in writing. Pietruszka puffed up with anger. "Don't plan. Don't write. Do something!"

13
•
Trial Run

PIOTROWSKI KNEW he was not alone in wanting Popieluszko silenced. The further up the chain of command, the more bureaucratic roadblocks were encountered. To Piotrowski it was as though each of his superiors, while loudly demanding that something be done about the troublesome priest, was simultaneously searching for reasons to avoid action. Wolski wanted to reduce the mission to a paperchase. And Pietruszka was no better. For all his vitriol about the priest's unhindered travel, Pietruszka showed himself to be ideologically hidebound. His clogged bureaucratic jargon reflected his paralysis. "Educated in the rigors of socialist humanism, we respect the principle that political opponents should be limited; more, they should be fought with the help of political and social argumentation, not with power or fists." But Pietruszka discovered those principles months later, when he was fighting for his own life.

At the very top level of the ministry was a different kind of blockage. General Czeslaw Kiszczak, the interior minister, had read exhaustive reports on Popieluszko's activities. He understood the frustrations of Department Four functionaries; understood and sympathized more than they knew. At one time Kiszczak had been presented with a detailed proposal for eliminating Popieluszko during a train trip. Two agents would follow the priest to the Warsaw station. One would get into the same compartment as Popieluszko; the other would wait at the end of the carriage, where the lavatory was located. When Popieluszko got up to use the lavatory the agents would overpower him and throw him from the speeding train. The proposal was minutely detailed, including a copy of the train schedules from Warsaw to all the major cities Popieluszko was expected to visit in the next few months. Kiszczak reviewed the plan and sent it back to the deputy minister, Wladyslaw Ciaston, with a handwritten notation at the top: "I'd love to, but . . ."

The ellipsis said more than the words. Kiszczak had become interior minister because General Jaruzelski knew he could be trusted to keep the police out of political power games. Kiszczak and Jaruzelski had known each other since their army days. When martial law was declared, Kiszczak tried to keep separate police and army units. His style of leadership within the ministry offended many agents, who looked back wistfully to the days of his predecessor, Miroslaw Milewski. Kiszczak imposed dozens of army counterintelligence officers on the Interior Ministry, ensuring that his most trusted advisers would run the notoriously truculent secret police according to his instructions. By contrast, Milewski, who now sat on the Politburo, had always been popular with both the uniformed and the secret police. He kept in close contact with the ministry's key personnel and, in private, would mock Kiszczak and his indecisive approach. Calling him the "General's general," and "Mr. New Minister," Milewski let it be known time and again that if he was still running the office of Rakowiecka Street, Popieluszko would be behind bars by now.

That was the kind of leadership Piotrowski liked. What he had instead were only hints and suggestions from Pietruszka of what should be done. On September 9 came a clear message that Piotrowski and the others could only interpret as holy writ. Izvestia, the official newspaper of the Soviet government, printed a "Letter from Warsaw" by its correspondent Leonid Toporkov, entitled "A Lesson Not Understood." For the first time, the official press of the Soviet Union mentioned Popie-

luszko by name; for the first time it condemned him specifically
for his sermons and his "hatred of socialism." It said:

Chance gatherings turn into divinely inspired political
meetings at the parish of St. Stanislaw Kostka in Warsaw,
from a hall ringing with prayers to impudent demands for
the "return" of Lvov and Vilnius. Not long ago the Polish
Roman Catholic Church's militant Father Popieluszko addressed himself to the amnesty for prisoners. He issued a
call which said: "Relax, don't struggle. Devote more energy to cunning than before. Most important: don't be
afraid. Convert your apartments into storehouses of illegal
literature. Cooperate closely with hard-core counterrevolutionaries. . . ." So the question arises more and more often
among the Polish mass media: Can Popieluszko and other
"clergymen" like him really be allowed to preach such de-
structive politics against the will of determined church-
goers?

To Piotrowski nothing could be clearer: the Kremlin was
calling for Popieluszko's removal. Just in case some Poles chose
not to read the official word in Russian, another article with the
same theme and conclusions appeared ten days later, on September 19, in the popular weekly *Tu i teraz* (Here and now).
The Polish government spokesman, Jerzy Urban, writing under
the pseudonym Jan Rem, condemned Popieluszko's "seances of
hatred" at the church. "I receive very detailed reports of the
content of Father Popieluszko's sermons from an extraordinar-
ily faithful frequenter of those events," Rem/Urban wrote, in
what was certainly a resourceful and original way to describe
the secret police. "Orchestrated by Popieluszko, the feelings of
political hatred toward the Communist authorities and postwar
Poland in general that are brought into this hall by its fre-
quenters cease being repressed hangups eating away at them
from inside. So Father Popieluszko organizes sessions that are
politically rabid. If Polish TV could hire a modern-day Raspu-
tin, the idea would be worth examining. This is very sad but it
will remain true as long as Father Popieluszko has his clients
and his black masses." The tone was exactly the same as the *Izvestia* article. The only difference was that Rem had expressesd

the sentiment in straightforward Polish: this was open season on Jerzy Popieluszko.

Toward the end of September, Pietruszka called Piotrowski and Wolski into his office and said, "This would be a good time to kidnap and beat up Popieluszko." Wolski expressed shock at such careless talk but did propose a vague plan in which Popieluszko would be given acid-coated papers that would either burst into flame when he handled them or slowly eat their way into his bloodstream. The plan, he conceded, needed some refinement, but he would report back on his progress. Pietruszka turned on him with an anger that had been building up inside each time he heard about a new sermon by the priest. Piotrowski remembered the scene: "Pietruszka reprimanded Wolski for his sluggishness. I thought it unnecessary because his group might collide with ours and it would lead to our exposure." But the young captain saw that caution was not a much-admired quality in Pietruszka's office and decided he would not share Wolski's ignominy. He told Pietruszka of the three plans he had in mind for dealing with the priest. As Pietruszka listened to each possibility, his face brightened. Even Piotrowski's doubts about his ability to get away with the crimes he was proposing could not erase the smile from Pietruszka's face. "Never mind that," he told the captain. "I will take care of that. It will be a conspiracy within a conspiracy. We'll open our eyes wide and say, 'Gosh, someone has grabbed Popieluszko.'" And to Piotrowski, such confidence was not only convincing. It was contagious.

He knew he had chosen the right accomplices when he explained his plans to Chmielewski and Pekala. They might have hooted at his suggestions, or curled their lips in disgust. But they did nothing, and said nothing, as Piotrowski outlined the three alternatives he had developed in his mind for eliminating Poland's most troublesome priest.

The first scenario exploited Popieluszko's fear of water. The fact that he was a hydrophobe was in his police dossier but was not generally known. That offered intriguing possibilities for Piotrowski. He told the two lieutenants that they should find a bridge over the Vistula River, not too far outside Warsaw, where Popieluszko could be taken in the dead of night, trussed and gagged, and suspended from a rope a few feet above the water. It was never clear to them whether Popieluszko was to die or whether it was intended as a punishment and a stern warning for the priest. They made a dozen midnight journeys outside the capital, pulling their car over to the side of the road near various bridges and observing the flow of traffic. They settled on the bridge at Modlyn, only ten or so miles from the city limits, as the most practical site. Piotrowski then accompanied them to the bridge to see for himself. But the captain only became angry: there was too much traffic, he complained, someone would see them as they dragged Popieluszko out of their car and lowered him over the bridge. They needed, he said, a place where they would be alone, a place where no one ever went.

Chmielewski loved children. He and his wife had one son and were expecting a second child. Chmielewski, however, wanted contact with older children as well, and he volunteered to be a Boy Scout leader. Like scouts all over the world, his troop went on hikes and occasionally camped out under the stars. He had led several such expeditions in the Kampinos Forest, a sprawling woodland south of Warsaw that during World War II had been used by the occupying Nazis as bunkers. Many of those underground strongholds still existed, and Chmielewski and his scouts had explored them extensively. The one thing the lieutenant remembered from those experiences was the peacefulness, the sense of absolute solitude. When he mentioned this to Piotrowski, the captain's brown eyes seemed to glow. They would abduct Popieluszko and drive him to one of the bunkers in the forest. Depending on his attitude, Popieluszko might or might not first be beaten up. Once humbled, they would force a funnel down his throat and pour down a liter or two of vodka—no hesitation, bottoms up. The sudden ingestion of that much raw alcohol would probably render the priest unconscious. Then they would drive back to Warsaw and dump him in front of the episcopate on Miodowa Street or, even better, near one of the convents in Zoliborz. Let the blessed Father Jerzy explain how he had become so drunk that he passed out. Word of the scandal would spread, and he would soon be preaching to empty pews, Piotrowski said. They went so far as to buy a few liters of vodka with money from a police contingency fund. But by the time he finished outlining his plan, he was already revising it. They would take him to the Kampinos, yes, but once they arrived they would bury him up to his neck in one of the bunkers and interrogate him. Who were his contacts in Solidarity? What other priests were active in antistate activities? How much help was he getting from the Americans? Printing presses? Money?

But what if he doesn't answer? Chmielewski wanted to know. Then, Piotrowski said, we will smear his face with honey and leave him for the animals. It was the first time the two subordinates realized that Piotrowski was not only ready but eager to commit murder.

There were problems, however, attached to the forest venture. It was already the second week of October. What if temperatures plummeted and the ground froze so that they could not fill in the bunker where Popieluszko was to be buried? What if the falling leaves left a trail? For a while, Piotrowski fretted. Then Popieluszko himself provided an answer.

One of Department Four's informants reported that Popieluszko would be traveling to Gdansk on October 13 to celebrate mass again at St. Brigyda's. As usual, he would be driven by Waldemar Chrostowski. But this time, there would be another passenger: Seweryn Jaworski, who had been the second highest-ranking official of Solidarity in the Warsaw region. Jaworski was one of the militants of Solidarity. He was one of the last of Solidarity's top members to be released from detention under the July 1984 amnesty, and he was every bit as obstreperous now as he had been behind bars.

To Piotrowski, there could be no better proof of Popieluszko's feelings toward his country than this choice of traveling companions. Once again, he primed himself and his team for decisive action, the kind he knew "the top" wanted. His own casual approach to the operation was chilling. "I wasn't interested in Popieluszko as a priest. I thought that what he was involved in was outgrowing him. He used to be a very mediocre priest. I want to stress that none of us had any bloodthirsty instincts. I was simply convinced that we had all put too much effort into the preparations [not to follow through]. We just wanted to have it all behind us. I felt that way, at least."

If so, he gave a convincing imitation of an enthusiastic assassin. It was not easy obtaining materials of the sort that Piotrowski required. A series of journeys to the forests yielded a large sackful of fist-sized rocks. Using the Interior Ministry's special requisition forms, he also purchased twenty liters of gasoline, some string, several yards of adhesive tape, and a knife. Next, he visited the radio room and appropriated three walkie-talkies, effective only for short-range communication. The next day, he brought into the office some old socks, which he instructed Pekala and Chmielewski to fill with sand.

What for? Pekala wanted to know.

We'll use them as clubs if we have to, Piotrowski answered. This was too much for Pekala, who burst into high-pitched laughter. Piotrowski did not even pretend to smile. He did not like being mocked, and certainly not by Pekala. So, he pulled a five thousand zloty note out of his pocket and sent Pekala and Chmielewski to do some more shopping. They returned with two short shovels, three travel bags, a bedspread, three battery-powered flashlights, batteries, two cloth sacks, two plastic sacks, three woollen ski hats, two pairs of gloves, and a liter of vodka.

October 13 was an overcast Saturday. Piotrowski had been up early and received a report from Chrostowski. Jaworski and Popieluszko were on their way north before sunrise. He and his two adjutants were in no such hurry as they ambled along in a Polish-made Fiat 125 that Piotrowski had signed out at the department motor pool. When they pulled into Sopot, the Baltic resort where Popieluszko was preaching, they knew just by looking around that their target was still in the church. They bought three bottles of beer and drained them slowly. Piotrowski tried on the ski cap, looked at himself in the mirror. His face was unrecognizable.

They saw the crowd depart and waited confidently until Chrostowski's white Golf pulled up to the church door. Popieluszko and Jaworski got in, and the car began winding through the streets. "Slowly," Piotrowski instructed. He had come to worry about Pekala's penchant for hot-rodding, but there was nothing to be done about it now. Once they were outside the city, the Golf picked up speed. Pekala hung back, occasionally searching Piotrowski's face in the rear-view mirror. The captain

knew where he wanted to stage his confrontation; he had been
by the spot many times. After about an hour, Piotrowski leaned
forward and said, "Okay, racing driver, take them." Pekala accelerated the Fiat. They whizzed around the curves, up the
small hills, and finally caught sight of Chrostowski. Pekala
swept by the priest's car in a blur. All three men averted their
eyes. Pekala put several miles between himself and the Golf.
They passed the turnoff to the village of Olsztynek. A few miles
before the next turnoff, Ostroda, the captain told Pekala to slow
down. The road cut through a heavily wooded hillside. As they
mounted a slight incline, Piotrowski ordered him to pull over
and indicated a section just before a curve to the right. The big
captain was out of the car before it had come to a full stop. He
threw open the trunk and pulled from it the largest of the rocks
he had gathered earlier in the week. Chmielewski got out from
the other side of the car. Pekala, according to plan, swung
around in the road and headed back toward the approaching
Golf. A minute later, the walkie-talkie in Piotrowski's pocket
crackled. "Yes, yes, are they coming?" he asked. In response he
heard more crackling. Pekala was already beyond the range of
the instrument. With the confidence of a man in charge, Piotrowski stepped into the road and played with the rock until his
fingers found a comfortable hold. There was no noise for several
minutes, and then they heard the straining engine of the Golf.
Piotrowski pulled the ski cap down as far as he could over his
face. The Golf was at the crest of the hill. Piotrowski cocked his
arm and waited until the automobile was twenty feet in front of
him, then with a nasal grunt hurled the stone.

Inside the Golf, Popieluszko was dozing, Jaworski reading.
Chrostowski, though, had the steady middle-distance vision of
an excellent motorist, and he knew the man ahead of him was
not merely crossing the road or hitchhiking. When he saw Piotrowski's arm draw back, the reflexes that had served him during his days as a paratrooper clicked into action.

Piotrowski hoped to smash the center of the windshield and
hoped that the glass would spiderweb sufficiently to obscure
Chrostowski's vision. For that, he needed a bit of luck, but that
was not unreasonable; he had carefully planned everything else.
The passengers, Piotrowski assumed, would be seriously in-

jured, if not killed, by the crash that would ensue once Chrostowski lost control of the car. If the gas tank did not explode on its own, the three secret police would soak the wreckage with the twenty liters of fuel in the back of their own car, then set it alight. No one would ever recognize corpses that had been through that kind of fire. Pekala had proposed stripping the car and selling the parts rather than burning it. Piotrowski had given him a withering look and vetoed the idea.

Chrostowski saw the rock before Piotrowski released it. No sense trying to avoid it, he decided. The only thing to do was to scare the madman, ruin his aim. He swerved the car to the right, so that the man's masked face was directly between his headlights.

The last thing Piotrowski expected was to be run down. He panicked; tried to throw the rock at the same time as he lunged to his left to avoid the oncoming Volkswagen. The rock hit the car, skidded over the roof. Popieluszko opened his eyes. Jaworski clutched the dashboard to keep from toppling into Chrostowski's lap. There was a shriek of rubber on roadway, a monosyllabic oath filled the air, and the Golf was away, roaring down the middle of the road. In the back window, Piotrowski saw Popieluszko staring back at them.

Pekala, who had made another U-turn, now pulled up in front of the stunned Piotrowski. Chmielewski filled him in. Pekala got out of the car, chuckling. "I was wrong, Captain, you should have used your socks. They'd have been more dangerous." Chmielewski later remembered how Pekala larded on his abuse. "You don't try to throw it through the car yourself. Use the momentum of the vehicle." He grabbed one of the other stones, walked into the road, and tossed it up, underhanded, so that it fell in an arc. "That would have broken the windshield without all the grunting."

Piotrowski's color had gone from an embarrassed red to an angry white. "I'm sure you'd throw it underhand, Pekala. It's the way girls throw." Pekala was undeterred. He had taken harassment of that sort before. They got into the car, drank another beer each, and headed back to Warsaw. The beer helped cool tempers, and by the time they reached the outskirts of the capital, Piotrowski was talking about another mission. Popieluszko had a very busy traveling schedule, the captain informed his men. Home to Okopy on Monday, then Stalowa Wola for a mass, and on October 19, to Bydgoszcz. Pekala, still feeling confident, was skeptical. He's just been to Bydgoszcz. He won't go back again.

Yes, he will, said Piotrowski. He'll go back one last time.

14
•
"It's the Water for Him"

FATHER JERZY felt terrible. He had one of the worst colds he could remember. His temperature was over a hundred, he felt dizzy when he stood up, and swallowing was painful. Moreover, his head ached, and his stomach protested against a heavy meal the night before. His doctor had cautioned him countless times to eat fewer fatty foods and more protein. His liver, severely affected over the years by Addison's disease, had lost its ability to process the grease and cholesterol that makes up a major portion of the Polish diet. Father Jerzy knew the problem, and when he visited the doctor's family she made sure the dinner she served was low in fats, high in energy. But the majority of his friends could not afford to be so particular about their food. And he could hardly rebuke them for poverty. He knew that his mere presence gave them the will to fight on.

On this day, though, he gladly would have traded some of that charisma for a head that felt as if it belonged on his shoulders. The very thought of driving for four hours to Bydgoszcz made him feel faint.

Chrostowski knew he was speaking into a void even as he said: "Call Father Osinski. He'll understand."

"Yes, he'd understand only too well." Father Jerzy glanced at the local Solidarity sympathizer, Marek Wilk, who stood expressionless by the door of Kostka's priest's house. Jerzy Osinski was the parish priest of the Polish Brother Martyrs Church and one of the few priests whom Father Jerzy knew was devoted to the ideals of Solidarity. Osinski's original invitation for October 19 had been for Father Popieluszko to say mass at 6 PM and, of course, to deliver the sermon. But Osinski had been visited on Thursday by the chief of the local secret police and told that if Popieluszko celebrated mass the chief could not be responsible for what might happen afterward. Osinski knew better than to call his bluff. He sent Wilk to Warsaw, first as an outrider for Popieluszko and Chrostowski and to tell his brother priest that he would say mass; afterward, Popieluszko should lead the recitation of the Sorrowful Mysteries of the Rosary.

As Father Jerzy eyed Wilk, he knew he had no choice but to make the trip, regardless of his state of health. Failure to turn up would be interpreted as fear of the SB. In the past week he had experienced a strange and recurring phenomenon: an icy finger, as one close friend described it, that touched the top of his spine at the most unexpected moments.

After officiating at the wedding of a Warsaw-based correspondent from an American television network, Father Jerzy remarked that it was probably the last marriage he would perform. It was not the cars parked outside the priest's house at Kostka that annoyed him, although the police had ceased any attempt to disguise themselves. Nor could he find refuge in his small apartment on Chlodna Street. Just days earlier, on October 17, he and Chrostowski had taken two secondhand chairs. They had also installed a makeshift room divider—little more than a screen—between the kitchenette and the fold-out couch. Joanna Sokol, his close companion, remembered that the young priest visited the downtown apartment regularly on Wednesdays, when his parish duties were lightest. Often, she met him there, and they spent numerous afternoons in its cramped anonymity. Father Jerzy, she said, acted as though he was hiding from the world when he was at his "bachelor's lair," as it was called by the official press. "What does priest Popieluszko do in his bachelor's lair that he could not do in the residence provided by the Church?" newspapers asked archly. Popieluszko had shrugged it off, but Joanna knew how it bit at his pride. The implication that he carried on illicit activities in a secret residence was intolerable for a man of his moral fiber. She, as its most frequent female visitor, also felt a flush of anger at the newspaper's hint of sexual wrongdoing. Joanna was unaware that the nextdoor neighbor knew the identity of the thin man who turned up only occasionally, dressed in blue jeans and a T-shirt. And when the neighbor saw him accompanied by a pretty woman, he drew the worst possible conclusions.

But by October, the relationship between Father Jerzy and Joanna had settled into a regularity that surprised both of them. When Popieluszko traveled, Joanna cared for his dog Tanjiak, even to the point of bathing the black and white mongrel every other day, as was his master's custom. On this Friday morning, she came by at about eight-thirty. She greeted Wilk, who made a bad first impression on her, then went to fetch Tanjiak's lead. She was surprised that the dog shied away from her when she approached him; usually he relished the long walks they took. On this day, he whined and tried to hide behind his master. Father Jerzy picked up the dog and nuzzled him. "Ah, Tanjiak, you're such a good friend." He handed the wriggling dog to Joanna and said in a conspiratorial tone: "They're on me non-stop now. Eventually they'll succeed."

"Be calm," Joanna said. "You have people around you all the time."

Father Jerzy smiled, but she sensed bravado. "You're right. Let them worry."

He reached out once again to hold Tanjiak. "I kiss your nose. Be good to Joanna."

They pulled out of the parking lot at Kostka's at 9:32 AM, Chrostowski driving the Volkswagen Golf that he had used to go to Gdansk six days earlier. They assumed that their departure was being noted by the two men in the Fiat 125 with a license plate that read WAB-6031. One had short light brown hair combed straight back. The other, on the passenger side, had black curls and a mustache. And although their instructions from Piotrowski were clear and vital to his plan, Leszek Pekala and Waldemar Chmielewski failed to notice the Golf as it left.

They were quarrelling about the white hat that Chmielewski held on his lap. It was the kind used by traffic police in big cities, but not the sort that the militia used on the open highway. Pekala was angry. If you are going to disguise yourself, why not do it right? he asked. Chmielewski conceded the point but was not interested in hearing criticism. He had to pick up the uniform jacket at the Interior Ministry warehouse. The cap had come from Piotrowski, and that was the end of the discussion.

Equipping themselves for the operation had been an awful experience. Piotrowski had seemed to regard the acquisition of tools, disguises, and provisions as too minor to concern him directly, yet became incensed when his subordinates did not meet his expectations. "Get a policeman's outfit and cap," he told Chmielewski airily. "Also some handcuffs." The young lieutenant stared like someone hearing a language for the first time. "Where do you think I'll get things like that?"

Piotrowski flipped the back of his hand, the gesture of a superior. "You're a policeman. Investigate. Just find them." Later Piotrowski told Chmielewski to visit the Interior Ministry's main warehouse. He had arranged for a friend to provide the uniform and cap. Thinking back on the episode, Piotrowski said, "I just asked him informally to let me borrow a uniform. Normally a lot of red tape is involved in getting one. I also mentioned that I'd need a jerry can for gasoline and a militia hat. Why he gave us one with a white top is something I still wonder about."

On Thursday, October 18, Chmielewski met a fellow secret police agent, Henryk Chojacki, and asked about handcuffs. Chmielewski offered no explanation for the request, and Chojacki demanded none. That night, he handed over a pair of rusty manacles with the instructions to give back the same pair. Chojacki did not mention that the teeth on the cuffs were badly worn and probably would not hold fast if tested. But just as Chmielewski did not volunteer the reason for borrowing them, Chojacki did not mention their defect. It was the way business was done in the Interior Ministry.

Pekala's contribution to their arsenal came from the only supplier he trusted completely—himself. On the same day that

Chmielewski was begging handcuffs, Pekala brought into the office old undershirts that he had been storing in a bookcase in his apartment. Pekala told Chmielewski that the sand-filled socks Piotrowski had wanted to use to beat victims were useless. Instead, he said, they would use the undershirts as sheaths around some clubs that Pekala promised to collect. The purpose, he told Chmielewski, "was to break the resistance of the kidnapped man." He also had two sacks, large enough to cover half a man's body. He told Chmielewski they would be used to cover Popieluszko's and Chrostowski's heads. Chmielewski swallowed hard but said nothing.

Nor did he betray his anger when Piotrowski, inspecting the pair of handcuffs that evening, said only, "Get another pair. We might need them." He phoned Chojacki at home. "I'm not a warehouse," snapped the agent, and Chmielewski could not fault him for running out of patience. "Go down to the Rozyckiego market," Chojacki said. "You can pick up a pair there for about ten thousand." Rozyckiego was an open-air market for secondhand tools, household items, furniture, and junk. Chmielewski had never been there and had no intention of going just to satisfy Piotrowski, who was becoming increasingly dictatorial as the date of the operation approached. When deciding how to cover their tracks on the operation, Piotrowski had suddenly decided to steal some license plates. He told Pekala to find some. Pekala refused, saying he was not a thief. Grumbling, Piotrowski said he would take care of it himself, and did. The plates bore the number CZK 3210 and belonged on a Fiat 126 owned by Marek Matysiak. Still not satisfied with his cleverness, Piotrowski altered the plates so that they read KZC 0423. The camouflage was hardly of professional quality but it did not matter, Piotrowski said. No one would notice their car.

Their first choice of vehicle was a Polonez sedan owned by the department. Piotrowski had used it numerous times and declared it to be in good condition. On the morning of the 19th, he found that the car was being serviced. Ignoring that bad omen, Piotrowski signed out a cream-colored Fiat 125 with the license plate WAB 6031. The mechanic at the garage made a point of showing Piotrowski that this particular car had a special handle under the dashboard for opening the trunk; when the catch was released a red light lit up. The mechanic was rather proud of the innovation. Piotrowski brushed him off, asked only if it ran well. Well enough, was the answer. Had Piotrowski asked, he could have told him that the car had an oil leak.

For all his careful planning, Piotrowski was free about informing other people in the ministry of his whereabouts that day. He had contacted Pietruszka on Thursday to report that Popieluszko would be going to Bydgoszcz. He also told his secretary, Barbara Story, a slightly adulterated version of the truth, saying he was going out on business and that Pietruszka knew all about it. Perhaps he felt that within the confines of his profession such information was safe. Or perhaps he felt he had no choice. For one thing, he needed Pietruszka's authorization to obtain a *laissez-passer* document, known within the department as a W pass, that gave the bearer immunity from police arrest. He also needed a superior to issue him gasoline coupons. He drew seventeen liters from the pump at the Interior Ministry garage, another twenty in the jerry can he had borrowed, and vouchers allowing him to purchase fifty liters more. He later recalled the circumstances. "I called Pietruszka and told him that Popieluszko was in Bydgoszcz. I asked him whether I was supposed to go since my deputy was absent. Pietruszka said: 'Go.'" It was only after this that Piotrowski considered how far the business on which he was embarking might lead. "In the car with Chmielewski and Pekala I said that it would be good to have our official guns since they were so impressive. I did not have mine at the office. I remembered that I had it at home. I took my P61 gun with me, with two magazines. I took them out. I hid them and I kept the gun in a holster under my sweater." After that, Grzegorz Piotrowski drove to the house of a friend, to repay him seven hundred zloty. He did not want anyone to think unkindly of him.

Piotrowski was tying up loose ends. A few days earlier he had paid a surreptitious visit to his eight-year-old daughter's school and sought out her teacher. He wanted to know how the girl was doing in her English classes. The reply was encouraging. She was bright and seemed to have an affinity for the language. Did Piotrowski want to discuss any other subjects, the teacher asked? No, that would not be necessary. The family was likely to be going abroad soon, he said, and it was important for his daughter to speak more than Polish. English was the most widely spoken and most important language in the world. He wanted the girl to fit in, wherever they went. The conversation was unusual enough for the teacher to remember it. Piotrowski spoke abstractly, as if he were having trouble concentrating. The teacher wondered if he was totally in control of himself.

Even with an unloaded gun, Piotrowski had reason to feel in command of the operation. He knew where the priest was preaching. He knew who was with him. He knew approximately what time Popieluszko had left and what car he was riding in. He had been given not only clearance but material support from his immediate superior and two subordinates who had demonstrated, if not great aptitude, at least a willingness to follow orders.

The three policemen began their trip on the northwest road to Bydgoszcz at 1:30 PM. They were in no hurry, and it was just as well. The car began losing oil almost immediately, even before the road forked: one highway led to Gdansk, the other branched off to Bydgoszcz. They stopped briefly near Lipno at a private service station, since no state-run garage would handle repairs on a stranger's car in less than half a day. The owner, Marek Debski, was glad to diagnose the leaky oil filter and offered to replace it, but was cut short by Piotrowski. Debski remembered the unpleasant encounter a few days later. At the village of Jezowo, Pekala hopped out of the car. A few minutes later he came back holding two long staves from a snow fence, each about a foot and a half long and two inches thick. Pekala had eagerly explained to his mates that the sticks could serve a dual purpose: first, "they could be used to fight Chrostowski in case he attacked us." Piotrowski stared in disbelief. Pekala eagerly wrapped the clubs with strips from the undershirt he had donated, talking excitedly about the things they would do differently this time, to prevent a repeat of the Gdansk road fiasco. Pekala was all for duplicating the Gdansk operation just outside a village called Studzienies, with a minor variation: waiting by the side of the curving road, hurling stones at the car, then beating its stunned passengers with the sticks. The difference, he informed Piotrowski, was that this time he would do the

stone throwing. Piotrowski listened to the lieutenant's prat-
tle and responded, "Sure, sure," but never took it seriously. He
knew exactly what was going to happen, and stones played only
a minor part.

They arrived in Bydgoszcz at 5 PM and went directly to the
local office of the Interior Ministry, where Bogumil Grazma
was on duty. With a brief flash of his identity card, Piotrowski
asked Grazma if there was a garage where the local Interior
Ministry cars filled up with gasoline. There was, Grazma said,
and he began to give them directions. Piotrowski cut him off
and picked up the telephone. "What's the area code for Warsaw?" he asked. No one knew, so the captain from the capital
placed the call through the local operator. All such calls are recorded. Piotrowski had the operator ring Department Four in
Warsaw. He spoke for a few minutes with the duty officer,
Ryszard Bedziak, to find out if Pietruszka had left any messages
for him. There were none. Then, rather than use the gasoline
coupons, they filled up their Fiat at the Bydgoszcz ministry
pumps and drove to the Polish Brother Martyrs Church. Piotrowski did not wear a trenchcoat; no mask was needed to conceal his identity. Who could tell that he was not another Polish
Catholic intent on hearing the celebrated priest from Warsaw?
He remembered the moment. "The church itself basically con-
sists of three smaller churches. In one of the smaller ones a choir
was singing. When I went into the other one, I saw a notice on
the board announcing a mass for working people. After the
mass a group of chosen people was supposed to meet there,
more than a dozen priests and Popieluszko. I went out and told
my colleagues that Popieluszko was there."

While Piotrowski was in the church, Pekala and Chmielewski
decided to change the license plates once again. They re-
arranged the numbers so that the Fiat now displayed plates
reading KZC 0423. They were pleased with their cunning.
How could you recognize a car when the license plates kept
changing? A similar question was puzzling two militia officers
who were walking their beat near the church. They had seen
the Fiat pull in earlier in the evening and discharge one of its
passengers. They made a note of the license number as they did
of all the cars that parked outside the Church on this particular

night. They too knew that the celebrated Father Popieluszko was in their town, and they were under orders to identify those who attended his service. Now the same car, with the same two men, had picked up the same third passenger long before the rosary service was over. And the car had new license plates. One of the policemen walked over to the car and read the new numbers out loud. His companion recorded them in his notebook. Inside, Pekala and Chmielewski were petrified. They had been discovered before they did anything. When Piotrowski came out, they told him what had happened. He merely shrugged. "Let them write." His confidence was complete. He was acting on the orders of people far above pavement-pounders in Bydgoszcz. For one of the few times in his life, Piotrowski was less concerned with the opinions of his fellow police agents than he was with the plans of a servant of God.

As each Hail Mary droned out, Father Jerzy's soft voice grew more muted. His fatigue and sickness were taking hold of him. He was concentrating his energy not on leading the group of twenty in prayer but on his short commentaries in between decades of the rosary. That night they were reciting the Sorrowful Mysteries: the Agony in the Garden, the Scourging at the Pillar, the Crowning with Thorns, the Carrying of the Cross, and the Crucifixion. Each cruelty endured by Jesus during his martyr-dom was said to have pierced the heart of his mother, Mary, like a sword. Father Jerzy had once confided to a close friend that he liked the Sorrowful Mysteries better than the Glorious or the Joyful Mysteries because they seemed to him more appropriate to life on Earth. And it was just that, adapting the sad journey of Jesus to the conditions that he and his fellow Poles saw around them, that he was doing on this night. Father Jerzy, his voice strained with a high temperature, tried to help make sense of the human condition. "One has to live out one's life in dignity, for we have only one life. Please God, let us retain our dignity through each day of life you grant us. Our Father, Who art in Heaven. . . .

"In order to defeat evil with good we must take care of the virtue of bravery. It means overcoming your weakness—fear. A Christian should remember that there is only one thing for him to fear—betraying Christ for a couple of pieces of silver of futile peace. For a Christian it is not enough just to condemn evil, lies, hatred, and force. A Christian must himself defend justice, truth, and goodness. Hail Mary, full of grace. . . .

"The most glorious struggles are those of human thoughts and ideas; the most miserable are those that involve force. Ideas which need weapons to stay alive are dying by themselves. Ideas which survive thanks to force only are deviant. Solidarity was able to astonish the world because it never used force, because it conquers on its knees and with a rosary in its hands. It simply called for the dignity of man and his work, and it called for these values in a much stronger voice than it asked for bread. Hail Mary. . . .

"It is not easy today, when censorship eliminates the words of truth, bravery and crosses out the words of the primate and even the Holy Father . . . it is not easy since in the past few decades the seeds of lies and atheism have been planted in the soil of our homeland. A Christian's duty is to stand by the truth, even if truth carries with it a certain price." The prayers followed, and to Father Jerzy each one might have been a supplication for the service to be over. He glanced several times in the direction of Father Osinski, but the Bydgoszcz priest seemed deep in meditation. Finally each bead on their rosaries had been touched, each devotion voiced. Perhaps some of those present were disappointed. There was no real fire in his words. His final public words were: "Let us pray to stay free from fear, but most of all, let us pray to avoid revenge and force."

With weary resignation, Father Jerzy allowed himself to be coaxed into the priest's house for a small dinner. Swallowing food was in itself a test of stamina; conversation was beyond him. He felt dreadful, and Father Osinski saw it plainly. "I tried to make him stay the night, start out for Warsaw in the morning, but he wouldn't hear of it," the host priest recalled. Only the next day was the reason evident: Father Jerzy was scheduled to say the 7 AM mass at St. Stanislaw Kostka.

He did agree to let Marek Wilk drive ahead of them as a guide until they reached the main road leading back to Warsaw via Torun.

Piotrowski was both relieved and agitated. They had concluded that if Popieluszko spent the night in Bydgoszcz they would return home and wait for their next chance. Then they saw Chrostowski pull up outside the priest's house, behind the wheel of the Volkswagen Golf, license plate WUL 2473. So that was it! Excitement turned to anxiety, though, when Wilk got into his red Fiat. Staying about a quarter of a mile behind the two-car convoy, the three policemen followed. Later, Piotrowski revealed that, had it been necessary, they would have killed Wilk, too. But the Bydgoszcz man accompanied Chrostowski and Father Jerzy only as far as the turn-off to the highway, flashed his lights and sounded his horn, and turned off to the left. Chrostowski, who knew Poland's main roads like the hallway of his home, slid into the right lane and established a steady speed of ninety kilometers an hour. He was too wise to speed. There had been too many nasty, anonymous police demanding documents, checking his breath, searching the car, for him to make such a basic error.

Piotrowski's recall of the three hours that followed is highly selective. It is also fascinating for its grasp of detail and its personalization of the use of violence. No similar account exists of a political crime committed in the Communist world, making it as much a document of history as a legal archive.

> The Golf started to put on speed. We tried to keep pace with it and then somebody—perhaps it was me—said that we will have to stop them soon. The Golf was accelerating, the distance between us grew, then it slowed down again, as if playing with us. I sat next to Pekala. I told him to start flashing the headlights. The VW slowed down, we caught up with it, and Chmielewski was signaling with a torch. I had already given Pekala the handcuffs to be used on Chrostowski. We were wondering what we should do if Chrostowski fought us. I took a stick to try it out, but it was impossible because of the position of the headrests in the car. So the stick could not be used in the car. The Golf started to slow down then. We slightly overtook it, then we stopped. The Golf overtook us and stopped several meters in front of us.

Chrostowski wanted to make a race of it. "Father, the police do not have the right to stop us just by flashing their headlights.

We don't have to stop." Father Jerzy, who had said barely a
word since Wilk's car peeled off, just wanted to get home. "No.
Better stop. Otherwise, there might be trouble." They were the
last words he spoke to a friend.

"Chmielewski and I aproached the car," Piotrowski said later.
"Chrostowski was giving us his documents. Chmielewski told
him he would have to take a breath test. Chrostowski got out of
the car, got in ours, and I sat behind him. Pekala put the handcuffs on him then. I said: 'Waldek, open your mouth,' and
shoved a gag in as far back as I could. Chrostowski started to
wheeze. I thought he was suffocating so I pulled the rag out a
little bit. Then I think I tied the rag around his head with a
piece of string, like a bridle."

Piotrowski forgot to include the bit of black humor he exhibited at that moment, but Pekala recalled it. "He said to Chrostowski, 'This is for you so that you don't make a noise on your
final journey.' " Piotrowski, carrying his cudgel, returned to the
car to confront the man he hated so deeply and had pursued so
intently.

"I asked Popieluszko to get out of the car for an identity
check. He was reluctant. I slipped the stick into the open window so he could not close it. Then he unfastened his seat belt
and got out. I told him we were looking for some criminal, or
something like that. I took him to our car, gently holding his
hand. We went to the back of our car, and I led Popieluszko in
front of me. I wanted him to get in but he wouldn't. I was still
holding him, and he started to speak: 'I won't get in. What is the
problem? Who do you think you are?' et cetera."

The pretended courtesy ended then. Chmielewski, shivering
with fear, saw it happen. He had been sitting inside the Golf,
trying to find the switch to switch off the headlights. Having
done that, he could not locate the door knob and for a full minute was trapped inside the car. He blundered into the knob at
last, scrambled out of the Golf in time to hear Piotrowski call
him. "Waldek, come here, he doesn't want to get in to our car."

"I asked the priest, 'Why don't you want to get in?' Popieluszko said, 'Because this gentleman [Piotrowski] is pushing
me.' Then I saw Piotrowski push the priest in the direction of
the trunk. I saw Piotrowski hit the priest with his stick, some-

where on the back of the head. He certainly hit him more than once. He beat him on the back, too, near the head. The priest was falling to the ground. I remember this moment because I was frightened. He was limp. We carried him to the side of the road. What happened there, in the bushes, I do not know."

"That was where the whole catastrophe began," Piotrowski later said. "It was while Chmielewski was saying something to him that Popieluszko tried to wrench away from me, with surprising force. I think he lost his balance. I hit him with the stick on the left shoulder and then probably again on the head. Chmielewski brought me rope from the car. I remember tying Popieluszko's hands. I think I remember putting something into his mouth. He didn't move. We seized him and put him into the trunk. We closed the lid. It was all very quick."

Not quick enough for Pekala, who was training Piotrowski's P61 pistol on Chrostowski. He had no idea whether the gun was loaded, or what he would do if Chrostowski tried to escape. He was not sure that he had put on the handcuffs correctly. He had never done it before. He need not have worried. At that moment, Chrostowski's biggest problem was breathing. The gag that Piotrowski had pushed into his mouth was working its way down his throat. Disturbed by the liquid noise of his prisoner's struggle, Pekala turned on the car radio. Even the music, though, could not drown out the sounds coming from outside, the crunch of wood striking flesh, the splatter of skin, the impact of an inert body as it fell to the ground. Chmielewski was at the driver's window then, telling Pekala to pull the special lever that opened the trunk. As he did a red light came on. In the glow of the light, Pekala saw Chrostowski's eyes widen. There was another thud, the sound of a heavy weight being dropped into the trunk. The car springs groaned and settled under the new weight. Twenty minutes had passed since they left the church.

Both back doors seemed to open and close at the same time. Chmielewski sat behind the driver, Piotrowski was behind the handcuffed and gagged Chrostowski. Pekala was told to step on it, he turned on the engine, and they pulled out on to the road, heading toward Torun. For a while he kept to the speed limit, but then Piotrowski was shouting from the rear, "Faster." Pekala felt there was something wrong with the car and tried to tell Piotrowski, but he seemed to have enough on his mind. The captain remembered: "I still had the keys to Popieluszko's car in my hand. His documents were given to me by Chmielewski. I put them in the pocket of my trousers. When the car started, Pekala gave me back my gun. Incidentally, there were never any cartridges in it, I had them in my pocket. I helped Chmielewski out of his uniform. Chrostowski started to make some strange movements. I said, 'Waldek, be quiet.'"

Everything was going according to plan. They were driving at a steady eighty kilometers an hour, they were less than five miles from Torun, and both their prisoners were bound. Piotrowski ordered Pekala to turn into the first road leading into the woods. They approached a gentle curve to the right. "We were coming up behind a Fiat, but we couldn't overtake it," Piotrowski said. "Eventually it slowed down and we did overtake it. That's when I noticed Chrostowski opening the door and jumping out. Leszek slowed down. I noticed the sparks from the handcuffs when Chrostowski hit the pavement. I looked back and saw him kneeling in the road. I told Pekala to step on it, to drive as fast as possible. We were wondering whether anything happened to Chrostowski. I said that it was just as well that he jumped out. Now we didn't have to worry about what to do with him."

Chrostowski knew he was a dead man if he stayed in the car. He considered trying to grab the steering-wheel, create an accident, a chance to run. But his kidnappers would probably be able to jump out; he and Popieluszko would be the ones most seriously injured. He nudged the passenger door with his right shoulder. It squeaked. Chrostowski had driven Polish-made Fiats. He knew they were about as tough as tinfoil. He leaned forward. No one noticed. He worked his manacled right hand slowly toward the door. His little finger touched the handle. Gently, painfully, he wrapped the finger around the black plastic door handle. The red taillights of the Fiat ahead beckoned like a lighthouse signal. Chrostowski only hoped the kidnappers would overtake it. If they did, he would try to hurl himself out in the road in front of the Fiat. The only problem, of course, was that Pekala would accelerate to overtake, meaning Chrostowski would hit the road at a higher speed. But he had no choice.

Pekala pushed the pedal to the floor, and the coughing car rumbled ahead of the red Fiat. The baby-faced driver slowed down to negotiate the curve to the right that loomed ahead. Before fully thinking out his action, Chrostowski had jerked the door handle and threw the weight of his body against the door. A hand grabbed his shirt, and Chrostowski's abiding memory is the sound of his clothes ripping. Part of the shirt stayed in the car. The majority came with him. His body had aged since his days as a paratrooper, but he remembered the basics of breaking a fall: contact, tumble, roll. He tucked his right shoulder in when he felt the hard surface of the road. He ended up, ironically he would later think, on his knees, as if praying. He was waiting for the sound of the gun, the sting of the bullet, and the screech of the brake as his kidnappers came after him. Instead, he watched dumbly as the cream-colored car pulled away. Next he became conscious that his hands were no longer bound. The teeth of the handcuffs that Chmielewski had obtained were so worn that the one around his right wrist gave way with the first violent contact. A second later, he was aware of the lights of the red Fiat they had passed just before the turn. Like an apparition, Chrostowski waved wildly, trying to flag down assistance. Even as he did so, he was thinking, "Would I stop for a man on a strange road, late at night, who had just jumped from a car, and was wearing one handcuff?" The car buzzed by him, and rude gestures were exchanged. Chrostowski walked less than one hundred yards before he saw lights in the distance.

He knew nothing except that he was alive, that his hands were bleeding and hurt terribly, and that Father Jerzy was missing: hardly prime material for the role of key witness to the most spectacular kidnapping in Poland's modern history. But he would do. Like a man possessed, Chrostowski began running.

Piotrowski was running out of patience. Pekala worried that Chrostowski had heard someone calling him by his first name, Leszek, and would remember Pekala's face. Chmielewski was wondering aloud whether the priest's driver had been seriously injured during his escape. Worse still, the car began making loud noises. They seemed to be coming from the back. Chmielewski, panicky, cried, "If it's the wheel, we're done for." Pekala said that it felt like the axle to him.

"I had to drive the car to Torun. I told them to stop, and we stopped in some parking lot. There was a second, louder noise. We all jumped out of the car. We looked at the tires, and we were going to look at the engine. But Pekala opened the trunk instead. Suddenly I saw Popieluszko running through the square. I ran after him," Piotrowski said.

The doctors would later say that Father Jerzy had already sustained critical injuries from Piotrowski's first beating. But shock, adrenaline, and force of will can be powerful stimulants. While he was still inside the trunk, the priest had managed to loosen the ropes that Piotrowski applied, removed the gag in his mouth, and begin banging on the trunk. As soon as Pekala inadvertently released the lock, Father Jerzy was on his feet and running. "Help people, save my life," he screamed. Neither he nor his abductors knew it, but the car had stopped just behind the Hotel Kosmos, whose restaurant was doing a flourishing Friday night trade. Several people later remembered hearing the shouts. But frantic cries from patrons too drunk to make sense were common. No one paid any attention.

"I caught up with him and hit him on the head several times with the stick," Piotrowski recalled. "I hit him near or on the head. He fell limp again. I think he must have been unconscious. And then, I became . . . never mind, it doesn't matter."

Chmielewski thought Piotrowski had gone mad, so wild were the blows. He watched the priest being beaten up the way one might witness a public flogging, repelled and fascinated. Finally, he could stand no more. He turned his back, went to the empty trunk, and took out the car's original license plates: WAB-6031. He went around to the front of the car, removed the stolen plate, and replaced it with the original. He was so disturbed by the sounds of the beating a few yards away that he forgot to do the same with the back plates. The car bore two different registrations.

Heaving with the effort, Piotrowski finally stopped the punishment. He ordered Pekala to bring new ropes and a new gag. This time, they took no chances. While Piotrowski tied the priest's hands and feet, Pekala stuffed a fist-sized piece of white cloth into his mouth. He took a roll of two-inch adhesive tape and wrapped it around the victim's head twice, covering both his mouth and his nose. He tore the adhesive with his teeth when he had enough. He inspected the bonds Piotrowski had tied. Pekala knew about knots. He took a six-foot length of blue plastic cord, tied one end around Father Jerzy's neck, slipped it through a loop, bent his legs up at the knees, and ran the cord down to the priest's feet. He tied it around his ankles, brought it back up, and fixed it in a double knot. If Popieluszko tried to straighten his legs, the noose around his neck would tighten. It was a death knot.

Somewhere between Bydgoszcz and Torun, the cap of the Fiat's oil valve had been lost. While Popieluszko was being beaten senseless, Chmielewski had taken one of the cloths intended to sheath the clubs and jammed it into the oil pipe. But once they were underway again, with Popieluszko back in the trunk, the car continued to stutter. They drove through Torun cautiously, picking their way like the strangers they were. "Where are we going?" Pekala kept asking. Piotrowski responded only in grunts until they reached a bridge at the edge of town that crossed the Vistula River. Then Pekala's heart nearly stopped. A blue and white militia car was parked at the side on the road. An officer was waving a torch, signaling them to halt. The Fiat slowed, its motor complaining. Two officers, both dressed in militia gray, came to the driver's side window. "Have any of you been drinking?" asked one. Pekala shook his head, made a point of putting his head out the window so the policeman could smell his breath when he said no. He was terrified the police would want to inspect the trunk. The cops waved them on after warning them that it sounded as if they were having engine trouble. As they pulled back on to the road, the oil light in the dashboard came on. Pekala fretted. Piotrowski cursed. They saw a gas station ahead on the left. "Drive past it," Piotrowski ordered. Pekala brought the car to a stop about eighty yards down the road. Piotrowski jogged back to the station, where he bought two half-liter cans of oil. He used a pocket knife to open them. As he poured the oil into the leaky valve, he heard a commotion in the back. The priest had, incredibly, prised open the lock of the trunk. He could no longer run, or cry for help—his bonds were holding fast. But what if they were stopped again by the militia and Popieluszko began to make a noise?

With a fury even he did not understand, Piotrowski slammed down the hood and went to the back of the car. Chmielewski was already there, sitting on the trunk to prevent it from springing open. Piotrowski told Pekala to drive a bit farther away from the gas station. They stopped about fifty yards farther down the road. The trunk popped open. Piotrowski jabbed at Popieluszko's face with the end of his stick, then took a healthy swing. The club hit the frame of the car. Piotrowski's hands stung and he cursed. He got out the bedspread that had been stuffed into a corner of the trunk and ordered Pekala and Chmielewski to carry the priest into the woods. They laid him out on the spread, delicately, Chmielewski recalled.

Piotrowski looked his prisoner in the eyes and said calmly, "If you make one more sound, even one, I will strangle you with my bare hands." He took out his gun and pointed it at Popieluszko's head. "I'll shoot you if I hear you again." He replaced the gun and lifted the club. It came down on the priest's nose, but instead of the sound of cartilage breaking, there was a plop, like a stick hitting the surface of a puddle. They added more ropes around his neck and wrists, more tape over his mouth, and wrapped him in the bedspread before dumping him into the trunk. No one spoke until they were underway again. This time Piotrowski told them to drive southwest, toward Wloclawek.

Chmielewski, sitting up in front with Pekala, told him: "I am so scared right now that I would strangle him myself to get it over with." Pekala looked back in the rear-view mirror and asked, "What are we going to do with him?" Chmielewski suggested that they dump him in the forest. "He won't live as far as Warsaw."

At that moment, Piotrowski's mind showed itself. The trunk was partially open—Popieluszko's struggling had jammed the lock—so the captain could see his victim lying in the back. "I saw the face of Popieluszko. I thought it was the face of a dead man. I have seen many dead people, my mother, and people in hospitals, so I knew Popieluszko was dead. I said, 'We shouldn't leave a dead man on the road.' " He added: "It's the water for him."

Then came the second nightmare. At a crossroads which Chmielewski still sees when he closes his eyes ("I remember one detail; a roadsign bearing the inscription 'Lipno 18 kilometers' ") a militia patrol stopped them. Pekala was about to become hysterical. The militiamen crowded around the driver's window and asked for identity papers. Piotrowski, the professional, snapped out the W pass like a man in a hurry. The militiamen inspected it, smiled, saluted. Pekala released his breath.

The reservoir at Wloclawek lies between a chemical plant and a row of warehouses. The town has a pleasant enough square and a salubrious drinking establishment. Nothing else. The twenty-mile-long reservoir that begins in Wloclawek put the town on the map. Completed in 1969 with help from the Soviet Union, it is one of Warsaw's main water reserves, leading directly into the Vistula. A bridge spans the water, which is placid nearly all of the time. Signs at both ends of the bridge warn visitors they may not take pictures, since a reservoir is considered of potential military importance.

Piotrowski's W pass gave them a feeling of freedom. They drove across the bridge, from the warehouses to the plant. Then they drove halfway back, until they were between the fourth and fifth spans of the bridge.

"Stop here," the captain ordered. They all got out and filed like pallbearers to the trunk of the car. Chmielewski thought that Piotrowski was no longer making sense. He opened the trunk and pointed to the two canvas sacks filled with stones that he had packed in the car. For no reason that he can remember, Piotrowski used a diminutive form of the word for stones, a kind of children's play term, when he issued his deadly command, "Put the stonesies on his feet." Chmielewski and Pekala hesitated, stared openly at each other. Piotrowski became annoyed. "Come on, am I supposed to do the whole job for you?" This touched some sort of nerve in the underlings. Each affixed a bag of stones to the inert priest's ankles. Together the bags and stones weighed twenty-three pounds. All three of them lifted the body out of the car.

Pekala said: "I saw the priest's forehead and the big drops of perspiration on it, and I got the impression he was cold. I touched his hand and it was certainly cold. There was no talk about whether the priest was alive. We lifted him out of the trunk." The time was 11:50 PM.

Chmielewski can remember how he shrank away from the touch of the priest's body. "He was in a vertical position when we tossed it into the water. We simply put the body over the barriers and let it go, all together. There was no talk, no signal."

Piotrowski recalls only the facts. "I cannot say who held which part of the body. We took it out and threw it into the water. We drowned him. Then we drove off. Pekala said, 'Popieluszko is dead.' I said, 'That's right.' I cannot describe the atmosphere in the car."

Pekala asked Piotrowski to open the bottle of vodka. They downed a half-liter among them. Pekala remembers that, as he drank, he thought: "Now we are murderers."

The journey was not over. As they entered Warsaw, at about 2 AM, they were stopped by a militia patrol. Piotrowski showed the W pass and they were waved on. As they turned off the road that runs parallel to the Vistula River, on to Tamka Street, they were stopped a final time. The W pass saw them through.

They drove to Rakowiecka Street, and near the Interior Ministry building Pekala got into his own Fiat 126. Chmielewski took the wheel of the cream-colored 125, and they drove separately to Piotrowski's flat on Bernardynska Street. They threw their wooden clubs into the bushes across the street. Piotrowski produced a canvas sack. They filled it with their equipment: a shopping bag, part of the towel they had torn up to use as a gag, three ski caps they had taken along to disguise themselves, three gloves, two of Pekala's undershirts, six pieces of rope, Chmielewski's mud-caked shoes, two socks filled with sand, the bedspread on which Popieluszko had been beaten, the stolen KZC license plates, two stones, and one brick. They drove to Czerniakow Lake nearby and parked under the bridge. The bag was doused with gas, lit, and tossed into the water. At the edge of the lake they burned Chrostowski's identity documents.

Piotrowski could smell the fear in his colleagues. "Leszek said that Chrostowski would recognize him and that he would become the scapegoat. I said that wasn't true. That we had our guarantees. I said that if the body was not found, then we should keep silent about everything. I felt it was my duty to cheer them up."

The cheerleader arrived back at his home between 3 and 4 AM on October 20. He did not bother taking a shower to wash Popieluszko's blood from his body. He was tired, and he had to be at work early in the morning.

15
•
End of
the Chase

LEGENDS SPRING from the grave. At the height of the national
hysteria that followed, Father Jerzy was portrayed as a flawless
priest. He said mass every day after his ordination and was un-
failingly punctual. These were exaggerations. However, Father
Jerzy's nonappearance at the 7 AM mass on October 20 provoked immediate alarm. It never occurred to anyone that Father
Jerzy might have overslept, or been hung over, or had forgotten
his duty. He was simply not that sort of priest. And so as they
sat on the hard wood pews and the minutes ticked past, the parishioners wondered what had become of the young priest with
the long sideburns, the smooth high voice, the steady cool gaze.
Reluctant to leave until they knew, they sat in the courtyard inside the church gates, gossiping innocently, their eyes flicking
regularly to the priest's concrete house where Popieluszko's
room was located upstairs. It was still too early to disturb the
other priests of the parish, and the other priest, Father Bogucki,
was in the hospital with a heart condition. Some decided to wait
until nine o'clock, by which time Popieluszko's driver, Waldek
Chrostowski, would surely have arrived. They could ask him.

Chrostowski had been through an ordeal. Still in shock from
his own abduction and painful escape, and frantic with worry

about his friend, he had run toward the only light visible from the road. It turned out to be the regional Center for Agricultural Progress, a combined school and self-help cooperative for farmers and would-be farmers. The center also housed newly released convicts. As on most Friday nights, the residents of the center were having a small party; that is to say, they were blind drunk by nightfall. The arrival of an apparition whose face and hands were caked with blood, who had manacles hanging from one wrist, and who kept raving, "They've taken him!" was considered the comic highlight of the evening. To Chrostowski it seemed as if there was not a sober man in the house. Did they not speak Polish? Did they not know who Father Jerzy was? Finally, a sparrowlike woman emerged from the back room. Ewa Affelt was the receptionist. As Chrostowski blurted out his story, Affelt began to wish he was just another harmless inebriate. At five past ten she called the duty officer of the police station in Torun and relayed Chrostowski's story. The officer in turn dispatched a policeman to the agricultural center. It was a wasted trip. Chrostowski was on his way to Torun, in an ambulance, to have his injuries treated. The doctor in the ambulance knew Chrostowski was in no great danger from the abrasions to his face, the lacerated hands, and the bruised shoulders and back. But the dazed look on his face was worrisome. When Chrostowski asked to be taken to a church, the doctor responded with professional deference: "In good time." The patient's religious inclinations were his own business. Chrostowski became wild: he wanted to see a priest, now. More to calm him down than anything, the doctor told the driver to stop off at the Church of the Holy Virgin Mary in Torun. The doctor went to the priest's house and rang the bell.

Father Jozef Nowakowski usually retired early on Friday nights. Weekends were the busy part of his work schedule, and he needed his rest. He was on his way upstairs to bed when he heard that he had visitors. Slightly perturbed, he answered the door. Could he see a sick man who wanted a priest? Nowakowski wondered if the illness was caused by badly distilled moonshine, especially when he saw the unfocused eyes, bruised face, and heard Chrostowski speaking gibberish. Which Father Jerzy, what Fiat, who was carrying a club, what driver named

Leszek? The answers were not reassuring. Jerzy Popieluszko, a man in a militia uniform, a thud in the trunk of their car, guns, gags, handcuffs. Nowakowski began to fear he was the target of police entrapment. Nowakowski first called the Torun police station. Yes, they knew about Chrostowski. No, they did not know that he was Father Jerzy Popieluszko's driver. Nowakowski heard a new, ugly tone on the other end of the line. He promised Chrostowski he would inform everyone necessary, then told him to go before the police arrived. Nowakowski did not know that the driver would spend the next few days exclusively with the police.

A call to the episcopate, where Nowakowski encountered a sleepy and unappreciative secretary, began the most elaborate manhunt in Poland's history. For eleven days, men and women who met in the street, on buses, in homes, in churches, in every place where people gather, asked each other, at first, "What do you think has happened?" and later, "Do you think he is still alive?"

Grzegorz Piotrowski was one of only three persons in a country of thirty-six million who knew, with certainty, the answer to the second question. And the first question, he hoped, would never be answered in precise terms. It was this point he wanted to impress on Chmielewski and Pekala when they arrived in his office late on Saturday morning. Pekala was fretting about the use of his first name during the kidnapping; Chmielewski was trembling visibly and seemed unable to string words together. Piotrowski gave them a soldier's talk. They had nothing to fear, he said. The priest's driver was in police custody and was being interrogated. But his testimony was rambling and useless. What the two lieutenants must do, Piotrowski stressed, was construct watertight alibis for their whereabouts the previous day.

Piotrowski had already been to see Adam Pietruszka that Saturday morning. The colonel had been in his office until ten o'clock on Friday evening and then had gone home. Next morning, he was especially irritable when the priest's murderer walked in. Piotrowski handed him the W pass that he had used four times. Pietruszka put it in his bookcase and asked for a report on the mission to Bydgoszcz. Before Piotrowski could answer, the telephone on the colonel's desk rang. Pietruszka grimaced. He hung up delicately and said to Piotrowski: "This will have to wait. Platek wants to see me right away."

For most of that Saturday, October 20, the phone rang on General Kiszczak's desk. The interior minister knew within eight hours of the kidnapping that something was amiss. As the news came in from Torun, it became clear that Father Popieluszko had been abducted, perhaps killed, for political motives, and somehow his ministry was implicated. For some weeks the inner circle of advisers around Prime Minister Wojciech Jaruzelski had been expecting a stunt by hardliners. Preparations were underway for a session of the Communist Party Central Committee on October 26, and the word was that General Jaruzelski would force the resignation of some members of the law-and-order lobby, perhaps even Miroslaw Milewski. After the amnesty of political prisoners, Jaruzelski had wanted to initiate a new policy of conciliation with the West. Western European foreign ministers were already lining up to reward the general for freeing the 670 detainees. But phone intercepts and gossip within the Party had alerted the Polish leader to the growing discontent of the dogmatic Marxists. They were angry not only at the amnesty but also at the soft line toward the Church and at the return to a policy of seeking favor with capitalist states. Kiszczak expected the hardliners to pose some kind of challenge to Jaruzelski before the Central Committee meeting. It might be little more than an open letter—as in the past—or a protest petition circulated within the Party *apparat*.

But the Popieluszko kidnapping far surpassed this kind of lobbying; it was a direct threat to the future of General Jaruzelski. Perhaps the hardliners hoped to spark off virulent clashes between Solidarity supporters and police. Perhaps they were simply trying to make Jaruzelski take the question of public order more seriously. In any case, Kiszczak quickly identified the Party patrons behind the crime. Marine commandos, the trusted elite of the Polish army, were dispatched to Torun to mount a twenty-four-hour guard on Chrostowski, the only witness. The Army Internal Service and the military police were put on red alert. Patrols were intensified around the important state administration buildings and television headquarters. The special Guards division stationed behind Party headquarters had its leave canceled.

The interior minister called the head of Department Four, General Zenon Platek, to his office and told him to establish a crisis task force to investigate the abduction. Platek suggested that his deputy, Colonel Pietruszka, be named to the task force as well.

The same questions that concerned the country's leadership were also being asked in the courtyard outside St. Stanislaw Kostka. Who gave the orders, and how high up did the conspiracy go? There had been no official announcement about Father Jerzy's disappearance, but by mid-afternoon more than a hundred of his parishioners knew about it and had congregated at the first place that came to mind. "There was nothing to be done, but then again, there seemed nowhere else to go," recalled one of the priest's closest friends. As word of the mysterious disappearance spread, various rumors sprang up to explain it. Father Jerzy had been arrested suddenly and sent forcibly to the West; he had been picked up and taken to Mostowsky Palace for more interrogation. Seweryn Jaworski, the former Warsaw Solidarity leader who had been with Father Jerzy on October 13 when their car was stoned, turned up suddenly to announce that he had evidence the priest had been spirited to Moscow, whence he would be sent to a gulag. Because nothing was known for sure, nothing could be discounted. Father Jerzy in a gulag? The murmurs grew in volume and intensity. An ugly mood emerged as more and more of Father Jerzy's friends, parishioners, and casual acquaintances flocked to the church. There were other people in the courtyard by mid-afternoon— the same men who had listened to Father Jerzy's sermons, taken notes, made tape-recordings. Now they picked up these potentially violent vibrations and reported to Rakowiecka Street. Kiszczak was consulted and, after him, Jaruzelski's (damage control) lieutenants, Jerzy Urban and Deputy Prime Minister Mieczyslaw Rakowski. How should the government respond? Not everybody on the Jaruzelski team was sure Popieluszko's abduction was a provocation by the party hardliners, intended to send the nation into civil revolt and bring down the government. One minister suggested it was a trick by the Catholic Church to mobilize antigovernment opposition. Another speculated, totally without foundation, that the Solidarity underground might have kidnapped Popieluszko and would blame it on the authorities. There was also a theory that the U.S. embassy had dispatched agents to kidnap the priest and play out the same kind of scenario.

By early Saturday morning it had been decided to announce Popieluszko's disappearance on the main news at seven-thirty. The government thus acknowledged Popieluszko's status as an important cleric. There was only one bit of specific information in the news item: near the abandoned Golf in which Popieluszko had been riding, the police had found a silver badge in the shape of the Polish eagle. The badge was the kind worn by traffic police on their white caps.

Within an hour, participants in the vigil outside St. Stanislaw had grown to a thousand. At 10 PM, the first of more than a hundred Holy Masses was offered for Father Jerzy's safe return. Some of the vigil-keepers left after that mass. Others stayed on for a while; a handful would not leave the courtyard for the next eleven days. They dozed in the church, or in the hallway of the priest's house. They dashed to the corner of the road to buy quick snacks, then darted back to the church.

In Okopy the parents of the missing priest, Wladyslaw and Marianna Popieluszko, were watching the evening news on that Saturday night. It was unusual for them; what did they care what the people in the government were saying? But on Friday night, Marianna had been unable to sleep peacefully. She dreamt that one of her sons—she could not tell which—was being tortured and maimed. Stanislaw, the youngest, was safe in the other room of the broken-down cottage. Jozef, the eldest, was in West Germany, trying to buy machine tools that he could bring back to Poland and resell at a profit. And Jerzy? They seldom knew exactly where he was.

When he saw the evening news and heard about the discovery of the militia badge, Lieutenant Waldemar Chmielewski was panic-stricken. Sitting in the living-room of his apartment, bouncing his son on his knees, Chmielewski had been congratulating himself silently for keeping a tight rein on his emotions.

His wife had casually asked him why he was so late coming in the night before. He found himself stuttering the reply and finally sidestepped the question. He had no idea of how to construct an alibi for the hours of the murder. Nor was he impressed by Piotrowski's resolute cheerfulness. Chmielewski was intelligent enough to realize that on the whole, the operation had gone badly. There had been too many slip-ups, too many unforeseen events.

When he heard about the eagle emblem, he nearly dropped his child. He had planned to return the cap to Piotrowski on Sunday, when they were to meet again. Frantically, he rushed to the bedroom closet where he had hidden it. The eagle had gone. As he stared at the white headgear, punctured by two small holes where the badge had been pinned, Chmielewski felt the muscles in his right cheek twitching involuntarily.

Sunday, October 21, was the kind of day on which families huddle in their homes. There was no longer any Father Popieluszko to deprive them of their Sundays, but his ghost now haunted Piotrowski, Chmielewski, and Pekala. Shortly before noon, the three assassins met outside the Moskwa cinema, within sight of the Interior Ministry. Pekala later remembered watching the young men and women standing in the queue and wishing he could join them inside, to escape reality for a few hours. Instead, he and Chmielewski followed Piotrowski across the street to a cafe. Piotrowski told them that he had been in contact with "certain organs" involved in the search for Popieluszko. In fact, a special task force had been created to direct the investigation. Its members included Leszek Wolski, head of the Warsaw special branch, and Adam Pietruszka. Their investigation into the priest's disappearance was being conducted by "good men."

Chmielewski asked Piotrowski what he should do about the missing eagle. Not only was Piotrowski unconcerned about the evidence, he smiled. Later, Chmielewski wondered if the captain—who, after all, had obtained the cap—knew the eagle would fall off, indeed had loosened the pin holding it to the cap, to throw suspicion on to the regular militia.

There was nothing to be done about that, Piotrowski said. They could, however, mislead the investigators, by making them believe Popieluszko was alive and being held for ransom. They walked to Czerniakowska Street, where Piotrowski gave Pekala the telephone number of the Warsaw Curia. Pekala deposited a two-zloty coin in the phone and dialed.

"Curia. Hello."

"Hello. I want to speak to someone about Father Jerzy Popieluszko."

"About who?" There was unmistakable tension in the voice.

"Popieluszko, the missing priest."

The line went dead.

"He wouldn't listen," Pekala said.

"They'll listen," Piotrowski responded grimly.

On Sunday, Chmielewski, with painstaking effort, printed a letter addressed to Bishop Miziolek which said that Popieluszko had been kidnapped and was being held for fifty thousand American dollars ransom. Pekala drove to Poznan, three hours west of Warsaw, where he dropped the envelope in a mailbox near the main post office, and returned to Warsaw.

Pekala and Chmielewski were unaware that their actions on Friday night were being unraveled with surprising speed by the task force. By Saturday afternoon, the transcript of Chrostowski's interrogation was sent to the Interior Ministry in Warsaw. One of the first people to read it was General Zenon Platek, who as Pietruszka's immediate superior was in overall charge of secret police operations against the Church. Platek was a graying man with black horn-rimmed glasses who had taken the directorship of Department Four in the hope it would speed him up the bureaucratic ladder. He was no specialist in Church affairs; that was Pietruszka's ground. Platek had a good relationship with the deputy minister, Wladyslaw Ciaston, and a nodding acquaintance with Kazimierz Barcikowski, the Politburo member ultimately responsible for reporting to the Party on Church–state relations.

Platek had known about and approved the plan to kidnap Popieluszko and Chrostowski. Although he later denied it, Platek had twice spoken from Warsaw to Piotrowski directly over the two-way radio in the kidnappers' Fiat. The first time was just before the October 13 attempt to stone Popieluszko's car. The second time was Friday, October 19, when the three killers were on their way to Bydgoszcz. In neither case had Platek identified himself, but Piotrowski had no doubt. "It looks like the director is playing with the radio," the captain had told his subordinates. Both times, Platek's message was the same: No change in plans. Carry out your mission.

Platek was alarmed, not so much by what he read in the interrogation report, but by the accuracy of Chrostowski's description of his abductors. That was not his only concern: the two Bydgoszcz policemen had reported sighting the light-colored Fiat with two different sets of license plates. The fact had been sent along to Warsaw when it became known that Popieluszko was last seen in Bydgoszcz. The whole operation was being uncovered with a speed Platek would not have believed possible.

Within an hour of receiving details of Chrostowski's interrogation, Platek dispatched two special agents, Colonels Stanislaw Lulinski and Waclaw Glowacki, to Torun. Their assignment was to monitor the official investigation of Popieluszko's disappearance and report privately to him.

The two officers were experienced troubleshooters. They assumed that Popieluszko's disappearance was not accidental and was probably permanent. They were not prepared for what they learned almost immediately upon their arrival in Torun. The official investigators had already spoken to the militiamen, to the attendant at the gas station where Piotrowski purchased two cans of oil, and to the driver of the red car that was behind the Fiat when Chrostowski escaped by hurling himself on to the road.

Everyone to whom they spoke remembered the car. Both officers gave precise descriptions of the three men they saw in the car outside the church. The gas station attendant described Piotrowski unmistakably. Before leaving Warsaw on Saturday, Lulinski had heard talk in the corridors of Rakowiecka Street: something major had taken place in Torun the night before and Department Four was involved. Lulinski decided to call General Platek.

"Hello?"

"General, this is Lulinski in Torun. I apologize for calling so late."

"What do you want? It's late."

Lulinski thought the voice on the other end of the line sounded disoriented, but he had no doubt that Platek knew who was calling. Lulinski quickly summarized what he had learned, taking care to spell out the license plate number of the car that had been spotted: WAB-6031. Both men knew that number belonged to the Interior Ministry. It had taken the police about eighteen hours to ascertain what had happened to Popieluszko, to determine what car had been used, and to obtain a detailed description of the kidnappers.

Piotrowski was no longer in touch with reality. Somewhere in the final days before he killed the priest, he actually began believing that he was performing a dangerous and patriotic service that would be lavishly rewarded. If he had misled the two lieutenants under his command, given them a distorted view of the crime they were committing, it was probably because he too believed it, or wanted to believe it.

On Sunday, Piotrowski's world fell apart. His superior, Colonel Pietruszka, who had planted in his mind visions of heroism for the fatherland, turned on the captain for the oldest of all reasons: to save himself. By Sunday morning, Pietruszka knew that the operation he had approved was a disaster. The speed with which the tracks of Father Popieluszko's murderers were being uncovered shook him. When he arrived at work that Sunday he saw, sitting in the parking lot behind the police headquarters, the Fiat bearing the number WAB-6031.

When Pietruszka walked into his office, the telephone was already ringing. It was General Platek, who was also at his desk. "Listen, when I passed the parking lot, I saw a car with the plates WAB-6031. They were seen in Bydgoszcz. Call Piotrowski and tell him to take it away so it doesn't stand out, until this is cleared up."

The colonel hung up and called Piotrowski at home. He had decided that the captain and the two lieutenants would have to be sacrificed.

Piotrowski remembered that call. "Sunday morning I was urgently called to work. Pietruszka told me that our car was seen in Bydgoszcz and that it was now standing in the courtyard right in front of his eyes. He told me to change those license plates immediately." It was only then that Piotrowski realized the extent to which he had been used by his superiors. Why should Pietruszka be concerned about their car standing in the ministry's parking lot? Wasn't the entire operation sponsored by the ministry? Why should he have to change the license plates immediately? He rushed to Rakowiecka Street, opened the trunk of the Fiat, and took out the KZC license plates that they had used for part of the mission. He took off the WAB plates, put the others on, and went home. In a few hours he had to meet with his accomplices and convince them that they were still safe. He did not know what he would tell them.

The end of the chase had begun.

Leszek Pekala's nerves were frayed. Two days after the crime, he had stopped believing Piotrowski's assurances. During that long weekend, the fey lieutenant came to the conclusion that he was being set up as a sacrificial lamb by his colleagues. By Sunday, when he, Chmielewski, and Piotrowski met outside the Moskwa cinema, Pekala wanted to know what steps were being taken to protect them. Without knowing why, Piotrowski said, "Look, at the very worst, they'll give us new names and new faces and send us out of the country."

The two lieutenants gawked at him. "They'll do that?" Chmielewski asked.

"Certainly." But, Piotrowski said, they should squeeze out as much money as possible. He gave Pekala an out-of-town telephone number and told him to go to the Forum Hotel. From the lobby telephone, Pekala called the headquarters of the secret police in Torun. As soon as the phone was answered, Pekala said: "I have information about Popieluszko."

"Who is this?" said the officer in Torun.

"Do you want the information or not? On Friday night, I was visiting my girl friend on Fordonska Street. I saw a light-colored Fiat 125 with two or three men in it. One of the men got out at the Church of the Polish Martyrs. He went in a side gate. I saw him. He was wearing a militia uniform."

Without waiting for questions, Pekala hung up.

Piotrowski, meanwhile, decided that the Church could actually be of use to them. He rifled his address book and found the private number of Bishop Miziolek, who had supported Popieluszko during his conflict with Cardinal Glemp.

"I'm calling from Torun," Piotrowski said. "We have Popieluszko alive and well. If you want him to stay that way, get together fifty thousand American dollars. I'll call again with more details." He hung up. Miziolek, who the next day would receive the ransom letter posted by Pekala in Poznan, never considered complying with the demand. That night on the television news, a rough pencil drawing was flashed on the screen showing a dark-haired man with broad cheeks and glaring eyes. The portrait was a police artist's sketch based on a verbal description by Waldemar Chrostowski of the man whom he had seen lead Father Jerzy to the back of the Fiat. The news reader said that progress was being made in the search for the missing priest.

People at Department Four tried to avoid looking directly at Grzegorz Piotrowski on Monday morning. Almost everyone had worked through the weekend, and they had all seen the previous evening's news, including Barbara Story, Piotrowski's secretary. She knew who the televised sketch resembled. When Piotrowski called her into his office that morning she saw in his eyes the look of a hunted animal. Piotrowski wanted her to call the main militia station in Warsaw and say that she and her husband had been driving from Bydgoszcz to Warsaw Friday night. Their car had broken down, and when they tried to flag down another vehicle, they saw in its back seat a man who looked like the police artist's sketch.

While Story was lying to the police at her boss's behest, Piotrowski began leaving his own trail of deception. Early Monday, he went to the garage where the ministry's motor vehicles were kept and serviced. A mechanic was there. He too had seen the news the night before, and he regarded Piotrowski with suspicion.

"Take this," the captain said, shoving a piece of paper at the mechanic, who refused to touch it. Piotrowski grunted and walked toward the light-colored Fiat that had become the most sought-after car in Poland. He laid the paper on the front seat of the vehicle and told the mechanic that it might be needed later.

The mechanic was as curious as the next man. When Piotrowski had left, he went to the car, unfolded the paper, and read it. It was an official slip granting Piotrowski permission to travel outside Warsaw on Friday, October 19. The signature authorizing the trip was Pietruszka's.

General Platek and Colonel Pietruszka were trying to save themselves. They were on their way to the makeshift headquarters of the Popieluszko special task force, where they would be meeting the deputy interior minister, Wladyslaw Ciaston. Platek called Pietruszka into his office and said: "Listen, to keep the chronology straight, if anyone should ask, tell them that we only heard about the car this morning." It was a suggestion Platek would later regret making.

As deputy minister in charge of the secret police, Ciaston was one of the few people in Poland who knew how seriously the government viewed Popieluszko's disappearance. He knew about the extra army units deployed in Warsaw, about the special roving army trucks which were scouring the capital. He also knew that the two first secretaries for political affairs from the Soviet embassy had paid unpublicized visits to Jaruzelski's office over the weekend. They wanted to know why the kidnapping had taken place.

Ciaston was put in charge of ascertaining who knew what within the Interior Ministry. It was obvious that Department Four was at the center of events, and Ciaston decided to test the nerves of those responsible. On Tuesday, he called in all employees of Department Four and ordered each to prepare a written account of their whereabouts from Friday morning until Sunday night. The fifty or so people in the room shuffled their feet uncomfortably and looked surreptitiously around for Piotrowski. He was not there.

Like most men forever shut away, Piotrowski remembers his last moment of freedom vividly. "On Tuesday, General Platek told me that we were both going to see the minister. Kiszczak just asked me, 'What about Popieluszko?' I said I didn't know where he was. The minister then said I was under arrest. It was because Platek was present that I said nothing. If he had been absent I probably would have admitted it at once."

Why did Piotrowski hesitate to speak in front of Platek? It would take a while for investigators to work out what was going through the captain's mind. When they did, the pieces seemed to come together, showing a much larger and more intricate picture. Piotrowski realized how badly he had been used, how completely misplaced had been his trust. He knew that Platek had led him into this trap. He knew, too, that Platek also knew about and had approved the plan to kill Father Popieluszko. As Piotrowski later told a colleague from the ministry—a man he knew well, who had been assigned to his interrogation—"When everything goes well, they say, 'Go ahead, boys,' but if something goes wrong, you're all alone."

16
•
Laying Blame,
Laying to Rest

THE JARUZELSKI GOVERNMENT was in a state of coiled anxiety, not sure whether the party hardliners were trying to take over by triggering a revolution in the streets or if the turbulent priest had met with some other end. The government spokesman, Jerzy Urban, misleadingly injected a small dose of hope into the country when he casually announced, "The authorities have been tipped by informants that Popieluszko was seen after his alleged abduction." He insisted that the whole episode was either a publicity stunt or a provocation against the government. Urban was aware as he spoke that a suspect who worked at the Interior Ministry was about to be arrested.

Until that time, one possibility seriously considered was that Popieluszko had been abducted by a mysterious group known as Organization Anti-Solidarity, or OAS. Almost nothing was known about it, except that it seemed to be opposed to everything in Poland. On March 2, 1984, a Torun man and his girl friend were walking along a back street, five miles south of where Popieluszko and Chrostowski were stopped. A car pulled up, three men got out and forced the couple inside.

203

They were taken to a house in the woods outside Torun, where masked men stripped them, then beat them until the man admitted he had been a member of Solidarity and gave the names of people he knew who still supported the union. After that, the couple was forced to sign a pledge never to speak about the ordeal and thrown from a moving car onto a rural road. The man, deprived of his clothes for several hours, found a note inside his jacket pocket. It said: "Organization Anti-Solidarity has been born. The incompetent team of Jaruzelski and the bureaucratic security forces are unable to combat the cancer eating at our society. Solidarity is this cancer. We shall fight the beast. We will hit where we are least expected. We will use the names of different institutions, maybe even Solidarity. Beware. So far we have given only a sample of our power."

By the middle of the year, four identical kidnappings were reported by former Solidarity members. Each time, the kidnappers said they represented OAS. The organization's avowed distaste for Solidarity, and the proximity of Torun to the site of Popieluszko's disappearance gave everyone pause. Could OAS have grabbed the priest? Might OAS be an arm of the party hardliners?

Under interrogation, Piotrowski realized there would be no protection, no altered names and asylum in a foreign land. The secret policeman turned on his superior with the same lack of conscience he exhibited in bludgeoning Popieluszko. Colonel Adam Pietruszka was arrested by two uniformed police at his office on Thursday, October 25. A day later, General Platek was suspended from his position as director of Department Four. Around Rakowiecka the question hung in the air like smoke: How high will it go? Even Piotrowski could not answer that. He knew that he had been duped, but he did not know how high the deception stretched. For reasons known only to him, the captain chose to lie when he was asked where Popieluszko could be found. He insisted throughout Wednesday and Thursday that he and his subordinates had thrown Popieluszko, still alive, into the Vistula River near Torun. But he said he could not remember the exact spot. That elicited groans from Minister Kiszczak's office. The body might be anywhere between Torun and Gdansk, where the Vistula emptied into the Baltic Sea. A high-ranking team of five police frogmen, carefully selected for their Party credentials and past reliability, began searching the river surreptitiously, while a trawler dredged the water. Its crew was told it was looking for an escaped prisoner who was believed to have drowned. No one believed it for an instant. The secret police does not dispatch a captain, a colonel, and two lieutenants to look for a common criminal. When the divers turned up nothing after the first day, and then a second, they expected to be relieved by another team. Instead, they were lodged at a Torun hotel and forbidden to contact their families.

Leszek Pekala broke first. In the beginning, he claimed that he and Chmielewski had helped Piotrowski to kidnap the priest but had abandoned the operation while Popieluszko was still alive and conscious. His questioners were courteous, but they never let him forget that unless he cooperated he would never again walk the streets. Piotrowski, they told him, claimed that it had been Pekala who tossed the body into the Vistula.

"That's not true," shouted the lieutenant. "It wasn't just me." There was a long silence, then the sound of Pekala's sobs. "All right," he said quietly. "I'll show you where to find the body."

At St. Stanislaw parish, the vigil-keepers had taken over the entire churchyard as the week progressed. Hastily handwritten summaries of the latest news bulletins hung from the wrought iron fence. Most people merely glanced at them. If something important was discovered about Jerzy, they would learn it the way Poles have been informed for centuries: the grapevine. At the masses that were celebrated each hour throughout the day and night, sermons were brief: an abjuration of violent thoughts, a call for more prayers on Father Jerzy's behalf, then a thumbnail update on the latest rumors and speculation. Outside, in weather that alternated between numbing cold and needle-tipped rain, men huddled together and spoke of the dwindling chance of seeing Jerzy alive.

The regular police, even more than the SB, were at a loss to explain Popieluszko's disappearance. On Friday, October 26, the priest's older brother, Jozef, drove back to Poland from Cologne, where he had been trying to arrange a business deal. He had been aware of Jerzy's kidnapping but decided to press ahead with his business. Who knew when he might get permission to leave Poland again? Jozef recalled that it was not until he crossed the border from East Germany to Poland at Swiecko that he realized the true mood in his homeland. "The border guard looked at my passport and called over a major. He looked in the car and said to me, 'Did you leave your brother in Germany so they could say we kidnapped him?' He said Solidarity had kidnapped Jerzy." When Jozef arrived in Warsaw he went directly to his brother's church. Huddled in the rectory almost directly under Jerzy's room, Jozef was told in strictest confidence that information had been received from a psychic that Jerzy was alive and being held in a Soviet prison camp. The eldest Popieluszko brother withdrew, slightly disgusted. His disillusionment, however, was only beginning. Through one of Jerzy's fellow priests, he asked to see someone in the Curia. He was certain that if anyone knew the latest and most accurate information about Jerzy it would be the primate. He received his answer within hours. No one at the Curia could find time for him.

On Saturday, October 27, Minister Kiszczak would appear on television to address the nation on the search for Father Jerzy. The decision to put Kiszczak on the air had been made by government spokesman Urban and the minister himself and was considered a defensive maneuver. Kiszczak would have to announce that three SB officers had been arrested for the kidnapping and that the search for Popieluszko had produced no results. Urban later recalled wondering what effect Kiszczak would have and coached him on how to appear humble, distraught, sincere. A haughty or bullying approach could fill the streets with protesters.

Kiszczak rallied to the occasion. His appearance was calculated to catch viewers after darkness had descended and while they were eating their supper. His carefully chosen words emphasized the shared tragedy of Popieluszko's disappearance and his personal disappointment and humiliation that employees of the Interior Ministry were somehow involved. The performance was carefully crafted from the moment Kiszczak's face flashed on the screen until he bid his rapt audience good night, and it worked. To anyone skilled at reading the emotional barometer by which Poland is guided, it was clear that there was no spirit for revolution. There was only sadness.

On Tuesday, October 30, Pekala was driven to Wloclawek, handcuffed to an SB officer. He directed them, in monosyllables, to the bridge, said "Here" when they reached the halfway point, and stared dully as the divers, who had followed in a panel truck, put on their gear and waded into the reservoir from its shallowest point.

That October morning was overcast. The sky had the texture and coloring of damp brown gabardine. The team on shore huddled into the back of the van, drinking coffee from a vacuum flask. One of them was reading aloud a sports report when a shout came from the bank. They had found something! This time it was not a false alarm. In the early days after the kidnapping, hundreds of police and military reservists had scoured the countryside around Torun, like beaters at a shoot. And they had found bodies: decayed tramps wrapped in newspapers, skeletal traces of long unsolved mysteries. But not the man they were looking for.

Flopped on shore, he lay there like the carcass of a porpoise. Mud made a death-mask of his face, smothering his eyes and lips, concealing everything that endows a head with humanity. The commander looked at the picture that had been issued to hundreds of Polish policemen over the past eleven days. There was almost no resemblance. His hair appeared to have fallen out. The orders had been not to touch the body before filming it. But one of the policemen did so anyway, prying open the jaw. The tongue was reduced to pulp. Traced in blood on the muddied neck was a line where the noose had been attached. The clothes identified him, of course. He wore the garment of his profession. That was enough to radio, as instructed, directly to Warsaw and relay the coded signal.

The policemen joked nervously with each other. They felt no great sympathy for the man. Alive, he had been a problem. In death, he was going to cause even more trouble. The radio spluttered. The department in Warsaw wanted the men to start videotaping the body, limb by limb. A doctor would arrive soon. The camera was switched on and a police officer moved slowly down the body speaking into a microphone. Only the left hand still had rope tied to it. The legs were bent back like a collapsed deck-chair. The pockets were emptied and the contents spread on the grass: a large bundle of money adding up to three months' wages for a police lieutenant (the cameraman let out a low whistle); an honorary membership card of a wartime Partisan unit; some business cards; a permit for an air-pistol valid until the end of 1984; and—its writing blotched by water, the photograph curling and discolored—his identity card. One of the team read it aloud. Date of birth: September 23, 1947. Profession: priest. "Priest? That's a profession?" an officer asked. Address: Chlodna Street, Warsaw. Laughter again. That was where their colleagues in the secret police had planted explosives under his bed. The press had also tried to portray the flat as the love-nest of a lonely priest. The address brought back ribald memories.

The police officers forgot to erase the laughter from the soundtrack. When the videotape was shown at the trial of the priest's murders, in a darkened courtroom, the disembodied cackling turned the hearing into a macabre séance.

The mass at St. Stanislaw Kostka had just begun when one of the ushers slipped quietly from the sacristy and placed a sheet of white paper, folded once, on the altar. The priest did not read it immediately. He waited for a moment when the two thousand faithful in the church were reciting a prayer, the Gloria in Excelsis Deo, to flip the paper back. In hastily written pencil was the message: "TV has announced Father J's body found in Wloclawek reservoir." As he raised his head, the priest saw that the back of the church was already being flooded with the first arrivals who had heard the news.

"Brothers and sisters," he began. "Today, in the Wloclawek reservoir, the body of Father Jerzy ..." The collective cry of anguish drowned the rest of the priest's words, to be replaced by the sound of spontaneous keening. For a while, the priest let his feelings trickle down his cheeks, too. He could not, however, allow the Holy Mass that Father Jerzy had celebrated so many times at the same altar to dissolve. With great effort, he began to recite the Lord's Prayer, using its words as a physician might use salve. "And forgive us our trespasses as we forgive." He paused. "As we forgive ... as we forgive." Three times he repeated the command, until he was certain its message had penetrated. He finished the prayer, then said, "We must forgive."

By the time the announcement of the body's discovery was made, Father Jerzy's corpse was on its way to Bialystok, 150 miles east of Torun, and only a few miles from the priest's birthplace. The Jaruzelski government, by this time confident that there would be no *coup d'état* by the hardliners, had begun putting into action a plan to minimize the damage and the danger that it faced. The plan was simple but required cooperation. Since Polish law required any murder victim to undergo an autopsy, the inquest would be performed quickly in Bialystok. The body would then be turned over to the family, taken under escort to Okopy, and swiftly buried. The last thing the authorities needed was a public funeral, emotional eulogies, and memorial marches. Jaruzelski needed to demonstrate to a worried Moscow the stability of his leadership.

Word was sent to the primate that the government would view favorably a decision to bury Popieluszko in his home village. Glemp's response was cautious: he would consult with the family, whose interests had to be taken into account. If that was the primate's main concern, he hid it well. Jozef Popieluszko, who had tried in vain the week before to meet with someone from the Curia, recalled that even after his brother's body was fished out of the reservoir, he could not get information from the Church hierarchy about where it had been taken. It was the Forensic Center in Bialystok that finally called Jozef's wife to tell her that her brother-in-law's body could be claimed on Friday after the autopsy had been performed by Dr. Maria Byrdy. After that, said the caller, a funeral could be arranged in Suchowola, at the church where Alfons Alek Popieluszko once served as an altar boy.

Something about Marianna Popieluszko makes it difficult to imagine her heartbroken. Her son had been kidnapped, murdered, and dredged from a manmade lake. His body had been carted off and was in the hands of the police. Yet the aging woman did not grieve. She summoned her eldest son to fetch her and take her to Warsaw. The next morning, Wednesday, October 31, Marianna Popieluszko walked into the office of Cardinal Glemp's secretary and asked to see the primate. It was not a request to be refused. Glemp, embarrassed but attempting cordiality, sat the mother down, expressed stiff sympathies, and assured her that a high-ranking delegation from the Church would travel to Suchowola for the funeral. The mother assured the cardinal that they would find no one there. The funeral, she insisted, would be in Warsaw. "The shepherd's place is with his sheep," she said as though reading it from the Bible. A silence ensued. Glemp the pastor wrestled with Glemp the politician. The government had made clear it wanted Popieluszko eulogized and buried far from the capital. Yet already Glemp had been criticized for his meek response and lack of formal protest about the kidnapping. To shunt the corpse of the rebel priest off to obscurity was unthinkable. The hem of Glemp's surplice swished along the floor. He called in his secretary and gave orders for funeral preparations to be made at St. Stanislaw Kostka.

Jozef Popieluszko was cold. The storage room at the forensic laboratory was kept at 45°F. to retard the decomposition of its occupants. He remembered thinking he was in a very cold hospital ward except that behind the green curtains were not beds but stone slabs. "A cop was taking pictures of the body. On the other side of the curtain was a big crowd of people trying to look in. When they pulled the curtain back everyone would gawk." Jozef did not want to gawk, did not even want to look, but there was no other way to make a formal identification. The corpse ranged in color from green to a black as dark as the cassock that Jerzy used to wear. The body, bloated from eleven days under water, looked like a grotesque cartoon of his brother gone to fat. But the bloating did not conceal the terrible punishment that had been inflicted. The face was misshapen, the nose a pulpy flap, the lips torn to strips. His right index finger was missing its last joint, and the neck and wrists still bore clear marks from where the ropes had bitten. It took Jozef a while to realize he was being addressed. "I said, 'Do you identify him?' " asked the chief officer. "I remember walking over and looking at his chest. I saw the witch's teat, the double nipples, that he had been born with. I nodded."

Even in death Father Jerzy's movement was impeded. Outside the laboratory in Bialystok his parents waited. Minutes passed, nothing happened. Jozef and Father Stasz, the pastor of the Suchowola church where Jerzy had once served mass, asked for an explanation of the delay. Months later, Father Stasz shook his head in recalling the incident. "They told us they had lost the key to the gate through which the hearse would have to leave."

Word spread that Father Jerzy's body would not be released. Within an hour, more than a thousand people had massed around the laboratory building, and there was talk of opening the gate with dynamite. A police captain appeared. "Please, father, keep this crowd under control. I don't have enough men at my disposal to handle them." Father Stasz smiled at the irony of the situation, and said, "Okay, captain, leave it to me." Pointing at the embarrassed captain, Father Stasz shouted: "I have this gentleman's personal guarantee that the body will be released in five minutes. Once it is, please stay calm. Obey only the commands that are given by priests." The key was quickly located.

Jerzy Popieluszko's final return to Warsaw followed the same road that he had taken by bus nineteen years earlier to St. John the Baptist Seminary. This time, he was in the middle of a mournful caravan that included hundreds of taxis, private cars and trucks, and buses. It wound through small towns and farming villages, and as it passed, the residents of those places stopped, knelt, and blessed themselves.

At St. Stanislaw Kostka there was consternation. Father Jerzy's body had been expected to arrive at noon. Long before that, there were ten thousand people inside and around the church grounds, on one of the foulest days of that inclement autumn. They ignored the wind, the snow, the rain, and the certainty that some of the television cameras roaming about the grounds had been sent by the police and were certainly recording their faces for retribution. A gray resinous haze filled the air, for almost everyone had bought an extra votive candle the day before. November 1 was the Feast of All Saints and the traditional day for families to visit graveyards and honor deceased friends and loved ones by lighting a candle. On this Saturday, they brought a second candle and lit them around the wrought iron fence, along the sidewalks, on both sides of the streets that led to the church. The day wore on, the candles flickered out and were replaced. Occasionally, word rippled through the throng: the casket is expected at two, at three, at five o'clock. By six-thirty, the light was long gone, but the friends of Father Jerzy were not. A car rumbled up, two men wearing pins that displayed the image of the Black Madonna began clearing a path. The small van backed into the churchyard, its back doors opened, and the wooden coffin was carried inside and up to the steps of the altar from which Father Jerzy had preached.

Throughout the night, they filed past the closed coffin. A pause, a tear, and then each moved on, happier for having had a moment to share in the sadness. The church remained open until an hour before the funeral service began at 10 AM. Then, the doors were closed, and the family allowed to spend a few final minutes with Alfons Popieluszko, the son and brother who had made them proud.

There were four hundred thousand people at Popieluszko's funeral and not a policeman in sight. For as far as the eye could see from the steeple of St. Stanislaw Kostka, hands made the V sign, voices sang the defiant hymn "God Who Watches Over

Poland." It was the largest single gathering in Poland since the last visit by the Pope. It was also the first time Lech Walesa was permitted to address a public gathering of any size since before martial law. Dressed in a severe black suit, Walesa knew the truth, and spoke it. "Rest in peace," he told the tortured body within the coffin. "Solidarity is alive because you have given your life for it."

17
·
The Defendant, Popieluszko

THE MOST IMPORTANT trial to take place in Communist Europe in over three decades was staged in a flaking building that had been converted into a modern fortress. The initial scare that a mysterious group of hardliners was trying to dislodge General Jaruzelski had passed. But still no chances were being taken. To come within even one hundred yards of the Torun Courthouse one needed a special pass. To reach Courtroom 40, freshly painted for the television cameras, one had to pass through two metal detectors. Overhead, a helicopter gunship chattered incessantly. Commandoes splayed out and blocked the line of fire when the four defendants were led into court, rubbing their wrists to restore the circulation blocked by heavy manacles. But nobody was going to shoot or rescue the four secret police officers. Kept in the cold narrow cells of the turreted prison known locally as "The Little Barrel," they had time enough to contemplate their fate and the desertion of their protectors.

For Piotrowski the dominant question was, Will they hang me? The prosecutor would demand the death sentence for the captain, as the acknowledged ringleader. The two lieutenants and the colonel faced twenty-five-year jail sentences, the maximum imprisonment under Polish law. It would be a trial that would reveal intimate details of secret police activity and hold Poles in thrall. A trial that would show to a curious world how the secret police helps to run Church–government relations in a Communist state. It was a show trial, but there was a great deal of uncertainty: not about the outcome, but about the possibility that the defendants would overplay their roles. Everything depended on the level of desperation of the four police officers. Would Piotrowski, to save himself from the noose, implicate men at the very top of the Polish establishment? Naming names was the last line of defense.

It took the state nearly two months to prepare its case against Captain Piotrowski and Lieutenants Pekala and Chmielewski. Not until the end of November was Colonel Pietruszka charged with murder and ordered to stand trial. The Justice Ministry also said it would allow auxiliary prosecutors representing the Catholic Church and the Popieluszko family. With each public statement, the government tried to reassure the country that an honest and open trial would be conducted. Prime Minister Jaruzelski told a group of visiting journalists in November that no one in Poland wanted to get to the bottom of the truth more than he did. There were setbacks, to be sure. On November 30, the two senior officials compiling evidence against the secret policemen were killed in a car accident, provoking suspicions of foul play. But the accident was probably a tragic coincidence. The Justice Ministry quickly assured the public that no evidence had been destroyed. On December 4, it was announced that the trial would be conducted in Torun because the kidnapping had taken place within the city limits. Until then, Torun, founded in the thirteenth century, had been best known as the birthplace of Copernicus and gingerbread. A week later prosecutors for the Torun region filed indictments against the four defendants and subpoenaed eighty-four witnesses.

The chief prosecutor opened the trial on December 27 by painting a picture of four men who had conspired among themselves and deserved punishment. "They thought that Popieluszko was a dangerous man who had not abandoned his activities despite warnings and the granting of an amnesty," said the prosecutor. "They thought they would be promoted instead of being blamed for their act."

The two lieutenants looked pale and clearly frightened in the dock. Chmielewski had developed a twitch in his right cheek that made him look and sound like a village idiot. When he was asked by the court if he understood the charges against him, he stuttered, "Ye-eeeeee-esssss." His wife, eight months pregnant, sitting in the back row of the courtroom, burst into tears. There was no sign of sympathy from Artur Kujawa, the chief of the five-judge panel. He was a porcine man with spectacles and a gruff way of phrasing questions. "Were you born with the stammer?" he demanded. With agonizing effort, Chmielewski finally choked out: "No. Only since the Popieluszko affair."

Piotrowski's brown eyes gleamed defiantly at the court as he heard the detailed account of his brutality. There was not a flicker of remorse. Adam Pietruszka, the highest ranking of the defendants, kept his mouth frozen in disapproval. He kept looking at his watch, as though he had more important things to do.

The reading of the indictment took two and a quarter hours, and when it was finished, the one hundred people in the courtroom knew enough about the death of Jerzy Popieluszko to realize that these four men would certainly be found guilty. Nothing they could say would mitigate the court's judgment.

Leszek Pekala took the stand dressed in a sheepskin coat and dark jersey shirt. Without hesitation he pleaded guilty to the charges against him, but said he had never meant to kill the priest. For the rest of the day and most of the next, Pekala confirmed the details of the kidnapping and murder that were in the indictment. But he recanted parts of his pretrial statement in which he had said the murder had the approval of the highest echelons in the Interior Ministry. On the first day of the trial, Pekala said: "It only seemed that way to me." Sitting in the front row along with her youngest son, Stanislaw, Marianna Popieluszko listened to the account of Jerzy's torment, her eyes never giving Pekala a moment's respite.

The other lieutenant's performance on the witness stand was so pathetic that it might have seemed contrived had he not obviously been suffering. The prison doctors said he had suffered a nervous breakdown since his arrest and had lost motor control of his facial muscles and speech. He could hardly complete a word without stuttering, and his painful efforts to spit out sentences at first elicited compassion, then impatience and contempt from the court. Yet even with his stumbling speech, Chmielewski had the room hanging on his every word. He quickly moved beyond the facts of the murder and spoke of the people he believed had ordered it. In so doing he uncovered the limits of the government's interest in having a fair and informative trial.

After a New Year's recess, the testimony was no longer deemed suitable for general consumption. On January 7, Chmielewski for the first time in the trial introduced the name of a deputy interior minister, the head of the secret police. The lieutenant said that Piotrowski told him "that everything had been approved at the top. I took this to mean that the deputy minister, Ciaston, knew about our operation and approved."

Alarmed at such loose talk, Judge Kujawa interrupted. "Are you sure of what you are saying? You don't have to talk about these things." Chmielewski, though, would not be silenced. He remembered that he heard Platek's voice on the car radio before the October 13 stoning attempt, telling the team that there were no new instructions for them. After the killing, Piotrowski told both lieutenants not to worry about the special task force that was overseeing the search for Popieluszko. "He said that the people involved in the investigation were both good guys."

Kujawa interrupted again. "Who did he mean by 'good guys'?"

"Well," blubbered the witness, "in addition to Colonel Pietruszka there was General Platek and Colonel Zbigniew Jablonski." Like Platek, Jablonski was a department head in the ministry. If the witness knew what he was talking about, it meant that the conspiracy to cover up Popieluszko's kidnapping and death went beyond Department Four, which Platek headed. When he and Pekala were called in by Platek on October 23 and asked where they had been the night the priest was killed, said Chmielewski, "I panicked. Neither Piotrowski nor Pietruszka was there for me to ask what to do." The implication was that the lieutenant was surprised to be confronted by a general who he knew had sanctioned the operation from the beginning. All of those statements were censored from the Polish press.

On the sixth day of the trial, Piotrowski was called to the stand by the prosecutors. The captain was a two-edged sword in the case. Piotrowski said whatever came to mind as he testified. After confirming each of the bare details of Popieluszko's beating and death, Piotrowski paused, and said: "When I first hit him there in the forest, it was the first time in my adult life that I ever hit a man. Oh, there were schoolyard scrapes, of course. . . ." As he spoke about his adolescent scuffles, Piotrowski's face changed. For that instant, he was not a brutal murderer but merely a big man telling tales at a bar or a party.

Piotrowski seemed to be under the impression that there would be no harm in speaking freely about Platek's role. Perhaps in his prison cell he had not been told that "the top" which had sacrificed him would still protect Platek. The day after the kidnapping, "I got a call from Platek summoning me to his office. Pietruszka was there. Our conversation took about an hour because phones kept ringing in the boss's office. Platek asked me to find out about Popieluszko's meetings with the U.S. Embassy to see if one of those undercover meetings didn't end in his abduction. He also told me to investigate some of the people who hid fugitives in their apartments. I went down with Pietruszka to his office. He asked me, 'Is Popieluszko still around?' I said: 'It no longer depends on me.' It was all idiotic." None of his damning extempore remarks were ever printed in the Polish press.

Judge Kujawa called a recess in the trial, which clearly was getting out of hand. In the afternoon, Piotrowski returned, looking bewildered and shaken. His whole manner had changed. He had prepared notes and did not stray from them. The murderer began to indict his victim. "I had information about the priest's relationship with a certain lady. To put it vulgarly, I had this information because I planned to blackmail him. I could name hotels and other places and give the name, but I don't see any reason now." He didn't hate the priest. "There was never any hatred. I was born without hatred, only a reflex that wanted to see the law in Poland respected. My attitude toward Jerzy Popieluszko was indifferent, officially chilly. As a priest he really didn't interest me. Popieluszko was a tool. He found himself in the center of interest of a certain environment. I was aware that in the past two years citizen Popieluszko had lost his sense of perspective. He used to be a normal priest."

It was the Catholic Church, he said, which was responsible for the change in Popieluszko and, indirectly, for his death. "How could we keep calm when import duties were waived for priests, mostly for cars and luxury goods?" he asked. "How could we keep calm if, disregarding the law, youth were incited and educated to hate the state?" The job of monitoring the Church and priests like Popieluszko brought unbearable strains on him. "For the secret police, there were no Sundays. Children never saw their fathers because some priests decided to make trouble for us. The only thing that concerned me was that Popieluszko, as a tool of the Church, was breaking the law. I was convinced that all the talk about Popieluszko leaving Poland to go to Rome on a scholarship was fiction. He would never leave Poland unless the primate ordered him to do so. When I saw all of this, I agreed to undertake the mission [to kill him]. I was fully aware that the actions to which I agreed were unlawful, but for me, that was a necessary evil in order to prevent a greater evil."

This was something that no one had expected. The Church was effectively in the dock. The phantom of Popieluszko was the fifth defendant, a victim accused of his own murder. Whatever had been said to Piotrowski during the recess that first day changed the thrust of his testimony and the nature of the trial. Had Piotrowski made a deal? His attack on the Church and Popieluszko in particular, venting the anger of his colleagues in the secret police, was not interrupted by Judge Kujawa. It had obviously been decided to let the captain have his platform as long as he continued to embarrass the Church.

As the net tightened around General Platek, Kujawa tried to devise a legal escape route for him.

COURT: Think about the way you conducted the operation. You used a car that barely worked. You had to borrow a pair of handcuffs. Didn't that make you wonder about how high the "top" was?

PIOTROWSKI: I told myself, it can't just be Pietruszka who had approved this. It must go higher. Now it turns out . . . oh, it's not important.

COURT: Would you have taken on such an action without encouragement from your superiors?

PIOTROWSKI: It's hard to talk about encouragement. It was an assignment.

COURT: So without official inspiration you would not have undertaken the action of October 19?

PIOTROWSKI: With all certainty, no.

COURT: Does adherence to the wishes of superiors justify breaking the law?

PIOTROWSKI: I realized I was breaking the norms of the penal code. But I believed that was a lesser evil than the hostile activities of Popieluszko.

COURT: Did you intend Popieluszko to die?

PIOTROWSKI: I realize I am responsible for his death. I have already answered extensively. Please excuse me from answering again.

COURT: Who killed Father Popieluszko?

PIOTROWSKI: I don't know.

Edward Wende had a reputation for defending people and causes opposed to the Communist regime. An imposing man who favored English suits and Davidoff cigars, Wende was representing the driver, Waldemar Chrostowski. When Piotrowski's lawyer moved to include in the court record a copy of the police file on Popieluszko, Wende jumped to his feet to object.

Overruled, said Kujawa. Wende, reaching for a copy of the Polish penal code and rules of court procedure, began to cite a section in support of his objection.

"If you intend to read from that book, it is a waste of time," snapped Kujawa.

Just as fiercely, Wende replied: "Here, in this room, we use only the code in this book, and I have a right to draw on it." He lost the ruling, but had made his point.

Kujawa ruled that inclusion of Popieluszko's criminal record would help determine the captain's frame of mind on the night of the murder. But most revealing was a slip of the tongue by Kujawa at the end of Piotrowski's testimony. Turning to the captain's lawyer, Kujawa asked: "Are there any further questions from counsel for the defendant, Popieluszko?" An embarrassed silence followed. "Ah, I mean Piotrowski," said the flustered judge.

Alone among the defendants, Colonel Adam Pietruszka maintained his innocence. When he first took the witness stand on January 10, he reminded the court: "The rule of law demands that undeserved punishment should not be inflicted on an innocent person." But the cloak of protection shielding General Platek did not extend to the crewcut colonel. When he was asked to explain why, if he was innocent, he had refused to answer any questions during his pretrial interrogation, he said that he had been disoriented by the bright lights and strange people in his cell.

Pietruszka made a poor witness. He was unaware that Piotrowski had gone to Gdansk on October 13 to stone Father Jerzy's car, he said, yet admitted that his signature was on a pass authorizing the captain to make the trip. From the colonel's testimony it emerged that General Platek had delayed the release of vital information about the sighting of Piotrowski's car in Bydgoszcz. First of all, the colonel said, he had discussed the subject with General Platek two days after the murder. But then he backtracked. He did not know until three days later where Piotrowski had been on October 19. Wende, smiling broadly, pointed out the discrepancy.

The colonel was shown the travel permit that the murderers had used to go to Bydgoszcz. "Is that your signature?" asked the prosecutor. "Yes, yes, it is," he muttered. "But I never signed such a pass for October 19. Someone must have changed the date." An analyst from the police laboratory was called to testify that there was no indication the date on the pass had been altered.

After the abduction, when he asked Piotrowski where the missing priest was and was told the Vistula River, the colonel explained that he failed to pass on the information because: "I couldn't believe that a head of a section [of the Interior Ministry] could have done it. It was my mistake that I regarded this as unreal and on the verge of absurdity. I didn't believe such things could happen in this country."

The whispers and titters built until Judge Kujawa threatened to clear the courtroom. One thing was clear: Pietruszka would have to fend for himself.

Once the defendants had made their statements, the prosecution called its witnesses. Their testimony over ten days filled in the gaps left by the killers. Popieluszko's driver, Waldemar Chrostowski, identified the three men who had kidnapped him so convincingly that Piotrowski put his face in his hands and shook his head. While the state built an airtight case inside Courtroom 40, there were rumors sweeping the country about the fallout the trial was creating. It was said that Miroslaw Milewski, the former interior minister who was the Politburo's overseer of police affairs, was out. He had not been seen in his office since Piotrowski's testimony. The stain of complicity had spread too far, and someone would have to pay for it.

General Zenon Platek seemed to be wearing shoes with rounded soles. From the moment he took the witness stand on January 21, he swayed back and forth, back and forth, on the balls of his feet, as he delivered his testimony. At one point a stenographer complained that she could hear only every other sentence. The general displayed the arrogance of a man who has made a backroom deal. But he went too far. Confident that he would not be linked with the murderers, the general made statements so blatantly false that Judge Kujawa occasionally had to ask him if he did not wish to reconsider what he had just said. Platek denied everything that Pietruszka had said, beginning with the suggestion that he had ordered the removal of the light Fiat from the ministry's parking lot on the Sunday after Popieluszko's murder. "Are you saying you did not order it removed?" asked Kujawa heavily. Platek backpedaled. Perhaps he had done that, but his motive was not to conceal evidence. How could it have been, since he had no reason to suspect that any

Interior Ministry employees were involved in the priest's disappearance? Certainly, said the general, he had no conversation with Pietruszka about agreeing when they first noticed the car and "keeping the chronology straight." If Pietruszka knew something about the murder and did not volunteer it, said Platek, then he must have had a reason for wanting to hide it.

Wende, the lawyer representing Popieluszko's driver, rose. What would you say about someone who intentionally concealed evidence about a crime? Platek chuckled. "I'm not very good at the law," he said. "I finished my studies long ago."

Then why did he not immediately report the information passed to him by telephone by the two special agents he had dispatched to Bydgoszcz? Platek stopped rocking. "I ... I got that information late at night. I had taken a sleeping pill and I was drowsy. I must have forgotten about it."

This time, it fell to the state's prosecutors to try to help Platek out of the hole he had dug. The attorney asked the general if, as director of the Interior Ministry's Church monitoring department, he was aware of the role Father Popieluszko played during the May 1 demonstrations in Warsaw. Yes, said the general, picking up his cue at last. A journalist from the Communist Party newspaper, Mrs. Arbatowska, had written to him demanding that some action be taken against the rebel priest.

Wende asked that Mrs. Arbatowska be called to testify. Platek blanched. He had not anticipated that. It took some hours to establish that there was no journalist by that name. The cross-examination went on. After receiving information about Popieluszko's May Day activities, Platek said, a letter had been written to Primate Glemp complaining about the priest's antistate conduct. Like a hawk swooping down, Judge Kujawa ordered that the document be included in the court record. "These documents," he ruled, "have important meaning to the defense."

The ruling sparked a fierce court battle led by attorney Wende, who, in the end, lost. More importantly, the diversion allowed Platek to recover before he made more stupid errors. Later, in reviewing the trial, Wende would admit: "We lost the momentum." General Platek, caught in the web of his own lies, was saved only by the court's indulgence. A lawyer from a West German legal institute who was inside the courtroom later said that in any other country Platek would have been arrested as soon as he left the witness stand and charged as an accomplice to murder. Instead, the general walked out of the courtroom a free man. The hemorrhaging of information about who ordered Father Popieluszko's death had been staunched.

There was never a question of guilt or innocence. The issue of punishment, though, began to loom large as the trial wound down at the end of January. For more than a month, Courtroom 40 had been a stage on which a morality play was enacted. The country became anesthetised to the chilling facts of Father Jerzy's death. Dr. Maria Byrdy, the pathologist who performed the autopsy on his body, testified with scientific precision that the cause of death was impossible to determine. The seventy-five-year-old doctor, white-haired and bespectacled, looked out of place among the antiterrorist guards with their machine guns, the defendants, the lawyers. Yet, she became one of the lasting images of the trial as she calmly handled the prosecution's articles of evidence. She showed how the blood-stained rope had been attached around the victim's neck, pressed against her own mouth the foul-smelling gauze gag, swung the stick that Piotrowski had carried with vigor. The priest, she said, could have died from the beatings he endured, from strangling on the rope around his neck, from swallowing his own vomit and blood that were prevented from escaping by the tapes and gags, or from drowning in the reservoir. On the last full day of expert testimony, the courtroom was shown the videotape that had been made as Father Jerzy's body was dredged from the water. More than one member of the audience asked to be excused.

When the state prosecutor began his summation, it was difficult to know who he was suggesting should be punished. "The pride and conceit of Piotrowski and Pietruszka have directly led to a criminal and macabre act by which they tarnished the good name of the Interior Ministry." Captain Piotrowski, he said, "combined the functions of accuser, judge, and hangman." The prosecutor paused. Yet there were similarities between the hunter and his victim. "Father Popieluszko fell victim to people who, just like him, thought they could break the law with impunity. The extremist stand taken by Father Popieluszko was no less harmful than the crime which was committed against him. Like Popieluszko, Captain Piotrowski must be judged as an extremist."

The courtroom was silent. Attorney Wende and his client, the priest's driver, were openmouthed. Could this be happening? The prosecutor was attacking the victim. "Popieluszko stood in opposition to the state. He sowed hatred. He did not call for accord, but for struggle and hatred, for social unrest. As a citizen and a clergyman he undertook extremist action. He fell victim to people like himself."

In exhaustive detail, the prosecutor reviewed not Popieluszko's murder but his arrest in 1983, after the secret police planted literature and explosives in his flat, his dodging of summonses for interrogation, his antistate sermons. "Father Popieluszko's provocative activities continued right up until his death," said the state's lawyer. "He continued to abuse freedom of conscience and religion and to preach political sermons. These are undeniable facts."

"Your honors, I am familiar with the old adage 'One should not speak ill of the dead.' But it is necessary to do so here for the sake of Polish law and Polish justice. There is no moral conflict here, your honors. You are obliged to judge not only who took Father Popieluszko's life and how, but why they did it."

For an hour and a half it went on, the equating of priest and policeman. And just as he expressed no sympathy for Popieluszko, neither did he ask leniency for Piotrowski, the chief killer, or Pietruszka, the overseer. The captain should hang, said the prosecutor. The colonel and the two lieutenants should be put in jail for the maximum time allowed by Polish law, twenty-five years.

The world was turning upside down. The judge coached the witnesses and allowed the victim to be calumnized after his death. The prosecutor attacked the dead man and said it was necessary to serve Polish justice. The smug general could not keep his lies straight, and witnesses who could have challenged his testimony were not allowed to speak. On January 30 Edward Wende took the floor. He had not slept the night before. He wanted his summation to span his outrage as a Pole and his obligation as a lawyer. The result was one of the outstanding presentations in the country's judicial history, a speech that left policemen and priests alike in tears. Wende began by stating the obvious. "It seems probable to me that the world's chronicles of justice have never recorded a statement by a prosecutor which likens the victim of a crime to his killer. No sentence was ever passed against the priest, and none ever will be. No one has proved that the priest was guilty of anything. What danger did he pose? Why was he killed? Because he was a man who fought in a different way. Jerzy Popieluszko was not someone to nod approval, and that is why he was killed."

Next, Wende walked to the front of the room and stared straight at the judges as he asked: "The defendants should know that the bench representing the people should be much longer. It stretches to millions of Polish hearts and homes. They did not know that there are some people who cannot be killed— people whose graves are lit eternally. They should have known that."

There remained only one thing more to be said. The lawyer looked at Popieluszko's mother, his brother, his friends and supporters who had wedged themselves into the room. He turned and said: "Father Jerzy was opposed to the death penalty. He believed that no man has the right to take the life of another for any reason. I hope that the court, when it considers its verdict, will remember that, and take his wishes into account."

It did not surprise Wende when, four days later, the judges finally sided with him. Piotrowski would not be hanged. He and Pietruszka would be sentenced to twenty-five years' imprisonment. Pekala, who had admitted helping to tie the ropes that choked the priest, received fifteen years. Chmielewski, stuttering still, would be imprisoned for fourteen years.

The night the verdict was announced, Piotrowski's friends and secret police colleagues in Lodz, where he began his career, sat down in the town's best restaurant. They ordered champagne and toasted each other's health. They sang songs and told jokes. Some of them took out their service revolvers and fired bullets into the beams of the restaurant ceiling. Their friend would not hang. It was a night for celebration.

18

•

Who Ordered the Killing?

PIOTROWSKI WAS ALWAYS a dandy. Even in the Torun courtroom he managed to wear a blue worsted suit that could have
been bought only with dollars and a matching button-down-
collared shirt. No tie, of course, lest he hang himself. In prison
he now wears his gray flannel uniform with similar panache.
His marriage has broken down, but two women visit him regularly and this seems to keep him spry, aware of his looks. The
eyes bulge a little, as they did in court, because the prison diet
has been aggravating his thyroid condition. His complexion is
sallow from too much artificial light. There is no escape from
the murder, its memories and images: he shares the cell with his
faithful lieutenant Waldemar Chmielewski, the tall, twitching
accomplice. The lieutenant has pictures of his wife and children
pinned above his bunk, counts off the time to visiting day on a
pocket calendar. Both men work in the prison printing shop and
have the normal privileges of political offenders. Food parcels
arrive once a month, sometimes more frequently. In the evenings a black and white television set is carried into the cell and
the two murderers are allowed to watch the news. It is a banal
existence, but not uncomfortable.

The prison governor calculated that the other accomplices

would not share a cell with Piotrowski. Chmielewski retains some of the spaniel-like respect for his former boss. Piotrowski still dominates him, asks him for menial favors. Leszek Pekala, by contrast, could never cope with Piotrowski and his overbearing arrogance. During the hearings of their appeal the captain tried to burden Pekala anew. The Supreme Court rejected the appeals, but Pekala has not forgiven him. He is kept well away from Piotrowski, and there are no chance meetings in the corridor or the canteen. In any case the homosexual agent has his own problems: he has been beaten up at least twice by fellow inmates.

Colonel Pietruszka, once one of the most powerful men in the running of Church–state relations in Poland, has aged more noticeably than the other conspirators. He stoops a little, his normal pendantry has become the irritable obsessiveness of the prematurely old; for him, the twenty-five-year jail term was a death sentence. For hours on end he sits in an apathetic daze, not working, not reading. Only his hatred for Piotrowski, his ambitious young section head, keeps his heart hurting. The colonel's friends think he was framed. Piotrowski, they believe, did a deal with the authorities at Pietruszka's expense. The agreement, they claim, was that the captain would not point the finger at anyone more senior than Pietruszka. In return, Piotrowski would escape the noose demanded by the prosecutor.

Certainly, it was difficult for those in Courtroom 40 to forget the extraordinary cynicism of the captain when Judge Kujawa pressed home what was essentially the government case: "You mean to say there was no 'top' beyond defendant Pietruszka?" Piotrowski spread his arms out wide, a theatrical gesture of resignation, "Yes, if that's what's required, yes, there was no 'top'."

Who was the "top"? Who ordered, or inspired, the killing of Father Jerzy Popieluszko? General Zenon Platek walks free, suspended as director of the secret police religious affairs department, but in line for a new posting or early, honorable retirement. He lied at least three times in court, but there has never been any question of perjury charges. His deceit, usually clumsy, tried to disguise the fact that he knew of the involvement of his own department soon after the murder. Why cover up the facts? The charitable explanation is that the interior minister, General Kiszczak, ordered him to do so. Convinced that there was a plot to oust Jaruzelski, knowing that secret policemen were involved, Kiszczak wanted to buy time. Piotrowski and his two accomplices stayed free at least two days more than necessary because of Platek's ditherings and blunders. But perhaps Kiszczak was having the murderers followed and bugged to see whether the trail led further back into the establishment.

Perhaps. The more likely explanation is that Platek, who was an absentee director for most of 1984, stumbled into the middle of a conspiratorial bog and did not know how to escape. The general had been away on special secondment for much of the summer of 1984. His first deputy, Colonel Pietruszka, had become so accustomed to using the general's office that he held staff meetings there even after the general had returned. The evidence in Courtroom 40 strongly suggested that Platek had authorized the kidnapping of Popieluszko and that he knew his agents were planning to use violent methods. But the evidence leans heavily on the testimony of three men who are now convicted killers. "They were lying to save their necks": that was a defense of sorts for the unhappy general, but few people in Poland believe in his innocence.

Those who know General Platek—his bureaucratic blindness, his poor political sense—realize he could never have been the "top." Platek shared none of the frustration of his subordinates with radical priests: the Church department was for him only a rung on the administrative ladder. He was tipped as one of Kiszczak's candidates for the position of SB chief. He therefore had little to gain from inspiring a conspiracy of this political importance; his own neglect pulled him into the plot, his childishly stupid lies wedded him to the murder.

Platek is a red herring, the kind of character written into an Agatha Christie thriller to divert the reader's attention from more and less obvious suspects. Even Dame Agatha's sleuths would soon discard Platek and move on to the other suspects. The genre of the detective mystery suggests that a crime must be unraveled by establishing the instrument of murder, the suspect who was in the right place at the right time, and the motive of the killer.

The instrument of murder is plain enough: Piotrowski and his accomplices. The other factors suggest four main suspects, four possible explanations for the killing of Father Jerzy.

(a) The first is that the kidnapping was ordered by General Kiszczak and thus, implicitly, General Jaruzelski.

Popieluszko's private diaries shed some light on the first explanation. The priest was above all the victim of officially authorized persecution. The sheer scope of the police units involved—the ZOMO riot police, Wolski's secret police troublemakers, Department Four, counterespionage officers, the traffic police, and the regional headquarters in at least five cities—clearly indicate that Kiszczak, who has overall charge of all police departments, defined Popieluszko as a target of major importance. When one of Wolski's men threw a brick with explosives into the priest's house, no charges were brought against the agent. When Popieluszko was framed, when a ridiculous arms cache was put under his bed, General Kiszczak did not object. If the general had been seriously embarrassed, or kept in the dark about the operation, he would certainly have dropped the charges.

Instead the priest was interrogated more than a dozen times, was formally indicted, and was not amnestied until the last moment. This must all have had the direct approval of General Kiszczak. He wanted to teach the priest a lesson, and Department Four was happy to oblige.

The propaganda machine which whittled away at the priest had also received top-level clearance. Since July 1982 the propaganda controller of the Communist Party had been an ally of General Jaruzelski. An economic journalist and supporter of the general, Jan Glowczyk, replaced the thick-set figure of Stefan Olszowski, the hardline Party secretary in charge of propaganda. The attacks against Popieluszko, increasingly bitter in tone, were evidently not part of a hardline plot to wrong-foot Jaruzelski; rather they were part of a centrally organized campaign to put the Catholic Church on the defensive. It was Jaruzelski's own appointee as government spokesman, Jerzy Urban, who led the troops into battle against Popieluszko. From May 1984, after General Jaruzelski's summit meeting with Kremlin leader Konstantin Chernenko, there was an almost constant barrage. As soon as it was plain that the amnestied Solidarity leaders would find a platform and an audience in churches, and in St. Stanislaw Kostka in particular, the press started to bay like hounds in pursuit.

A typical sample:

JUNE 14: A party daily, *Trybuna robotnicza*, attacked Popieluszko for his "philosophy of disarray" and said that he was a "dishonest Christian." It quoted Matthew, chapter 7, verse 15: "Beware of false prophets, which come to you in sheep's clothing, but inwardly they are ravening wolves."

JULY 31: Of Popieluszko's masses for the fatherland, Urban wrote: "Do not confuse a mass, of any intention, with the functioning of a political club where incitement against the state takes place . . . that is the same kind of abuse as daubing a red cross on a rocket-launching pad."

AUGUST 8: Urban wrote: "We hope that the adventurist and irresponsible attitudes and statements of some clergymen, at all levels, will be curbed."

By September Urban is writing, under his pseudonym of Jan Rem, about Popieluszko's, "seances of hatred." This hatred, he said, was directed against "Communism, against the authorities, against everything that is postwar Poland."

That same month, only a matter of weeks before Popieluszko was murdered, the propaganda controller, Jan Glowczyk, addressed a meeting of Communist Party journalists and called on them to be more aggressive toward the Chruch, to muster the courage to battle with Church ideas and representatives in the columns of the official press. A young journalist from a woman's magazine stood and nervously challenged him. "That's all very well Comrade Glowczyk, but most of my readers live in places like Ursynow [a Warsaw housing project]. There is no school, so every morning the kids have to leave in the dark to cross Warsaw in buses and return in the dark, late in the evening. But on the weekend they can walk the few meters to their church with their parents and sit in Sunday School lessons, flicking through colorful books about Jesus. How can we fight against that? None of my readers will believe anything negative I write about the Church." Glowczyk was stumped for a reply. The authorities had thought no further than first base. It was clear that Solidarity leaders were finding support in some churches. The prosecutor had already warned union activists and advisers, Jan Rulewski, Wladyslaw Frasyniuk, Jacek Kuron, and Adam Michnik, about making political speeches in Church. The next step was obviously to confront the Church itself, especially long-standing enemies like Father Popieluszko. More profound questions of how to woo Poles away from their faith had to take second place to the front line of ideological warfare.

The steps against Father Popieluszko were thus in the mainstream of government policy and consistent with day-to-day SB tactics. The number of priests who have fallen victim to mysterious, never-detected, never-arrested assailants has continued to increase ever since Father Popieluszko's murder.

When in May 1983 a score of SB men broke into a medical aid center in the Warsaw Church of St. Martin and beat up some of the helpers, the authorities hardly raised an eyebrow. The investigation was dropped for "lack of evidence." A few months after Father Popieluszko's death, Father Kazimierz Jancarz from Nowa Huta, a steelworkers' parish near Krakow, had a large rock thrown through his windshield. Was it supposed to be another of the SB's "beautiful accidents"? Certainly the tall, bearded former railway worker was exactly the kind of cleric the Polish government wanted to stamp out: he too had started worker education classes in church, he too was holding masses for the fatherland. Six months after the death of Father Jerzy, another Solidarity priest, Tadeusz Zaleski, was roughed up by a gang of plainclothes men and repeatedly burnt with a cigarette end. An official investigation concluded that the wounds were self-inflicted, the result of an epileptic fit.

Despite this history of violence and despite the verbal attacks and the obvious anger of the Communist authorities, it is still difficult to argue that General Kiszczak directly ordered or in-

234 WHO ORDERED THE KILLING?

spired the murder of Father Popieluszko. The interior minister must have known there were various ideas being floated about how to deal with Popieluszko; he must have known that some of these ideas involved violence. General Kiszczak's culpability is that he did not set limits, did not scribble in the margins of proposed operations: "This is illegal" or "Do not use violence"; instead his comments were wistful attempts to sympathize with the frustrations of his subordinates.

But he could not have benefited from dragging his own ministry into the crossfire. He reacted intelligently to the murder, using the crisis to purge the SB of some three hundred agents. The killing of Father Popieluszko thus helped him to regain control over his secret police. But Kiszczak clearly did not order the murder of the cleric and risk the ousting of General Jaruzelski simply to supply himself with a pretext for a purge of the police. Neither Kiszczak nor Jaruzelski had an interest in bringing down their own government.

And this is what was at stake. The immediate effect, and presumably therefore the motive, of the murder was to destabilize Jaruzelski's leadership. It was a mark of the Jaruzelski regime's fragility that the killing of a single priest could push it to the brink of a major crisis. So much then for "normalization," that state of induced narcoleptic calm imposed on Czechoslovakia after the 1968 Warsaw Pact invasion and on Poland in 1981, when its own army in effect invaded and occupied the country. Who would want to expose the weakness of Jaruzelski's leadership in such a way? Solidarity, of course, had been waging its own modest war with the authorities since the imposition of martial law, and the purpose of its repeated demonstrations, staged in the face of huge police deployments, was to show the world that the general did not control the spirit of the people, that he was dependent on force to stay in power. But Solidarity had never used violence, never really tried to dislodge Jaruzelski, only, in the first instance, to persuade Jaruzelski to talk and listen to his people and change the system in a mutually agreed manner. A month before the murder of Father Popieluszko, Solidarity was in a conciliatory mood, buoyed up by the amnesty of political prisoners and trying, with the help of sympathetic priests, to work for a more pluralistic society: even the most cynical of cynical Marxists would find it difficult to argue that Solidarity was prepared to kill one of its outstanding heroes simply to embarrass General Jaruzelski. The enemy was within, not outside the establishment.

(b) The second: the crime was organized by a hardline faction, inspired by the disgruntled Politburo member Miroslaw Milewski. The purpose was either to overthrow Jaruzelski or to force him to adopt much tougher policies toward Solidarity, internal order, and the Church. Whatever the results—the fall of Jaruzelski or a tougher policy—General Kiszczak would have to go, thus realizing a long-term aim of the hardliners in the security *apparat*.

For Westerners it is useful to think of Communist leaders as either hardline "hawks" or moderate "doves." Nobody, however, is very clear what these terms mean. Sometimes "hardliners" are simply those who are out of, or who aspire to, power. Moderates, pragmatists, technocrats, liberals—the label is irrelevant—are the men who actually run the government. "I don't believe in a liberal wing of the Party," says the veteran dissident Jacek Kuron, "only the pragmatism of the people in power." In Poland, hardliners are said to be against private farmers, against private businessmen, against Jews in government, against income differentials in factories, against Solidarity or anyone other than the Communist Party, which claims to represent the workers, against flirting with the West, and against appeasing the Church. By the time of the 1984 amnesty, Jaruzelski had offended against all these principles. He had been aware since taking over as Party chief in October 1981 that there was a real threat from these "hardliners," and for a while he tried to steal their clothes.

The gestures did little to calm Jaruzelski's critics. He had bought Chernenko's approval for a wide-ranging amnesty but only on condition that positive steps were taken to blunt the political power of the Church, to win over Polish youth to Communism, and to guarantee adequate internal security. If the hardliners could expose Jaruzelski's failure in any of these areas they would effectively destroy his credibility with Moscow. The move, or series of moves, started in August 1984, as the freed political prisoners began to trickle home. Would it not be a good idea to pass an exile law, or at least an executive decree, that would banish Solidarity troublemakers to the West? The seed was planted by the hardliners, and soon enogh possible candidates were mentioned: Adam Michnik as the least tractable dissident; Jacek Kuron perhaps; maybe even—this was said with a shrug, a speculative glance at the sky—maybe even Popieluszko. When the Church leadership picked up these signals, it was put in a quandary. Parishioners and well-wishers were suggesting that the priest be sent to Rome for his own safety: could the primate not dispatch him to the Vatican? Later Glemp was to recall: "How could I order him to Rome when there was talk of banishment in the air?" So Popieluszko stayed at home, a natural target.

The second maneuver by Jaruzelski's internal enemies was to press for greater police powers. The amnesty had freed not only over six hundred "politicals" but also tens of thousands of common criminals. Praga, the rundown thieves' kitchen of Warsaw, was echoing with festivities, drunken homecoming parties in the long courtyards. Pickpockets, car thieves, safecrackers, fences, big- and small-time speculators were on the loose again. The respectable burghers of Warsaw began to panic. Grilles were fixed to windows, and a brisk trade was done in Alsatian dogs. The calls of Miroslaw Milewski for extended police rights became strident in and out of the Politburo. Milewski was head of the Law and Order Committee linking the Interior Ministry with all the government officers concerned with crime prevention—the Justice Ministry, regional prosecutors, judges. Why were juries not tougher? Why was the prosecutor not following up cases after the police had gathered enough evidence? Somehow Milewski managed to give the impression that Jaruzelski and Kiszczak were only barely able to keep order in the country. One spark and things could turn nasty.

The next step was to narrow the field of action to Popieluszko. This was straightforward: the Jaruzelski government had already played into the hands of the hardliners. The September article by Jerzy Urban, the government spokesman—under his well-known pseudonym Jan Rem—brought the official tub-thumping anti-Church campaign to a loud crescendo with one of most personal and savage press attacks ever launched against an individual priest. The hardliners saw their chance. Here was evidence that Jaruzelski was all talk, no action, seemingly paralyzed by fear of disrupting Church–state relations. Kazimierz Kakol, religious affairs minister during the Gierek regime, was a hard-bitten atheist and unhappy with Jaruzelski's style. Soon after Urban's article appeared he met Miroslaw Milewski, an old friend, and together they drafted a reply, a letter to the editor of the weekly *Tu i teraz* (Here and now) that effectively challenged the government: you can write nasty, now how about doing something? Urban was a lamb that was trying to roar like a lion, wrote Kakol. If Popieluszko was such a threat to the system, then why had he not been arrested and put on trial? That was precisely the point being made by Captain Piotrowski and his friends in Rakowiecka Street. Milewski had listened attentively to the complaints from the secret police: he knew what kind of assault would draw approval from his allies in the security *apparat*. The letter was sent to the weekly, set in print, but it never appeared. Instead it circulated privately (a proof was also stolen by the Solidarity underground, which was predictably indignant); and the opinion gained currency. A glance at Kakol's background shows how he was an ideal front man for a lance thrust at Jaruzelski. He had hoped for a university career but failed to win approval for his doctoral thesis, a necessary step for promotion to assistant professor. However, he was given a hand up by Mieczyslaw Moczar, who put pressure on Warsaw University. When Moczar attacked Jews and liberals in 1968, as part of a bid to topple Gomulka, the Party leader, Kakol helped to purge the universities. For these services he was appointed director of the Center for Journalistic Studies, the main training ground for Party propagandists. As religious affairs minister he was part of a secret commission whose function was to "contain" the effects of the Pope's 1979 visit to Poland.

The Moczar connection was crucial throughout Kakol's career, as it was for Milewski. By the time of the plot against Popieluszko, Moczar was an old man with no real hope of power. He was, however, a godfather, a *padrone*, who could still bring up his own men through the Party and, to a lesser extent, the state machine. Having given up his chance of winning the throne, he had settled on the role of king-maker, or possibly king-breaker. Milewski was his candidate for the leadership, the hardliners having lost faith in their previous champion, Stefan Olszowski. Milewski was an example of a protégé who had become more important than his patron. But the energy behind his quiet campaign for the leadership of the Polish Communist Party was supplied by Moczar; above all, it was the energy of hatred. It is difficult to underestimate the enmity that buzzes between Moczar and Jaruzelski's group of civilian advisers. It was Moczar's anti-Semitic campaigning in 1968 that first made a politician out of General Jaruzelski. As a young political officer, Soviet-trained and in the fast lane, Jaruzelski probably would have been content to be a professional spokesman for the army in the Politburo. But involvement in the invasion of Czechoslovakia—which taught him the limits of Soviet tolerance for Eastern European reform—and his growing anger at the way Moczar was manipulating the anti-Semitic card drew him into the fray. By refusing to order soldiers to shoot workers in 1970 he spelled the end of the Gomulka era, and, by backing Gomulka's successor Edward Gierek, he hoped to keep Moczar out of power. But in the long term the only way to neutralize Moczar was to depoliticize the secret police or at least ensure that it was a faithful arm of the leadership. Kiszczak as head of military counterintelligence helped Jaruzelski to spread army influence both in secret intelligence gathering and in broadening his civilian power base. The fall of Gierek and the Solidarity strikes in 1980 were Moczar's last opportunity to seize power, but General Jaruzelski moved quickly, helping to mobilize support for Stanislaw Kania.

Moczar could not forgive Jaruzelski. By September 1984 it was time for the old man and his friends to strike back.

Jaruzelski was entering the riskiest phase of his political career. Martial law had been lifted. If unrest broke out now it would expose the failure of the whole unorthodox approach of a Communist army temporarily displacing the Communist Party in a Soviet bloc state. General Jaruzelski had freed the whole of the political opposition. For the first time since the Solidarity revolution, the firebrands who had argued for the dismantling of Polish Communism or even withdrawal from the Warsaw Pact, were free. Few had changed their minds, most of them still had the courage to stand up in public and express their views. As if this germ of instability was not enough, Jaruzelski's government was again preparing to open its doors to the West. The guest list for the coming autumn was astonishingly long compared with the past three years of diplomatic isolation. Andreas Papandreou, the Greek premier and first NATO leader to break the boycott of Jaruzelski, was planning to come to Warsaw in late October; the Italian and Austrian foreign ministers, the junior minister at the British Foreign Office were all on the calendar, and the West Germans were talking of a visit. Jaruzelski wanted events to move fast: there had been too much paralysis. Only Western acceptance—for example in the form of membership of the International Monetary Fund—could revive the sickly economy and the tired nation. But the hardliners needed to move quickly, too. General Jaruzelski had to be blocked.

That view gained ground in the corridors of secret police headquarters in Rakowiecka Street. Later, as the observers at the Torun trial were to listen in amazement to the slipshod techniques of the secret police conspirators, the question arose: Why were Piotrowski and his men in such a hurry? After watching the priest slip out of their traps so many times, why could they not have planned more carefully, with more precision? The answer lies in the sense of alarm felt by the hardliners. After inching forward since the winter of 1981, the Jaruzelski government was accelerating in the wrong direction: westward. The counter-offensive had to be appropriately swift. There was no time to lose.

(c) Third suspect: Moscow. Either in cahoots with Milewski or independent of him, the Soviet Union or a faction of the KGB decided to remove Popieluszko.

How far did Moscow encourage or inspire the conspirators? The relationship between the Soviet Union and its allies is complex, an intricate web. Rarely is there a clear and unambiguous signal from Moscow because there are at least four channels of communication and the messages are often contradictory. Moscow has its voice in the normal diplomatic traffic, with the Soviet ambassador enjoying special access to the foreign minister of the allied country. Information—hints, warnings, ultimatums, and "friendly advice"—can also flow through the Communist Party, the military, and the police pipelines. The essence of stable leadership in Eastern Europe is to have control over all four channels. But with rapid changeovers in the Kremlin, the Brezhnev era giving way to the short, sharp shock of Andropov, and then to the brief reign of Konstantin Chernenko, no Soviet bloc leader could be entirely certain in the early 1980s that his country's policies were being understood by the big Eastern brother. Jaruzelski himself could only be completely sure of the military connection. By 1984 he had given up his position as defense minister, but the political command of the Warsaw Pact and the Soviet army was a good source of information about developments in Moscow. The ideological and Party contacts were dwindling in value by then. Although, two years before, the Soviet Party had been quite active in monitoring Polish politics—complaining that some Polish Communists were wolfish Social Democrats in sheepskin coats and worrying aloud about some of the reprimands handed out to Moczar's supporters in the so-called hardline "reality" clubs. And in the Solidarity era, the Soviet Central Committee tried to stamp hard on Party men who were going soft on socialism. But by 1984 the catchword was "consolidation"—keep the Party alive in the factories and the universities was the Soviet advice—the diplomatic link was difficult. The Polish foreign minister was Stefan Olszowski, who could not be accused, even by his friends, of excessive loyalty to Jaruzelski. The Polish ambassador to Moscow was Stanislaw Kociolek, ousted from the powerful job of Warsaw Party boss. General Jaruzelski, had, in the idiom of Madison Avenue, an image problem in Moscow. The combination of Olszowski and Kociolek was not exactly hardselling the Jaruzelski line. When the Soviet ambassador arrived for his regular briefing on Polish Cabinet and Politburo sessions, Olszowski knew how to distance himself from Jaruzelski, from the sluggish economic recovery, from the plans for an amnesty, that grand rabbit-out-of-the-hat gesture toward the West.

But the formal and informal connections between the KGB and the Polish secret police were the most important. All the indications are that the KGB has considerable respect for the SB. Most of the founders of the postwar Polish secret police were Soviet-trained, many of them early Communists who had spent the war in Moscow. Soviet advisers were placed in Rakowiecka Street, indeed, in most ministries. The civil war against the anti-Communist Home Army Partisans and Soldiers (thirty thousand of them disappeared) was orchestrated by the Russians. The Politburo man in charge of security, Jakub Berman, was in regular contact with Moscow. Although there were embarrassing moments—when the Moscow-trained Department Director Colonel Jozef Swiatlo defected, for example—the Russians were happy enough to give the secret police a degree of autonomy. It was, after all, a Pole, Felix Dzerzhinsky, who had founded the Cheka, forerunner of the KGB. Polish counterespionage agents worked closely with the KGB, and all Polish espionage operations abroad—notably, buying up hi-tech secrets in the United States—were coordinated with Moscow. The two civilian secret services and the Soviet and Polish military security services had worked together on the planning of martial law, which was an extraordinary detailed police operation.

In July 1981, when General Jaruzelski installed his friend Czeslaw Kiszczak at the head of the Polish Secret and Uniformed Police he expected trouble, trouble from the old guard within the SB and trouble perhaps from Moscow. But Kiszczak seemed, within two years of taking over, to be in control. Certainly no rumblings of discontent were reaching him. The Soviet leader and former KGB chairman, Yuri Andropov, was not only understanding about martial law, he also seemed to be preparing a purge of the Soviet secret police by trusted colleagues from the military. Andropov's new KGB chief, Vitaly Fedorchuk, later appointed interior minister, and his new deputy, Georgi Tzinev, both had military connections, partly as controllers (in Department Three of the KGB) but also in military counterespionage. There were thus parallels between what Andropov and Jaruzelski were doing to their security services: using men with army links to clean away dead wood.

Perhaps this had a paralyzing effect on the SB malcontents and slowed down their efforts to organize resistance to Kiszczak. If so, that effect swiftly wore off when Andropov's health started to fail. By November–December 1983, when the SB drafted and carried out its plan to frame Popieluszko, Andropov had almost no impact on internal Soviet policies, and his appointees in the KGB were losing clout. The death of Andropov and the succession of Konstantin Chernenko in February 1984 can only have encouraged the conspirators in the SB and their hardline supporters.

First, there was no more talk in Moscow of "reform," the watchword of the Jaruzelski regime. Andropov had talked much of change, though he usually meant little more than enforcing work discipline and raising productivity. The ruling team in Poland had been behaving as if they had the Kremlin's Good Housekeeping seal of approval.

Second, Chernenko was an old NKVD man. Andropov, despite all his years as head of the KGB, was first and foremost a man of the Party, not a professional agent. But Chernenko had, in a mysterious slab of his personal history, actually served with the wartime and postwar version of the KGB. It was the NKVD that was in the vanguard of the "liberation" of Eastern Europe, organizing the roundups and the political vetting. By a happy coincidence, Miroslaw Milewski was also an NKVD officer before joining the Polish secret police. His official biography states that he was involved in secret police work from the age of sixteen. It does not state, but it is well known in Rakowiecka Street, that he earned his spurs at the age of nineteen by betraying a whole Polish anti-Communist partisan unit to the Russians in the forests of eastern Poland. The relationship between the frustrated faction of the Polish secret police and the Soviet leadership thus gained an added warmth with the accession of Chernenko.

Hardly surprising then that in May 1984 the meeting between Chernenko and Jaruzelski was rather frosty. The information flowing to the Kremlin from Warsaw was not very encouraging: the Polish army was not modernizing its forces quickly enough, the Party was stagnating, young Poles were demonstrating and showing disrespect for the Bolshevik revolution (by ripping down red flags on May Day), and General Jaruzelski was preparing an amnesty for some hundreds of counterrevolutionaries.

But, above all, the Catholic Church was a nuisance. Despite special units set up in Moscow and Prague after the accession of the Polish Pope in 1978, the faith was spreading, and a certain type of priest was trying to make a bridge between this new fervor and national, anti-Communist ferment. Czechoslovakia, with some ten million Catholics, a high concentration in Slovakia, was worried and had acted accordingly, outlawing private Sunday school lessons, squeezing the Church leadership, trying, with indifferent success, to align the clergy to government policies through an organization called Pacem in Terris. The Czech equivalents of Popieluszko were banned from preaching. Vaclav Maly, the closest equivalent to a Solidarity priest, had to work as a boilerman in a rundown Prague hotel. The Czechs persistently nagged Moscow about the menace of the Pope making common cause with President Reagan and trying to infect the young generation. For the Soviet leadership Catholicism was only a problem in the Ukraine and the Baltic republics, especially Lithuania, which borders Poland. In Lithuania there were also aspiring Popieluszkos and enough unexplained murders and "beautiful accidents" to suggest that the KGB was not going to tolerate a connection between the clergy and the dissident movement.

After the Pope's second visit to Poland, Leonid Zamyatin, the Soviet propaganda specialist, had visited Warsaw to advise on how to contain the danger of "clericalism." Popieluszko was singled out by name. That was a significant nudge to the men in Rakowiecka Street, and not just the malcontents. It almost certainly persuaded Kiszczak to authorize the frame-up operation against Popieluszko.

The Chernenko–Jaruzelski summit led to new propaganda guidelines on the Church to be implemented after the amnesty. For Jaruzelski it was important not only to shatter the liaison between Church and Solidarity but also to show the world that he had not released the country's political prisoners because of pressure from the Church (or Solidarity or the West). At the same time, the amnesty created a good climate for doing deals with the Church leadership, or at least conjuring up an aura of stability and calm. A Catholic nation and a Communist state—but still at peace with itself. This was confusing for the professional propagandists. Do we attack the Church or are we to make our peace with it? That bewilderment was felt throughout the nation; somehow there seemed to be insincerity both in the press crusade against the Church and in the attempts to be nice to Primate Glemp.

It took the Russians to set things straight. When Polish Deputy Premier Mieczyslaw Rakowski publicly reminded the Church leadership that they should restrain "adventurist" priests, the Soviet TASS news service quoted him approvingly, and, in September, the government newspaper *Izvestia* pointed the way with its blast at Popieluszko. The time had come—that was the underlying message of the article—to be specific, to stop railing and ranting against "some" priests, and to state clearly who was the class enemy. This unquestionably aided the conspirators. But neither the nudge from *Izvestia* nor the earlier heavy hints add up to an order from Moscow. This may be naive, too narrow and textual an argument. The murderers of Popieluszko probably interpreted the article as thinking aloud, Moscow's way of saying: "Who will rid me of this turbulent priest," the effective death sentence for Thomas à Becket. Certainly when Moscow puts its criticisms of an ally into newspaper print it is a sign of frustration, a sign that other channels of communication are not working properly. Moscow was irritated, it was skeptical about some of General Jaruzelski's policies that it was listening carefully to his critics in the Politburo. But the fact is that the Kremlin had no interest in ousting General Jaruzelski. Chernenko wanted stability in Poland—that was the point of persuading Jaruzelski to crack down harder on the Church—and pushing out Jaruzelski would hardly serve that cause.

Certainly the natural suspicions of the Poles turned their gaze eastward. When the auxiliary prosecutor Jan Olszewski uttered his important, censored phrase in court he was articulating not only the vows of his clients, Popieluszko's parents, and the Catholic church, but also the freely offered opinion of many ordinary Poles as they traveled to work in trams or gossiped in their offices. The inspiration for the crime, said Olszewski, in his half-whispered delivery, must have come from centers opposed to Poland's vital interests—and every schoolchild knew where that was. That is as close as one can come in a Communist country to denouncing Moscow. Echoes perhaps of the letter to Pope Pius the Ninth from General Traugutt, the leader of the anti-Russian uprising in 1863. "Moscow understands that there is no way of getting along with Catholic Poland, so vents its greatest anger on our spiritual pastors." Popieluszko had quoted the phrase, with some glee, in one of his sermons.

The question of the Moscow connection was hotly debated within the Polish intelligentsia. Some speculated that the KGB had simply miscalculated. The Soviet secret agency encouraged the Polish police conspirators to dispose of Father Popieluszko, thinking that this would be a problem solved. The generals, Jaruzelski and Kiszczak, would act out of self-preservation and keep quiet about the killing. It would be another unexplained, probably politically motivated crime. The escape of the priest's driver, Waldemar Chrostowski, complicated the situation but need not have been an insuperable difficulty. His testimony about being stopped by traffic policemen could have been shrugged off, discounted as the ramblings of a deluded excommando, and the assailants explained away as a gang of disguised criminals.

It is dangerous, however, to build up an argument on the basis of KGB miscalculation. There is little evidence to support the theory. The family backgrounds of the murderers, for example, reveal nothing that would suggest an informal link with the KGB. Neither Colonel Pietruska nor Captain Piotrowski had Soviet training nor, it seems, friends in the Soviet Embassy.

This is a murky territory. All that can be firmly said is that Moscow did not withdraw its support from General Jaruzelski when the kidnapping and then the murder of the priest were made public. It was not, of course, very happy about secret police officers being put on open trial, but its concern from the moment of the murder was containing the damage rather than power-play. Soviet propaganda specialists were in touch with the allies by Monday, October 22, three days after the murder. Hungarian radio had already announced the kidnapping on October 20, but had played safe by taking over the official Polish version: Popieluszko, kidnapped by unknown assailants, had "preached against national reconciliation." The Soviet guidelines, drawn up by Leonid Zamyatin and Boris Stukhalin, urged silence until more was known about the kidnappers. Almost ten days after the event, Czechoslovak television announced the kidnapping for the first time. In the preceding week the Poles had arrested secret police officers and were preparing murder charges against them, but Czech television overlooked this and concluded that "people" were using the crime to whip citizens into rage and hatred against the Polish authorities. The overall impression left by the broadcast was that Popieluszko himself was in some way responsible for causing trouble again. Moscow broke its silence only after the priest's body had been discovered. The killing, said Soviet television, radio, and TASS, was a political provocation against the Polish authorities, who "ensure the country's tranquility." No mention of the secret police.

Citizens of the Soviet bloc found out quickly enough thanks to Western radio broadcasts, but Moscow was above all concerned that there should be no public anger against the police. It was therefore at Soviet initiative that the trial was deflected from being a general indictment of the secret police into an all-out attack on the Church and Popieluszko. The weekend before the state prosecutor was due to deliver his speech, Boris Stukhalin was in Warsaw, roaring through the streets in a black Chaika limousine. The script was ready. The style of the Kremlin's crisis management suggests that the murder was a surprise.

Before the trial began in December 1984, Jaruzelski summoned a meeting of the Central Committee and set out proposals that would become the basis of a purge of the secret police. Milewski kept his seat in the Politburo, but the criticism of the Communist Party cell in the secret police was so sharp that his eventual sacking was inevitable. From that month on, Milewski did not attend Politburo sessions. After the trial was finished, Milewski was thrown out of the Party leadership. Just over a year after the murder of the priest, Foreign Minister Stefan Olszowski was also levered out of power. Either of these men could have been Moscow's candidate for Communist Party chief in Poland. If it had really been the Kremlin's intention to replace Jaruzelski, then it had obviously changed its mind.

(d) Final possibility: the crime was solely Piotrowski's brainchild but his accomplices were senior officers in other SB departments. That is to say, the conspiracy did not have a vertical chain of command but was based on horizontal links between different secret police units.

Political speculation about Moscow connections inevitably leads to a dead end, stopping at the Kremlin Wall. General Kiszczak promised to keep on looking for the masterminds of the crime even after the trial was over. Not many people believed him. The trial verdict was so neatly packaged, so obviously designed to kill further questions about the "top," that it would have been foolhardy to continue turning up stones. The sacking of Milewski was the ideal coda to the Popieluszko affair. Technically he was fired because he did not properly supervise the secret police. In fact, so the Jaruzelski supporters would privately argue, he was thrown out because he was deeply implicated in the plot, although not to such a degree that it could be proved in a court of law.

But Kiszczak, against all expectations, kept his word. There was an investigation—not one that would lead eastward, or even very deep into the Communist Party woodwork, but a genuine inquiry within the secret police, carried out by trusted aides from the secret police internal control department. Two of them died in a car accident with a snow plow before the trial started in Torun. But the inquiries continued. Kiszczak had reached the conclusion, self-evident to anyone so closely involved with espionage work, that the four conspirators could not have acted autonomously within Rakowiecka Street. Piotrowski and his two accomplices were not a trained hit squad functioning smoothly in conditions of complete confidentiality. They were desk men who needed help. Nor could the Church affairs department of the secret police act in complete isolation from the anti-opposition department. On the contrary, there were regular consultations and many personal, informal ties between the two departments. To follow, persecute, harass, and frame Father Popieluszko because of his contacts with Solidarity, it was necessary to talk to the Solidarity experts in Rakowiecka Street. This was not just a matter of form but of operational necessity. The trial tried to camouflage these internal connections, and if many courtroom observers came away more baffled than illuminated about secret police activities, then that was fine by Rakowiecka Street. Piotrowski, out of both bravado and instinct, declared at the outset of the trial that he would not give the names of fellow agents. But those priests who had had contact with Piotrowski know him under a variety of different names: each agent uses a number of different identities when interrogating suspects. The four men were convicted under their real names: that much can be established from tracing their family histories. But other agents called as witnesses seemed to be allocated ranks and even named at random, deliberately to confuse the audience at home and in the West. Thus one witness was first introduced as a police driver but was later described by another witness as a colonel.

In this confused situation the main suspicion naturally fell on General Platek, the man immediately above Colonel Pietruszka in the departmental hierarchy. If a "top" was to be discovered in open court, then it would have to lead through General Platek. Platek survived, did not end up in the dock despite the legitimate doubts of many, in and out of the courtroom. But he served a useful purpose by diverting attention away from the possibility of a horizontal rather than a vertical conspiracy, a plot hatched between different parts of the secret police. The Interior Ministry has six deputy ministers, one of whom, General Wladyslaw Ciaston, is head of the secret police. Each deputy minister has approximately five department heads reporting to him. Each department head supervises several sections. The Church department, Department Four, has a staff of perhaps fifty. Despite this pyramid structure, there is a great deal of mobility between sections and between departments. It was said by the authorities that Piotrowski's section had developed an unusual degree of autonomy, floating freely in Church affairs. This was a necessary fiction, essential if the trial of only four conspirators was to make any sense.

But small discrepancies that emerged in the trial indicate that several secret police officers were in the know about the kidnapping plan. When Piotrowski left on his mission on October 19, 1984, he told his secretary Barbara Story to ring a certain number regularly within Rakowiecka Street. Piotrowski would telephone in to find out if there were any messages. Mrs. Story could not, in court, remember the number, though she knew it belonged to another SB department. Who was Piotrowski so anxious to contact on the day of the murder? And why was Mrs. Story not pressed by the judge to remember the extension number?

Another clue: when the priest's driver Waldemar Chrostowski was asked to identify the getaway vehicle he was confronted with five possible cars. It was difficult. But when he asked one of his police escorts to switch on the engines of each car he immediately identified the correct vehicle. "It was," he said, "simply that the engine hummed so nicely, that it was so obviously in good shape." Chrostowski, who drove thousands of miles with Father Popieluszko, knew about cars. Yet according to the getaway driver, Lieutenant Pekala, the car was in disastrous condition. There were problems with the oil pump, and the whole bizarre Keystone Cops nature of the mission owes its origins to the mechanical flaws of the car. There was no reason for the lieutenant to lie about this, and the facts were corroborated by other evidence.

Either someone made a mistake or, more probably, more than one car was involved in the operation. The existence of a second car would also shed some light on the problem of the changing number plates. The evidence given by the two lieutenants was supposed to explain why their car was spotted at different times of the fateful evening with different plates. Their version was credible if one believed that the agents were frightened, bumbling men, out of their depth and out of control. In court it was easy to accept this self-characterization. But a second car would immediately suggest a more professional operation. And a second vehicle means that more people were involved than the four men in the dock.

Kiszczak's purge of the secret police machine indicated that he also suspected a "horizontal" plot. His first move was to install his own men, usually former military counterespionage officers, in each department to investigate the activities of each employee in the months preceding the murder. Second, a "positive vetting" was carried out, with each secret policeman in Rakowiecka Street having to face a board. Nominally they were supposed to test the agents' loyalty to Jaruzelski and weed out supporters of Milewski, but sometimes the questions were more specific: Who was tied in with Piotrowski, with the lieutenants, with Colonel Pietruszka? Not surprisingly, few claimed any friendship with the murderers, but dozens, then several dozen agents were sacked, reprimanded, sent into early retirement.

It is inevitable that this book must end with questions unanswered. Even in the relatively open climate of Poland, some corners remain closed in a Communist state, some secrets stay locked. The German novelist Heinrich Böll, writing of a fictional police affair, concluded that he could "find no explanation, yet it was not inexplicable but almost logical." So it was, is, in the Popieluszko case. The four possible lines of investigation lead the thread into and not out of the labyrinth. The Agatha Christie detective is not able to turn, at last, and, with curled lip, announce the astonishing guilt of the least suspected of the suspects. There are no such certainties. But by collating the facts for the first time, it has been possible to demonstrate the logic of the murder of the hapless Father Jerzy: the anti-Church crusade of the Polish government vying with its own need to conciliate a Catholic nation; the apparently unlimited scope of action given to the security services; the need of a nervous government to return to Western favor and at the same time keep the trust of Moscow; the hardline security men, bound by intermarriage and clannish loyalty, and their unhappiness with the army; frustrated agents, men in love, falling out of love, hungry for promotion; and their target—a young priest, feeling his way into a political commitment, a fierce allegiance to an outlawed organization, his conflicts with the Church leaders, a man with a sense of national mission.

Father Jerzy Popieluszko is being considered for beatification. There are formal procedures involved and some politics too: it would be a defiant move to elevate the man who is already regarded as the martyr of Solidarity. But few doubt that Pope John Paul will do everything in his power to create this new Polish saint. Popieluszko's church, Stanislaw Kostka, has become a garden in a desert, a shelter for Solidarity, its ideals— still voiced in the masses for the fatherland—and its emblems. The wrought iron railings are smothered with banners in the blotchy Solidarity script: "With good we will defeat evil."

As the months become years, the traces of Popieluszko's killers will be obscured, brushed over. His death will be a matter of record: a murder, apparently solved, the killers duly sentenced. The notion of a puppet-master will fade, a matter of obscure speculation, the stuff of yellowing newspaper clippings. But this priest died a cruel, dirty death, and the background and the motives should not be forgotten. This book has tried to ask the questions, to leave nothing unasked, in the hope that answers will one day emerge.

About the Authors

JOHN MOODY is a correspondent for *Time* magazine and has worked in New York City, West Germany, and Eastern Europe. Previously he worked in Paris and Moscow for United Press International.

ROGER BOYES has been the *Times of London*'s Warsaw correspondent since 1981. He has traveled extensively throughout Eastern Europe. He previously worked for Reuters in Bonn and Moscow.